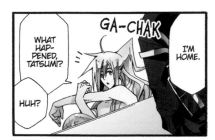

I'M HOME.
GA-CHAK
WHAT HAP-PENED, TATSUMI?
HUH?
SOME-THING GOOD HAP-PENED, RIGHT?
YOU LOOK HAPPY
YEAH...
YOU GOT A LITTLE EXTRA! THAT'S GREAT!
CLAP CLAP
YEAH, I CAN REALLY USE IT THIS MONTH.

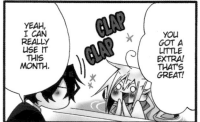

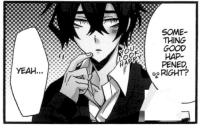

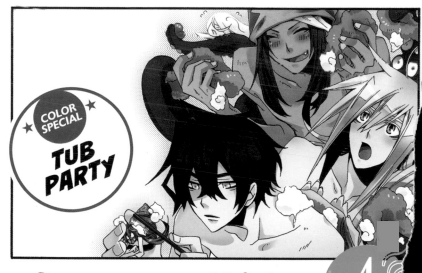

COLOR SPECIAL
TUB PARTY

Merman in My Tub 4

ORENCHI NO FURO JIJO

story & art by

ITOKICHI

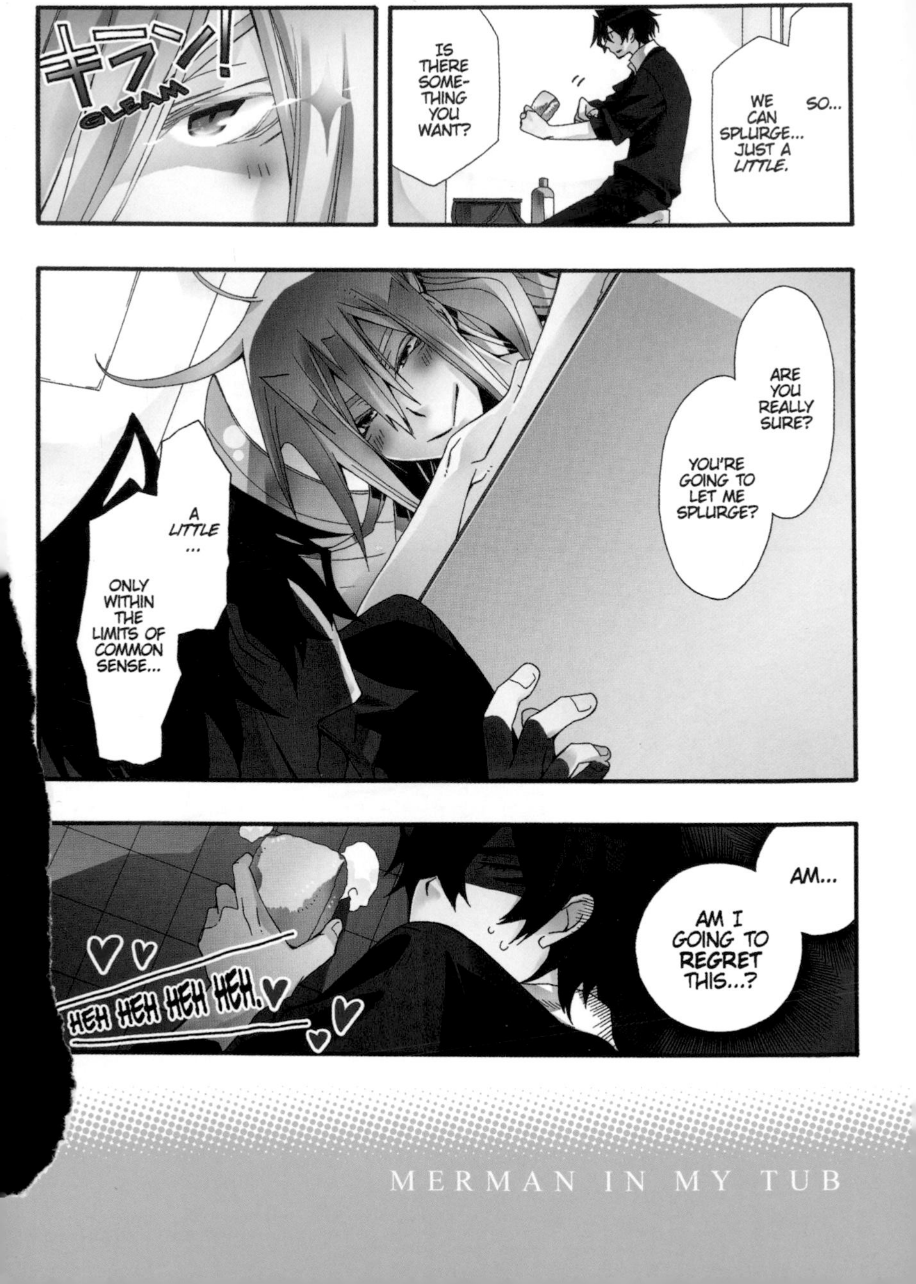
SO... WE CAN SPLURGE... JUST A LITTLE.
IS THERE SOMETHING YOU WANT?
キラン!
GLEAM
ARE YOU REALLY SURE?
YOU'RE GOING TO LET ME SPLURGE?
A LITTLE ...
ONLY WITHIN THE LIMITS OF COMMON SENSE...
AM...
AM I GOING TO REGRET THIS...?
HEH HEH HEH HEH.

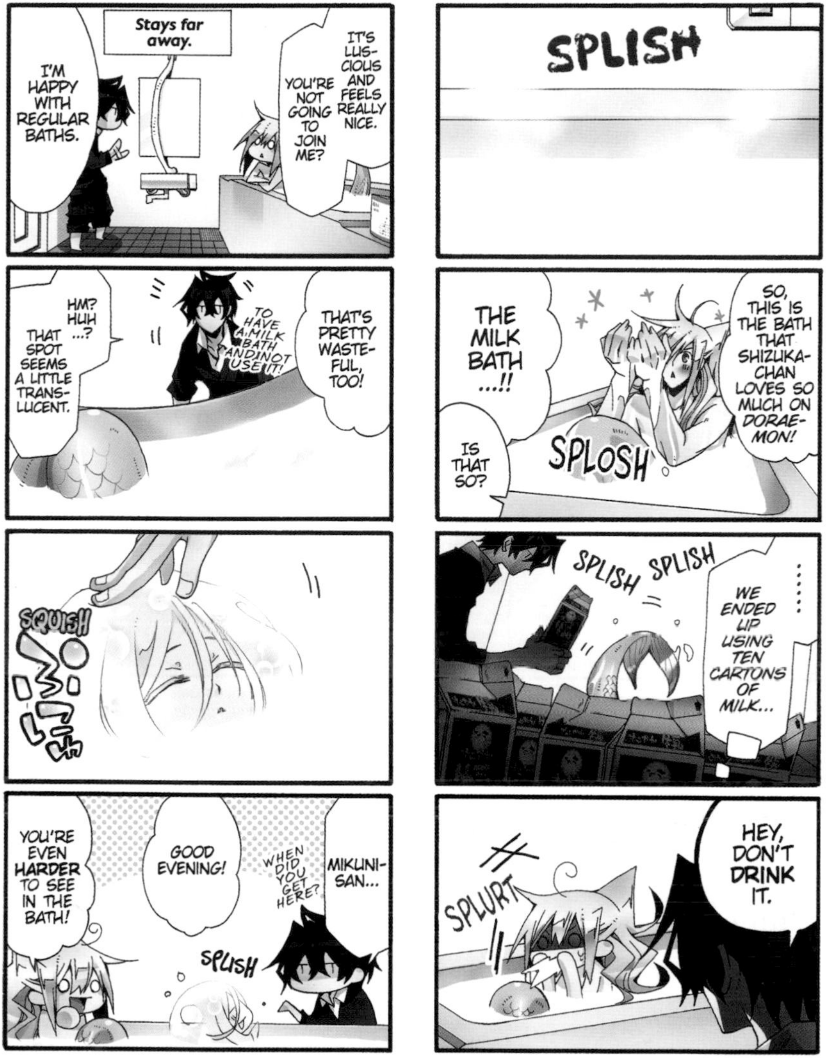
SPLISH
SO, THIS IS THE BATH THAT SHIZUKA-CHAN LOVES SO MUCH ON DORAEMON!
THE MILK BATH ...!!
IS THAT SO?
SPLOSH
......
WE ENDED UP USING TEN CARTONS OF MILK...
SPLISH SPLISH
HEY, DON'T DRINK IT.
SPLURT
IT'S LUS-CIOUS AND FEELS REALLY NICE.
YOU'RE NOT GOING TO JOIN ME?
I'M HAPPY WITH REGULAR BATHS.
Stays far away.
THAT'S PRETTY WASTE-FUL, TOO!
TO HAVE A MILK BATH AND NOT USE IT!
HM? HUH ...?
THAT SPOT SEEMS A LITTLE TRANS-LUCENT.
SQUISH
MIKUNI-SAN...
WHEN DID YOU GET HERE?
GOOD EVENING!
YOU'RE EVEN HARDER TO SEE IN THE BATH!
SPLISH

I HEARD YOU WERE HAVING A TUB PARTY AND DECIDED TO POP IN!
AND SO, I BROUGHT SOME SALTS MYSELF!
DID I EVER SAY SOMETHING LIKE THAT?
AQUARIUS
COFFEE
THESE... AREN'T BATH SALTS.
THEY'RE NOT?!
I THOUGHT YOU'D ENJOY THEM BECAUSE OF ALL THE DIFFERENT COLORS...
UNFORTUNATELY.
SHOOT...
WAIT, SO I WASN'T SUPPOSED TO USE THEM?!
NOW IT'S LIKE A CAFÉ AU LAIT...
EXPAND
WELL... DO WHAT YOU WANT.
I'M NOT THE ONE WHO'LL BE SOAKING IN IT.
SPLASH
SPLASH
YOU'RE TOO LENIENT!!
YOU'RE TOO LENIENT WITH MIKUNI!!
BLURB BLURB
SPLOSH
Coffee.
THE FEELING OF HARMONY...
Green Tea.
AQUARIUS IS THE BEST, AFTER ALL!
SO LENIENT!!
YOU JUST LET HIM DO WHATEVER HE WANTS!!
GULP...
Aquarius.

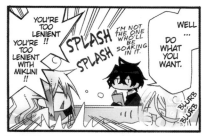

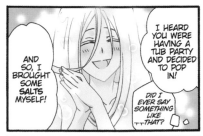

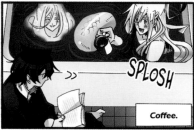

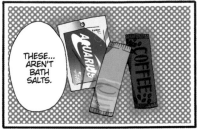

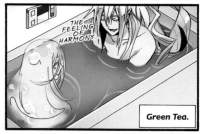

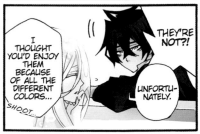

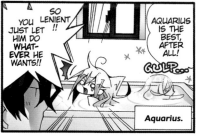

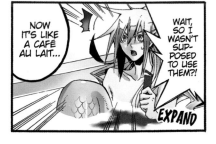

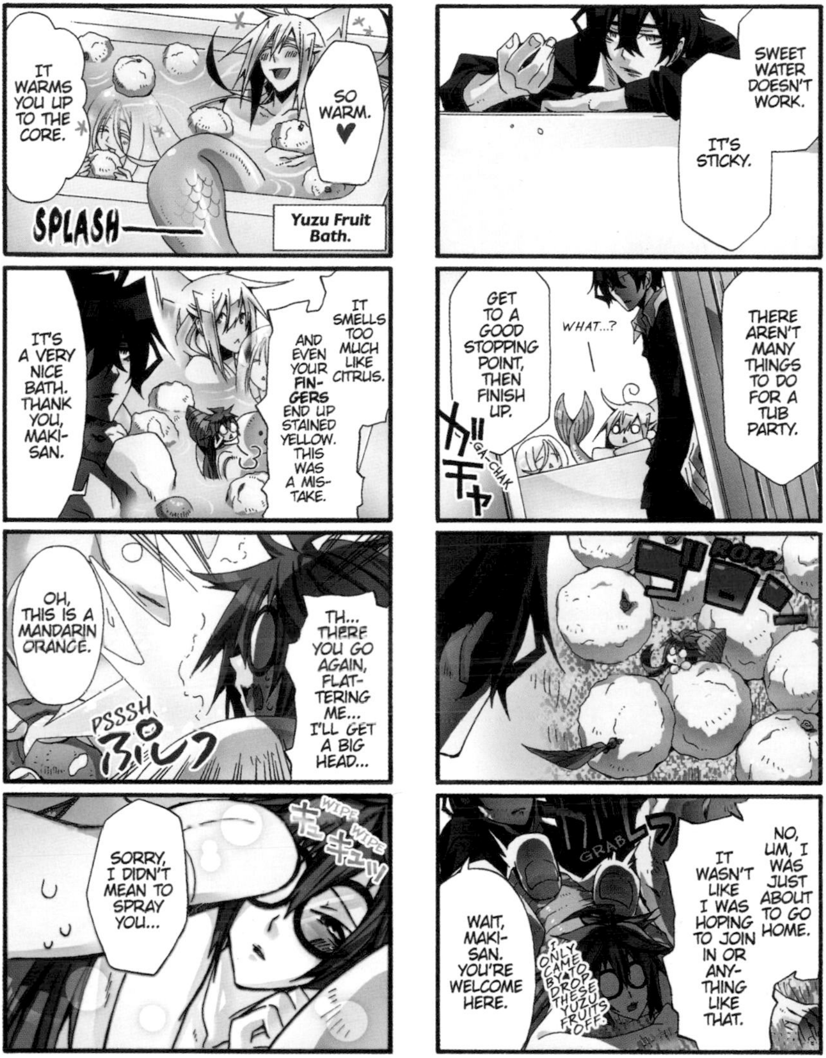
SWEET WATER DOESN'T WORK.
IT'S STICKY.
THERE AREN'T MANY THINGS TO DO FOR A TUB PARTY.
WHAT...?
GET TO A GOOD STOPPING POINT, THEN FINISH UP.
GA-CHAK
ROLL
NO, UM, I WAS JUST ABOUT TO GO HOME.
IT WASN'T LIKE I WAS HOPING TO JOIN IN OR ANY-THING LIKE THAT.
GRAB
I ONLY CAME BY TO DROP THESE YUZU FRUITS OFF.
WAIT, MAKI-SAN. YOU'RE WELCOME HERE.
Yuzu Fruit Bath.
SO WARM. ♥
IT WARMS YOU UP TO THE CORE.
SPLASH—
IT SMELLS TOO MUCH LIKE CITRUS.
AND EVEN YOUR FIN-GERS END UP STAINED YELLOW. THIS WAS A MIS-TAKE.
IT'S A VERY NICE BATH. THANK YOU, MAKI-SAN.
TH... THERE YOU GO AGAIN, FLAT-TERING ME... I'LL GET A BIG HEAD...
OH, THIS IS A MANDARIN ORANGE.
PSSSH
WIPE WIPE
SORRY, I DIDN'T MEAN TO SPRAY YOU...

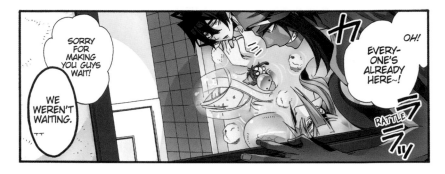

OH! EVERY-ONE'S ALREADY HERE~!
RATTLE
SORRY FOR MAKING YOU GUYS WAIT!
WE WEREN'T WAITING.
TA-DA~!
WINE, BEER, AND SHOCHU~!
DUUUN
I'M UNDER-AGE.
DU-DUUUN
JUST DON'T DRINK IT, THEN?

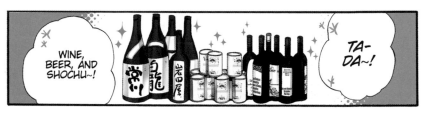

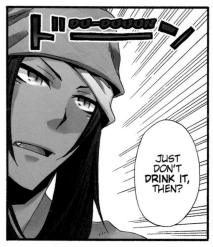

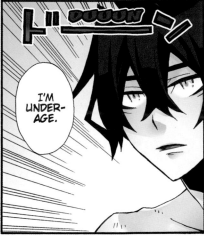

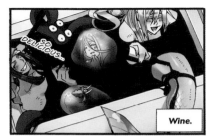

THAT'S NOT THE ISSUE HERE!
WHAT'LL HAPPEN IF SOME-ONE UNDER-AGE SEES THIS AND TRIES--
SPLASH
ざばっ
STARE
All adults here.
STARE ...
WE CAN'T...?
REALLY...?
※Even though they act like kids.
CLATTER
WE HAVE TO DO IT RESPON-SIBLY!
CHEERS!!
CLATTER
ARE YOU LISTENING, TAKASU?
These guys are not role models!! Do not go drinking near kids!!
SO DELICIOUS...
Wine.
Beer.
YOU HAVE TO CONSUME ALCOHOL, NOT BE CONSUMED...BY IT...!
Shochu.
TAT-SUMI ?!
DID HE OVER-HEAT ?!
BLECH
HE'S GOTTEN SICK JUST WATCHING THEM.

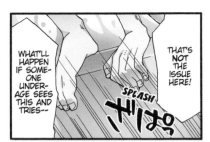

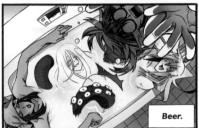

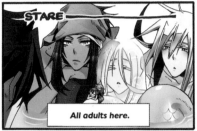

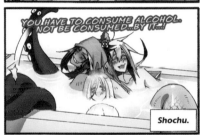

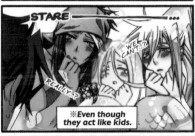

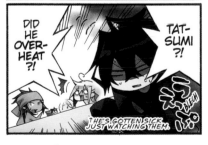

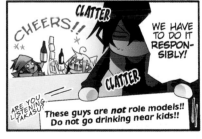

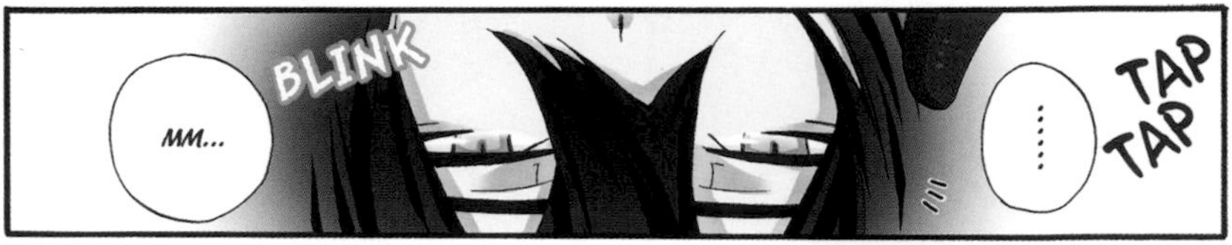
TAP TAP
......
BLINK
MM...

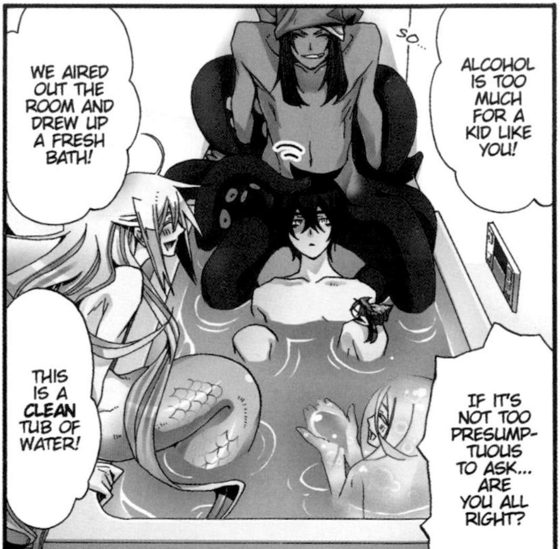
ALCOHOL IS TOO MUCH FOR A KID LIKE YOU!
SO...
WE AIRED OUT THE ROOM AND DREW UP A FRESH BATH!
IF IT'S NOT TOO PRESUMPTUOUS TO ASK... ARE YOU ALL RIGHT?
THIS IS A CLEAN TUB OF WATER!

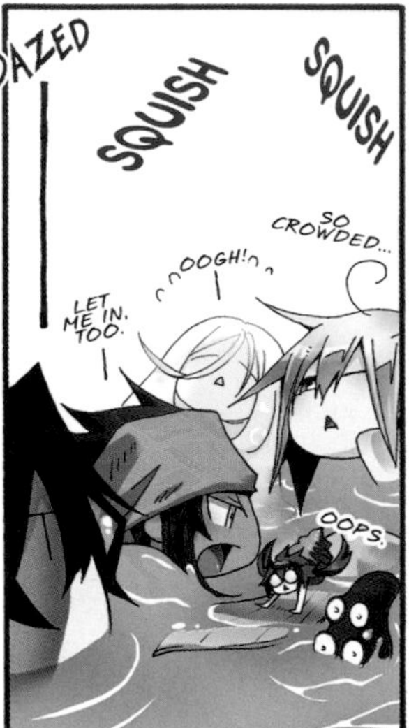
SQUISH
SQUISH
DAZED
SO CROWDED...
OOGH!
LET ME IN TOO.
OOPS.

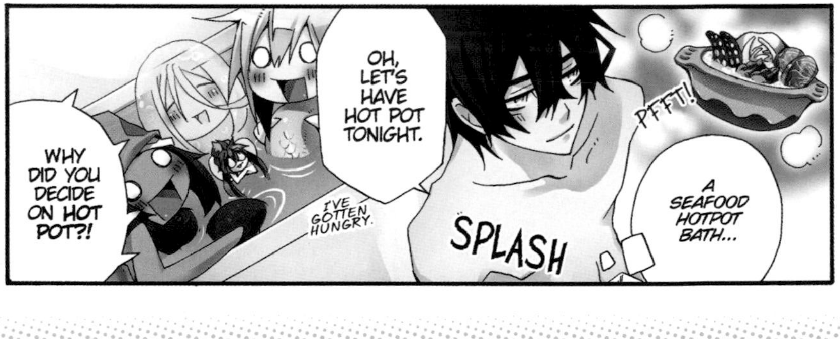
PFFT!
A SEAFOOD HOTPOT BATH...
OH, LET'S HAVE HOT POT TONIGHT.
SPLASH
I'VE GOTTEN HUNGRY.
WHY DID YOU DECIDE ON HOT POT?!

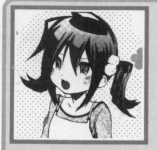

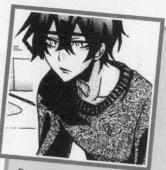

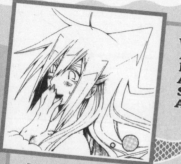

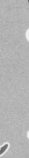

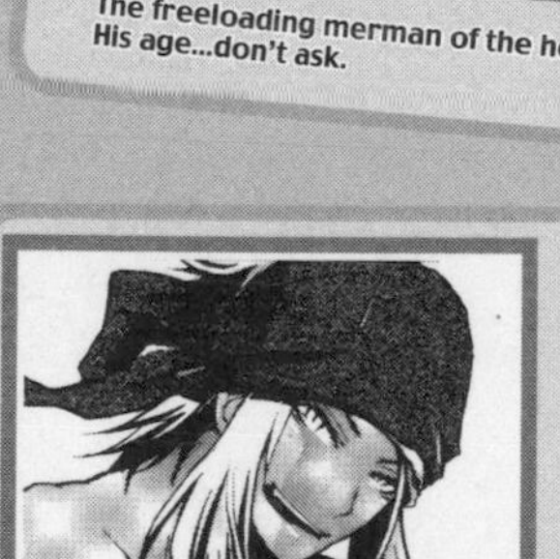

PICTURE BOOK OF LIVING CREATURES
(...or appearing characters)

T A T S U M I

The owner of the house. High school boy. He's good at cooking and household chores.

K A S U M I

Tatsumi's little sister. She loves her big brother very much. Her rival is Wakasa.

W A K A S A

The freeloading merman of the house. His age...don't ask.

T A K A S U

An octopus-man that sometimes appears at the bath. Seems to be longtime friends with Wakasa. He's good at massages.

HISATORA UNCLE

Tatsumi's uncle. He develops suspicious medicines and has Tatsumi test them out.

SOUSUKE

Tatsumi's friend. He has two older sisters.

GOROMARU

A starfish that appeared in the house who often goes unnoticed. He looks a bit like Kasumi and is skilled at clinging.

MAKI

A snail-man that appears quietly at the bath. Very nearsighted and self-deprecating.

AGARI

A shark-man that suddenly appears at the bath. It seems he is Wakasa's senpai.

MIKUNI

A jellyfish-man that wanders into the bath. His body is 99% water. He loves Aquarius.

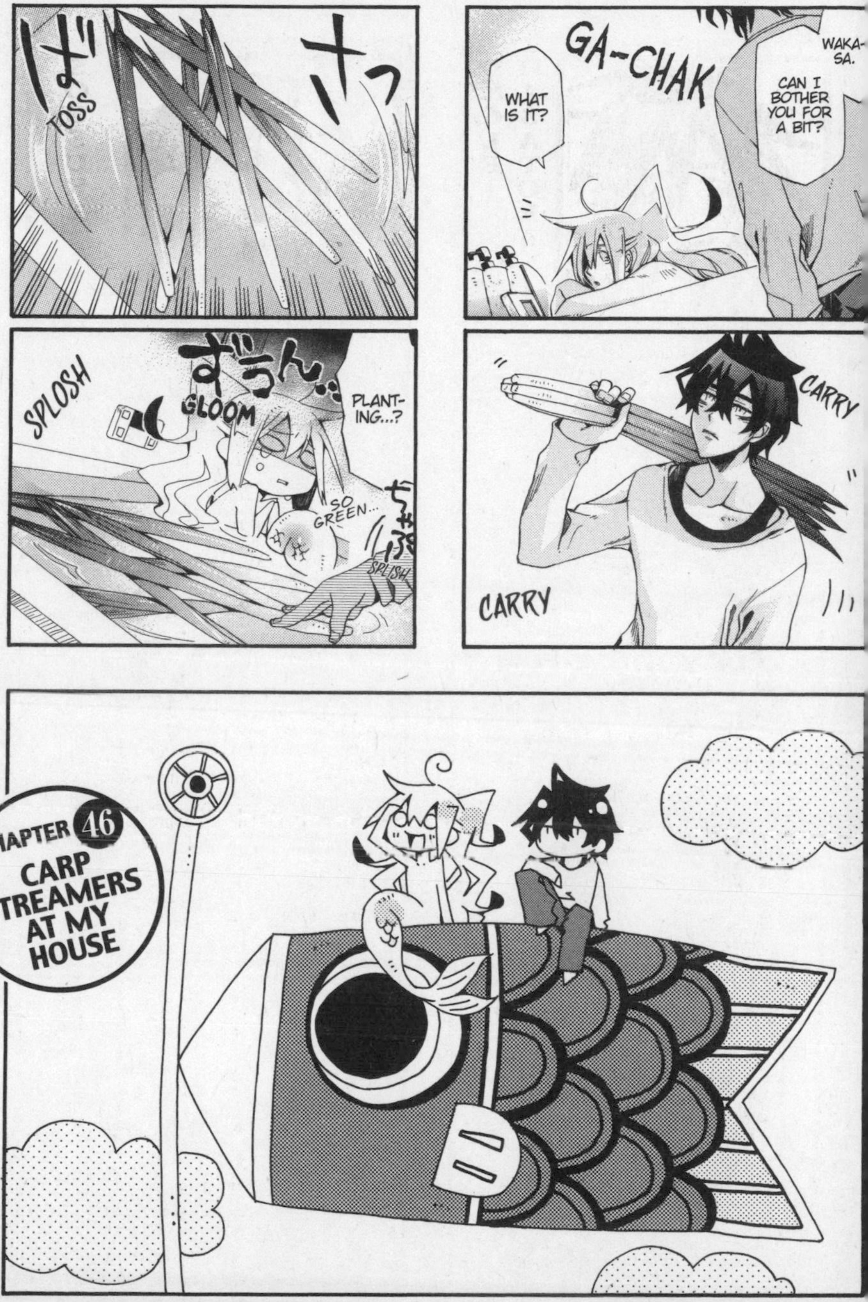
GA-CHAK
WAKA-SA.
CAN I BOTHER YOU FOR A BIT?
WHAT IS IT?
ばさっ
TOSS
CARRY
CARRY
SPLOSH
ずぅん…
GLOOM
PLANT-ING...?
SO GREEN...
ちゃぷ
SPLISH
CHAPTER 46
CARP STREAMERS AT MY HOUSE

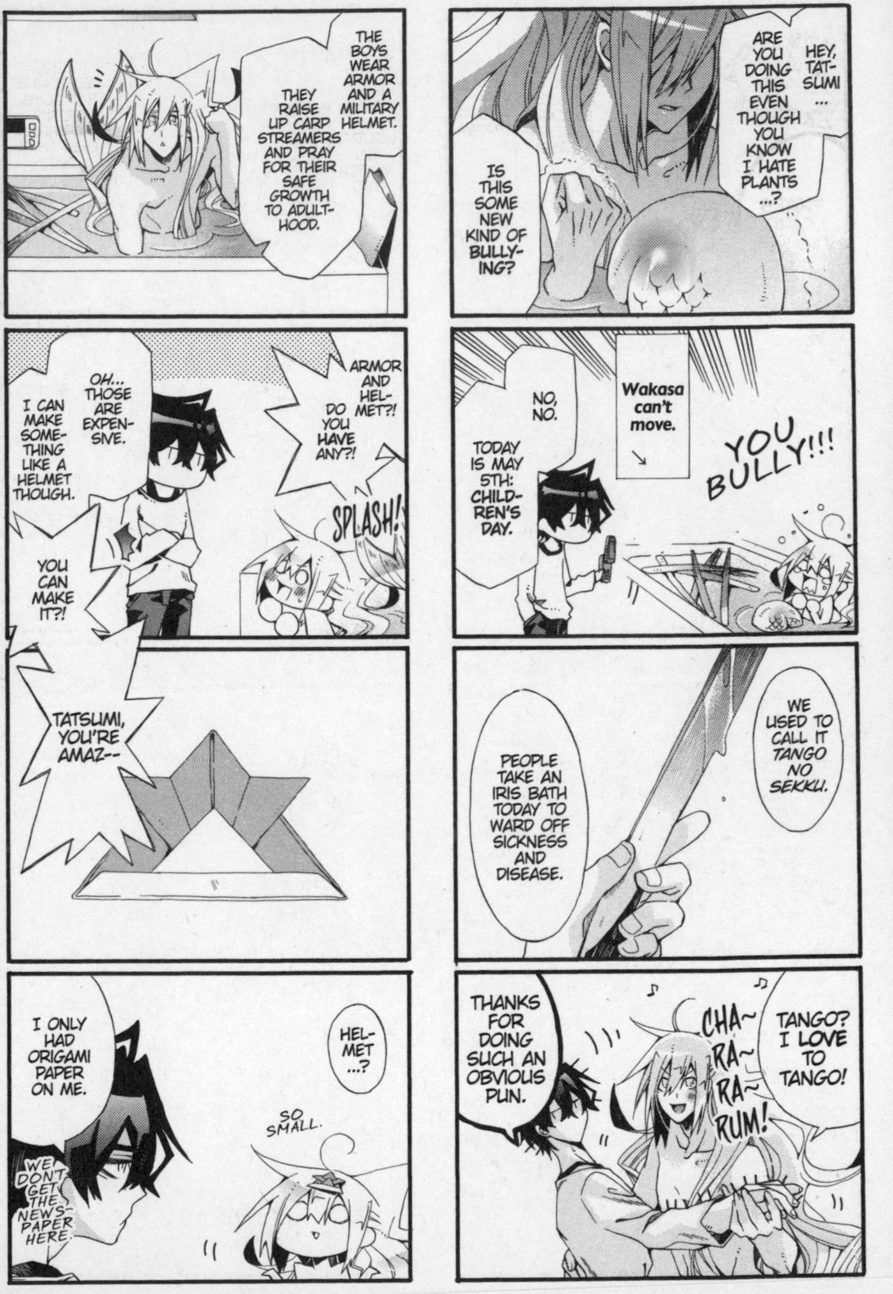
HEY, TATSUMI ...
ARE YOU DOING THIS EVEN THOUGH YOU KNOW I HATE PLANTS ...?
IS THIS SOME NEW KIND OF BULLYING?
Wakasa can't move.
NO, NO.
TODAY IS MAY 5TH: CHILDREN'S DAY.
YOU BULLY!!!
WE USED TO CALL IT *TANGO NO SEKKU.*
PEOPLE TAKE AN IRIS BATH TODAY TO WARD OFF SICKNESS AND DISEASE.
TANGO? I LOVE TO TANGO!
CHA~ RA~ RA~ RUM!
THANKS FOR DOING SUCH AN OBVIOUS PUN.
THE BOYS WEAR ARMOR AND A MILITARY HELMET.
THEY RAISE UP CARP STREAMERS AND PRAY FOR THEIR SAFE GROWTH TO ADULTHOOD.
ARMOR AND HELMET?!
DO YOU HAVE ANY?!
SPLASH!
OH... THOSE ARE EXPENSIVE.
I CAN MAKE SOMETHING LIKE A HELMET THOUGH.
YOU CAN MAKE IT?!
TATSUMI, YOU'RE AMAZ--
HELMET ...?
SO SMALL.
I ONLY HAD ORIGAMI PAPER ON ME.
WE DON'T GET THE NEWSPAPER HERE.

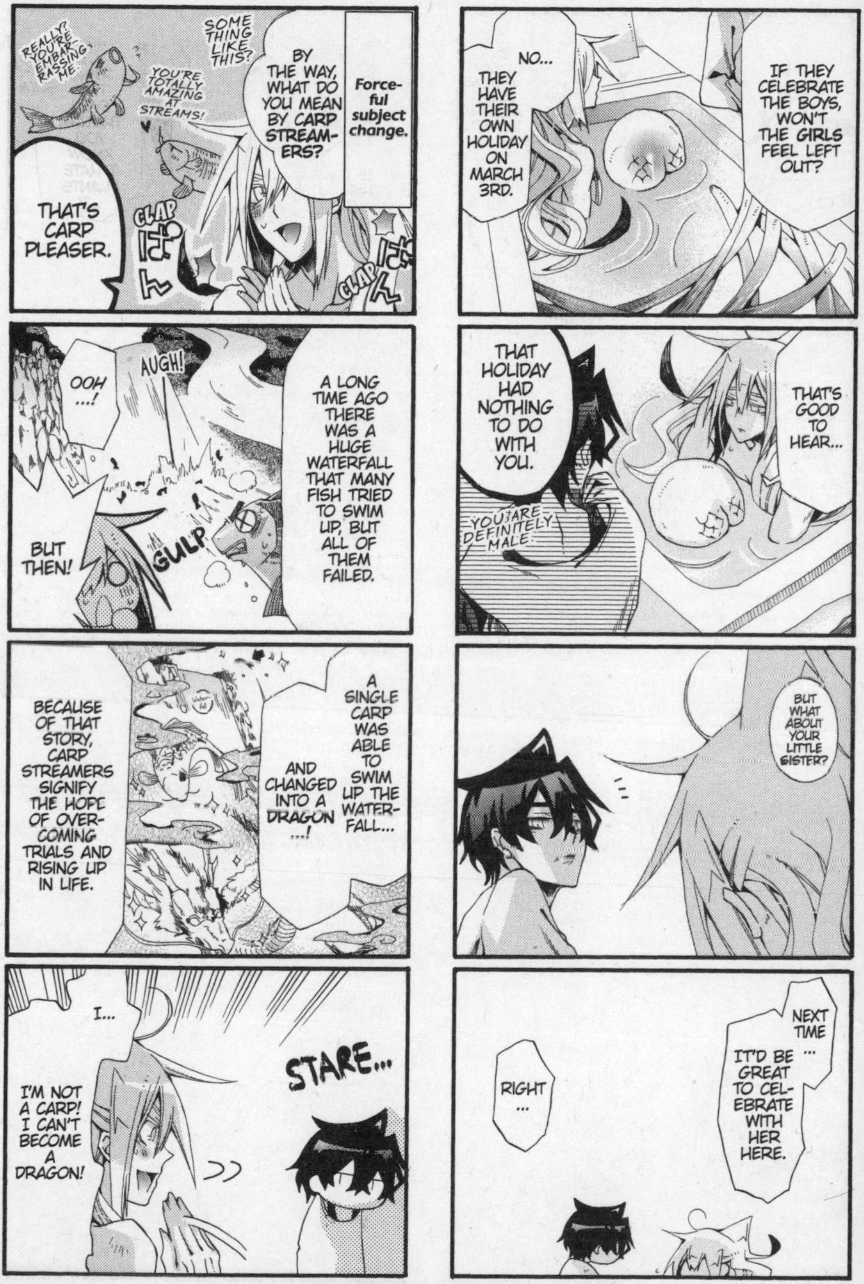
IF THEY CELEBRATE THE BOYS, WON'T THE GIRLS FEEL LEFT OUT?
NO... THEY HAVE THEIR OWN HOLIDAY ON MARCH 3RD.
THAT'S GOOD TO HEAR...
THAT HOLIDAY HAD NOTHING TO DO WITH YOU.
YOU ARE DEFINITELY MALE.
BUT WHAT ABOUT YOUR LITTLE SISTER?
NEXT TIME...
IT'D BE GREAT TO CELEBRATE WITH HER HERE.
RIGHT...
Force-ful subject change.
BY THE WAY, WHAT DO YOU MEAN BY CARP STREAMERS?
SOME THING LIKE THIS?
REALLY? YOU'RE EMBAR-RASSING ME.
YOU'RE TOTALLY AMAZING AT STREAMS!
CLAP ぱん
CLAP ぱん
THAT'S CARP PLEASER.
A LONG TIME AGO THERE WAS A HUGE WATERFALL THAT MANY FISH TRIED TO SWIM UP, BUT ALL OF THEM FAILED.
AUGH!
OOH...!
GULP
BUT THEN!
A SINGLE CARP WAS ABLE TO SWIM UP THE WATER-FALL...
AND CHANGED INTO A DRAGON...!
BECAUSE OF THAT STORY, CARP STREAMERS SIGNIFY THE HOPE OF OVER-COMING TRIALS AND RISING UP IN LIFE.
STARE...
I...
I'M NOT A CARP! I CAN'T BECOME A DRAGON!

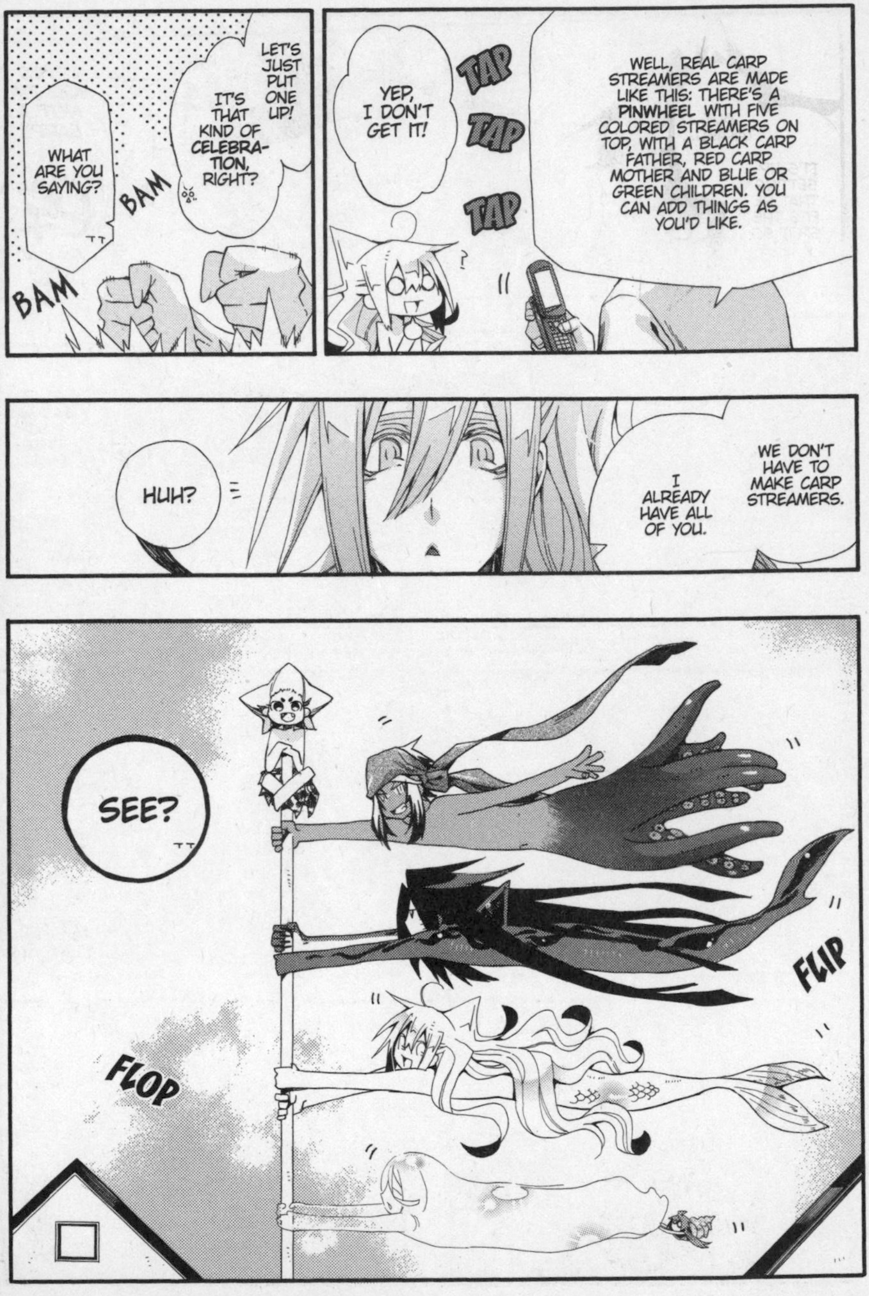
WELL, REAL CARP STREAMERS ARE MADE LIKE THIS: THERE'S A **PINWHEEL** WITH FIVE COLORED STREAMERS ON TOP, WITH A BLACK CARP FATHER, RED CARP MOTHER AND BLUE OR GREEN CHILDREN. YOU CAN ADD THINGS AS YOU'D LIKE.
TAP
TAP
TAP
YEP, I DON'T GET IT!
LET'S JUST PUT ONE UP!
IT'S THAT KIND OF CELEBRATION, RIGHT?
BAM
WHAT ARE YOU SAYING?
BAM
WE DON'T HAVE TO MAKE CARP STREAMERS.
I ALREADY HAVE ALL OF YOU.
HUH?
FLIP
SEE?
FLOP

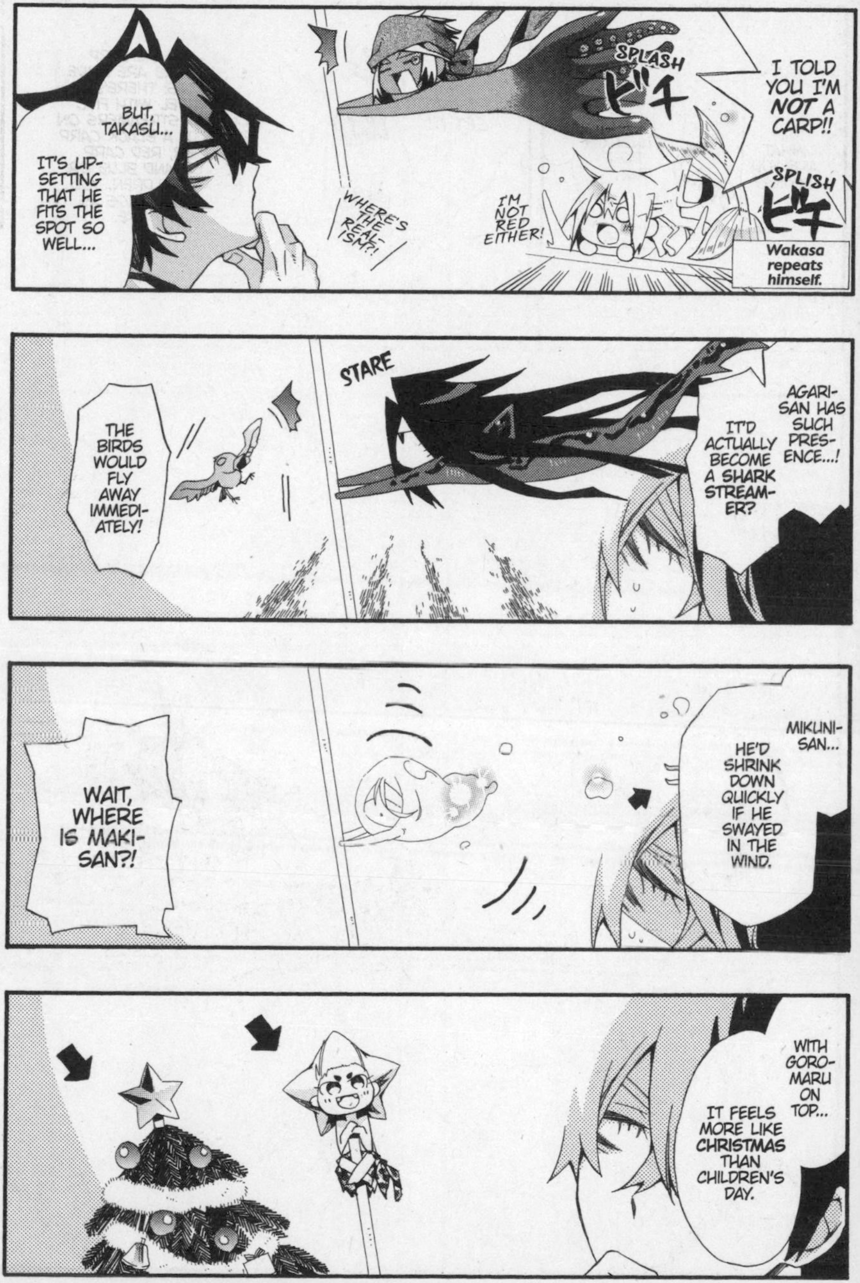
I TOLD YOU I'M NOT A CARP!!
SPLASH
ビチ
SPLISH
ビチ
I'M NOT RED EITHER!
Wakasa repeats himself.
WHERE'S THE REALISM?!
BUT, TAKASU...
IT'S UPSETTING THAT HE FITS THE SPOT SO WELL...
AGARI-SAN HAS SUCH PRESENCE...!
IT'D ACTUALLY BECOME A SHARK STREAMER?
STARE
THE BIRDS WOULD FLY AWAY IMMEDIATELY!
MIKUNI-SAN...
HE'D SHRINK DOWN QUICKLY IF HE SWAYED IN THE WIND.
WAIT, WHERE IS MAKI-SAN?!
WITH GOROMARU ON TOP...
IT FEELS MORE LIKE CHRISTMAS THAN CHILDREN'S DAY.

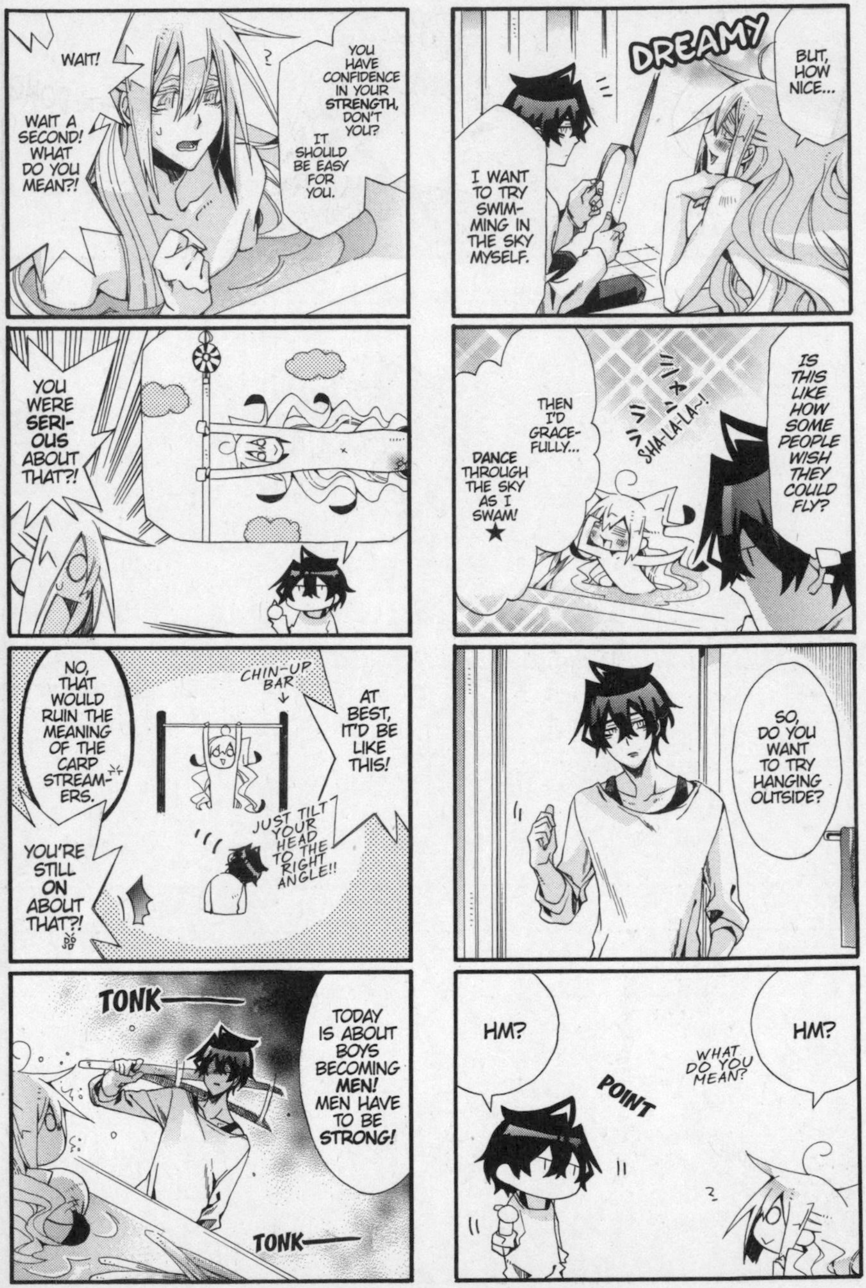
DREAMY
BUT, HOW NICE...
I WANT TO TRY SWIMMING IN THE SKY MYSELF.
IS THIS LIKE HOW SOME PEOPLE WISH THEY COULD FLY?
SHA-LA-LA~!
THEN I'D GRACEFULLY...
DANCE THROUGH THE SKY AS I SWAM! ★
SO, DO YOU WANT TO TRY HANGING OUTSIDE?
HM?
HM?
WHAT DO YOU MEAN?
POINT
WAIT!
?
YOU HAVE CONFIDENCE IN YOUR STRENGTH, DON'T YOU?
IT SHOULD BE EASY FOR YOU.
WAIT A SECOND! WHAT DO YOU MEAN?!
YOU WERE SERIOUS ABOUT THAT?!
AT BEST, IT'D BE LIKE THIS!
CHIN-UP BAR
NO, THAT WOULD RUIN THE MEANING OF THE CARP STREAMERS.
JUST TILT YOUR HEAD TO THE RIGHT ANGLE!!
YOU'RE STILL ON ABOUT THAT?!
TONK
TODAY IS ABOUT BOYS BECOMING MEN! MEN HAVE TO BE STRONG!
TONK

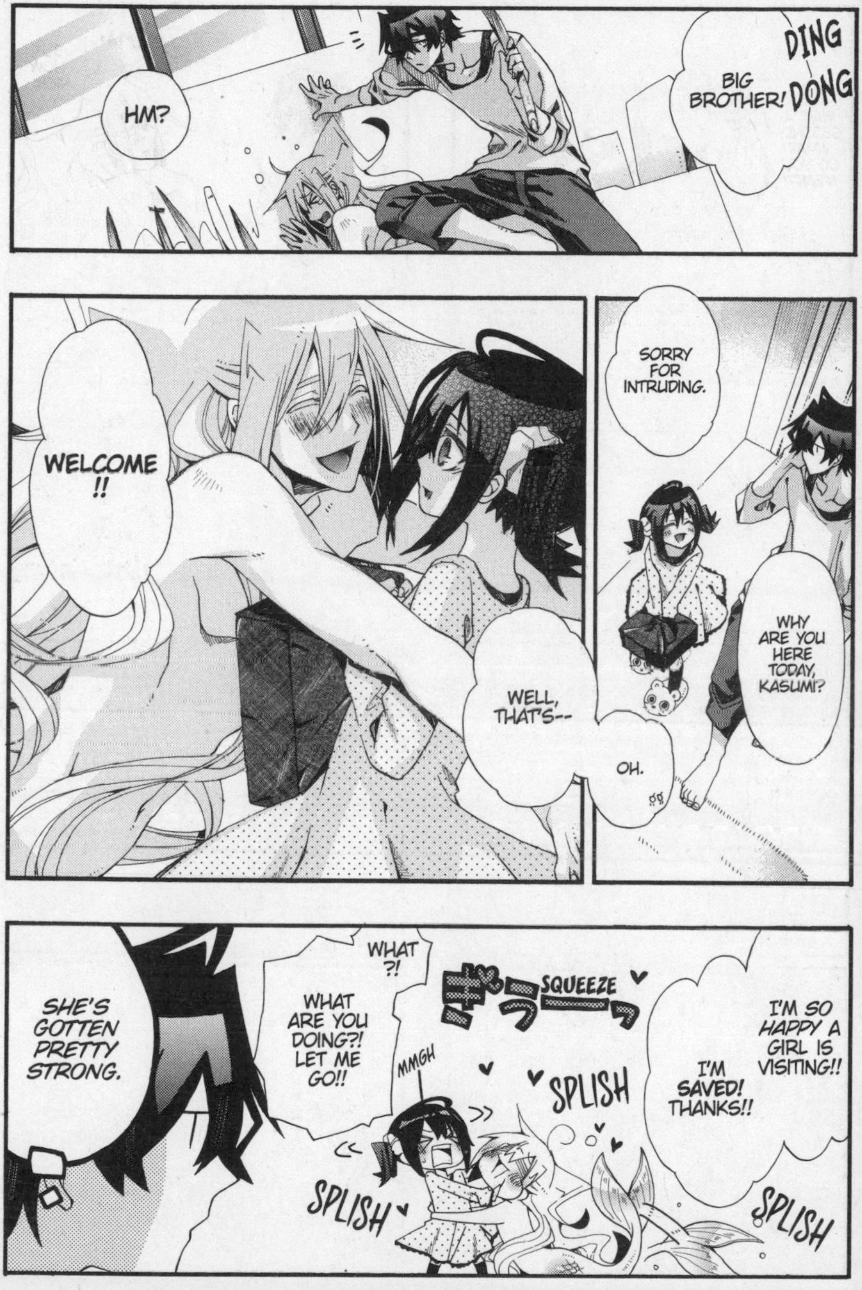
DING DONG
BIG BROTHER!
HM?
SORRY FOR INTRUDING.
WHY ARE YOU HERE TODAY, KASUMI?
WELL, THAT'S--
OH.
WELCOME!!
I'M SO HAPPY A GIRL IS VISITING!!
I'M SAVED! THANKS!!
SPLISH
SQUEEZE
SPLISH
WHAT?!
WHAT ARE YOU DOING?! LET ME GO!!
MMGH
SPLISH
SHE'S GOTTEN PRETTY STRONG.

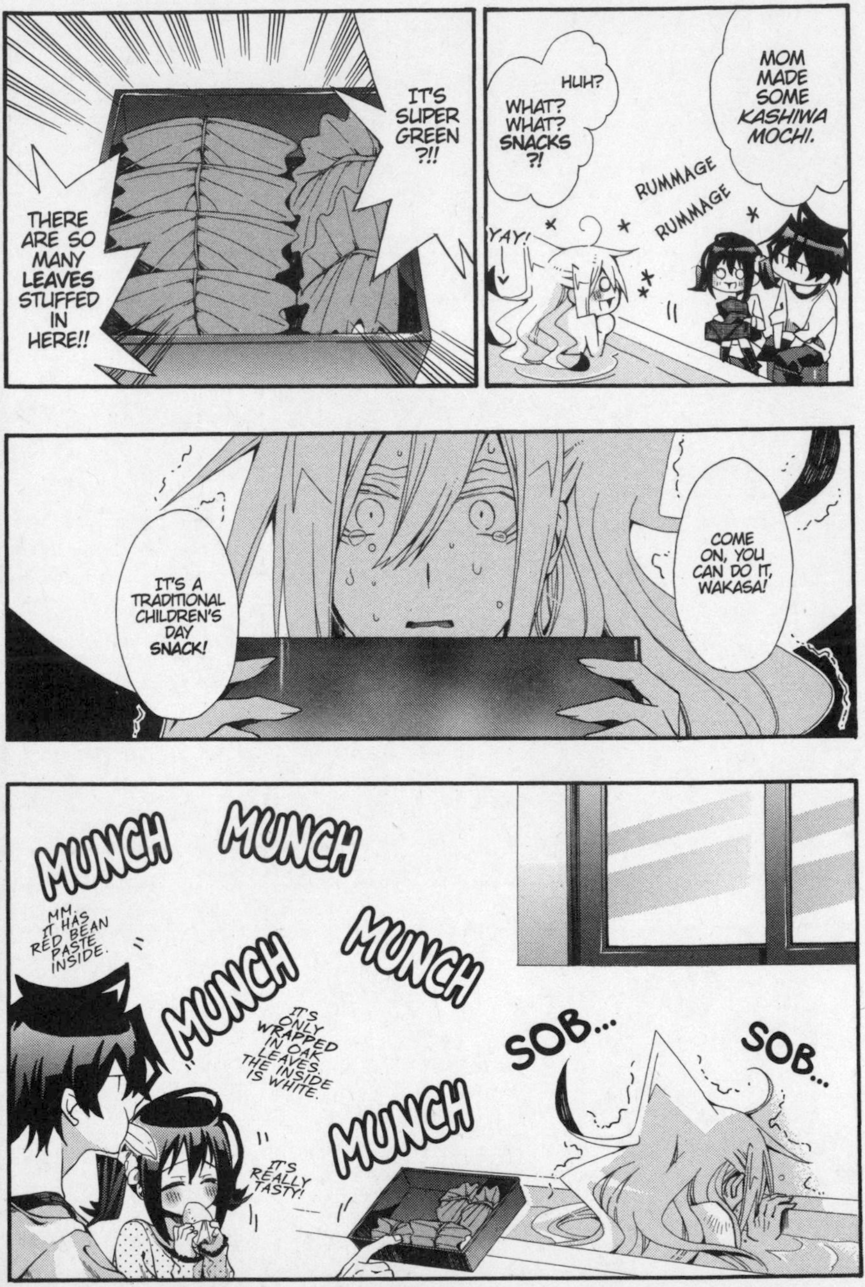
MOM MADE SOME KASHIWA MOCHI.
HUH? WHAT? WHAT? SNACKS?!
RUMMAGE RUMMAGE
YAY!
IT'S SUPER GREEN?!!
THERE ARE SO MANY LEAVES STUFFED IN HERE!!
COME ON, YOU CAN DO IT, WAKASA!
IT'S A TRADITIONAL CHILDREN'S DAY SNACK!
SOB... SOB...
MUNCH MUNCH
MM. IT HAS RED BEAN PASTE INSIDE.
MUNCH MUNCH
IT'S ONLY WRAPPED IN OAK LEAVES. THE INSIDE IS WHITE.
MUNCH
IT'S REALLY TASTY!

Merman in My Tub

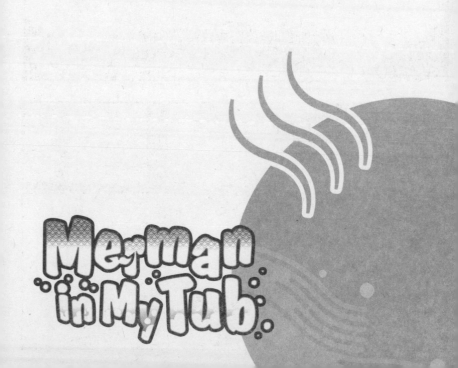

オレん家（ち）のフロ事情

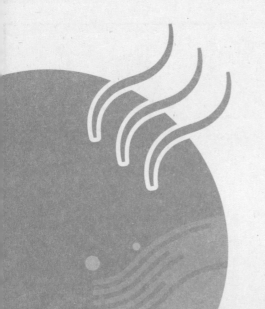

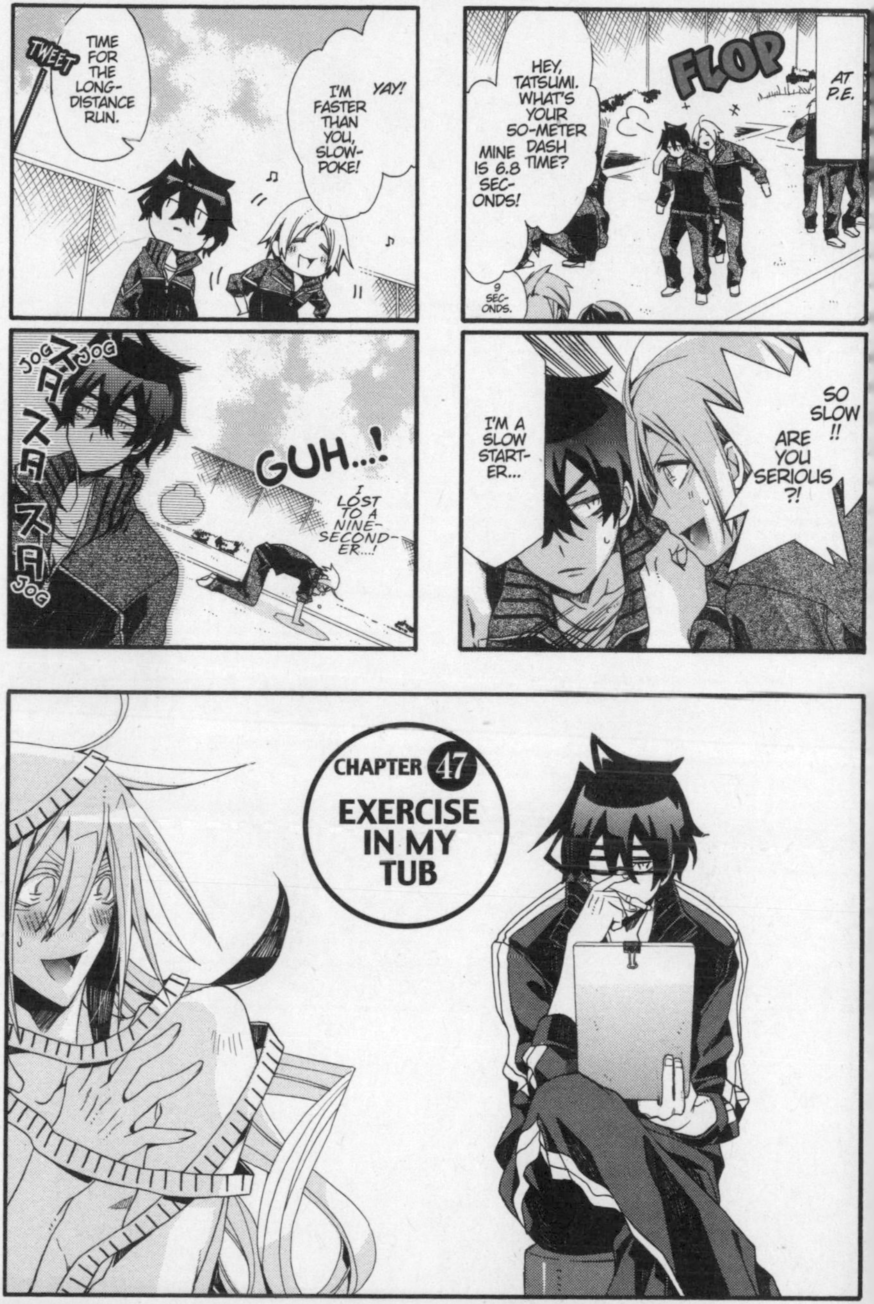
AT P.E.
FLOP
HEY, TATSUMI. WHAT'S YOUR 50-METER DASH TIME?
MINE IS 6.8 SECONDS!
9 SECONDS.
TWEET
TIME FOR THE LONG-DISTANCE RUN.
YAY!
I'M FASTER THAN YOU, SLOW-POKE!
SO SLOW!!
ARE YOU SERIOUS?!
I'M A SLOW STARTER...
JOG JOG
スタスタ
JOG
GUH...!
I LOST TO A NINE-SECONDER...!
CHAPTER 47
EXERCISE IN MY TUB

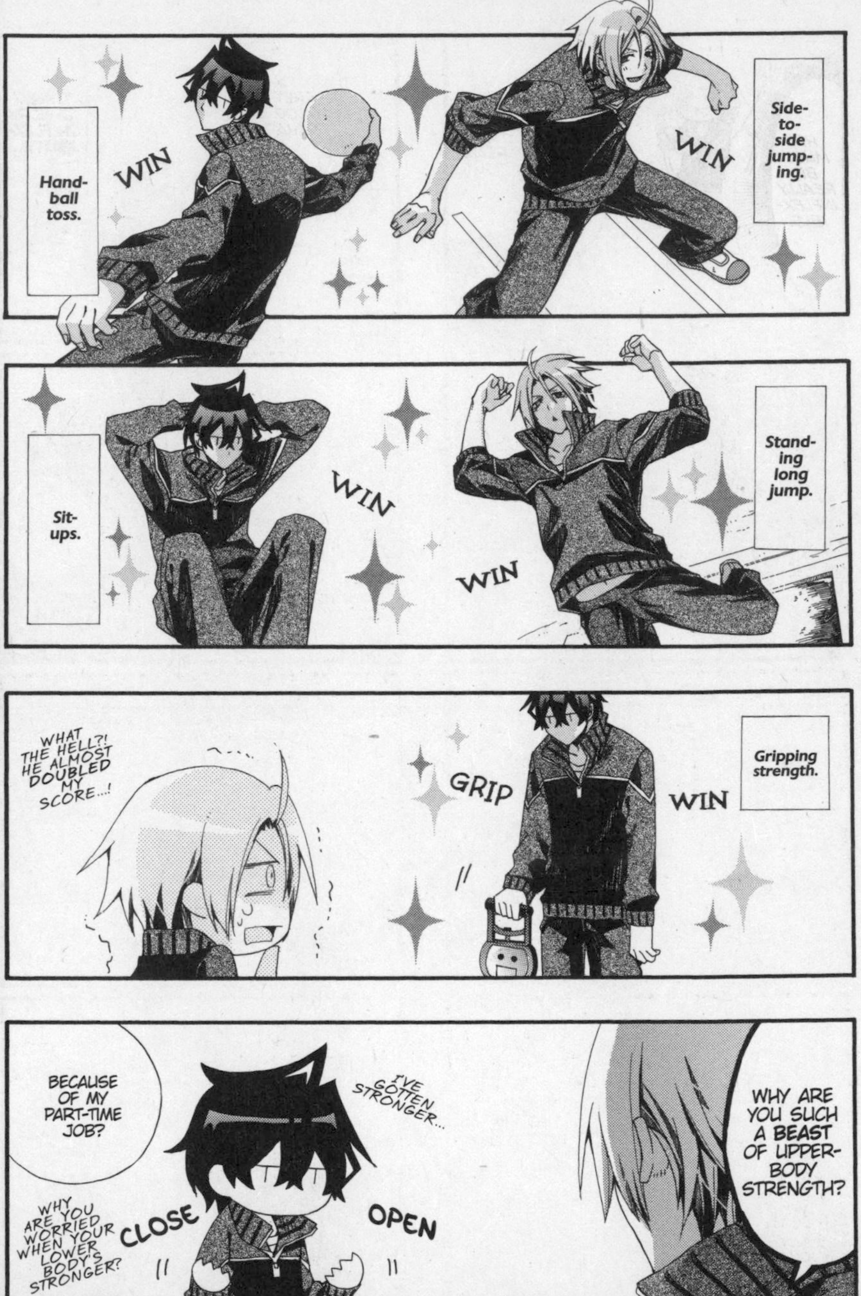
Side-to-side jumping.
WIN
WIN
Handball toss.
Standing long jump.
WIN
WIN
Sit-ups.
Gripping strength.
WIN
GRIP
WHAT THE HELL?! HE ALMOST DOUBLED MY SCORE...!
WHY ARE YOU SUCH A BEAST OF UPPER-BODY STRENGTH?
I'VE GOTTEN STRONGER...
BECAUSE OF MY PART-TIME JOB?
OPEN
CLOSE
WHY ARE YOU WORRIED WHEN YOUR LOWER BODY'S STRONGER?

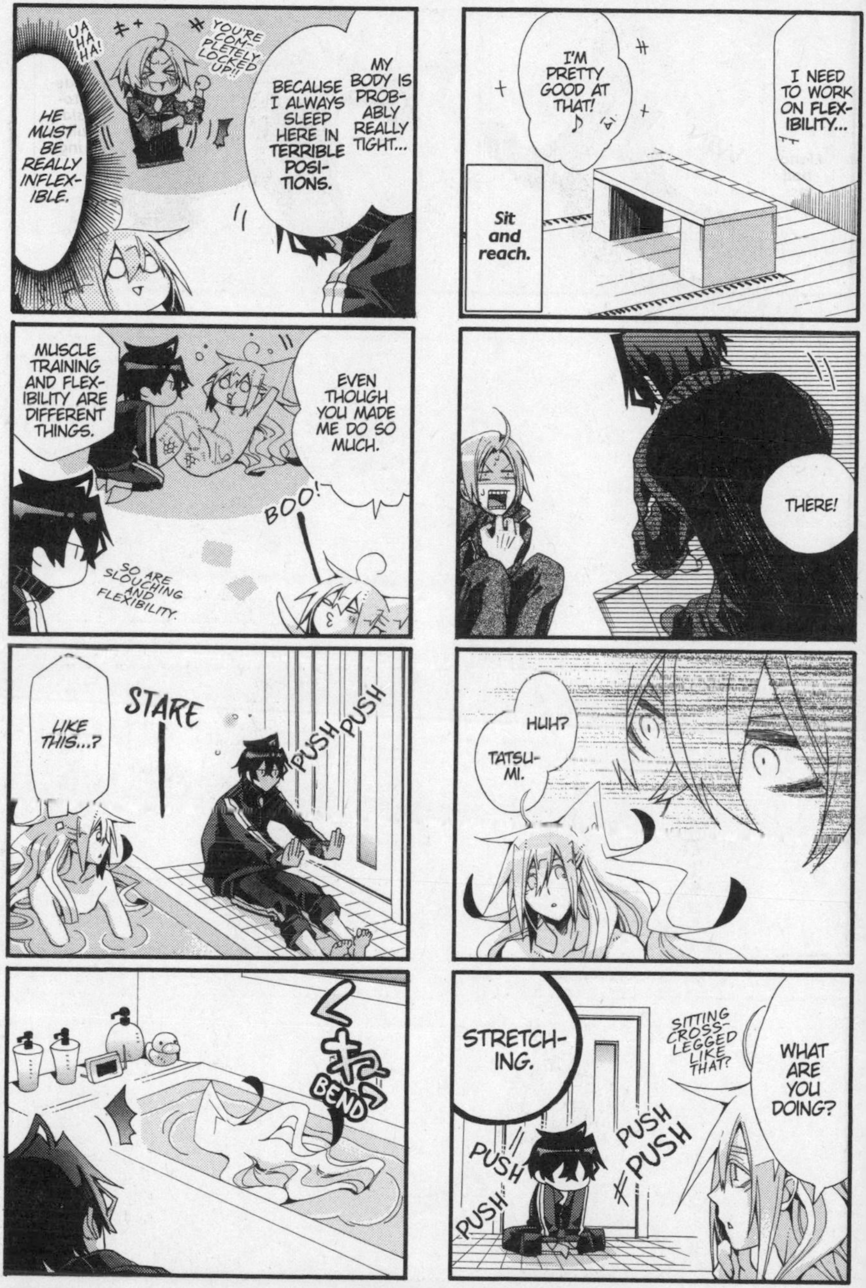
I NEED TO WORK ON FLEXIBILITY...
I'M PRETTY GOOD AT THAT! ♪
Sit and reach.
MY BODY IS PROBABLY REALLY TIGHT...
BECAUSE I ALWAYS SLEEP HERE IN TERRIBLE POSITIONS.
YOU'RE COMPLETELY LOCKED UP!!
UA HA HA!
HE MUST BE REALLY INFLEXIBLE.
THERE!
EVEN THOUGH YOU MADE ME DO SO MUCH.
MUSCLE TRAINING AND FLEXIBILITY ARE DIFFERENT THINGS.
BOO!
SO ARE SLOUCHING AND FLEXIBILITY.
HUH?
TATSUMI.
PUSH PUSH
STARE
LIKE THIS...?
WHAT ARE YOU DOING?
SITTING CROSS-LEGGED LIKE THAT?
STRETCHING.
PUSH PUSH
PUSH PUSH
BEND

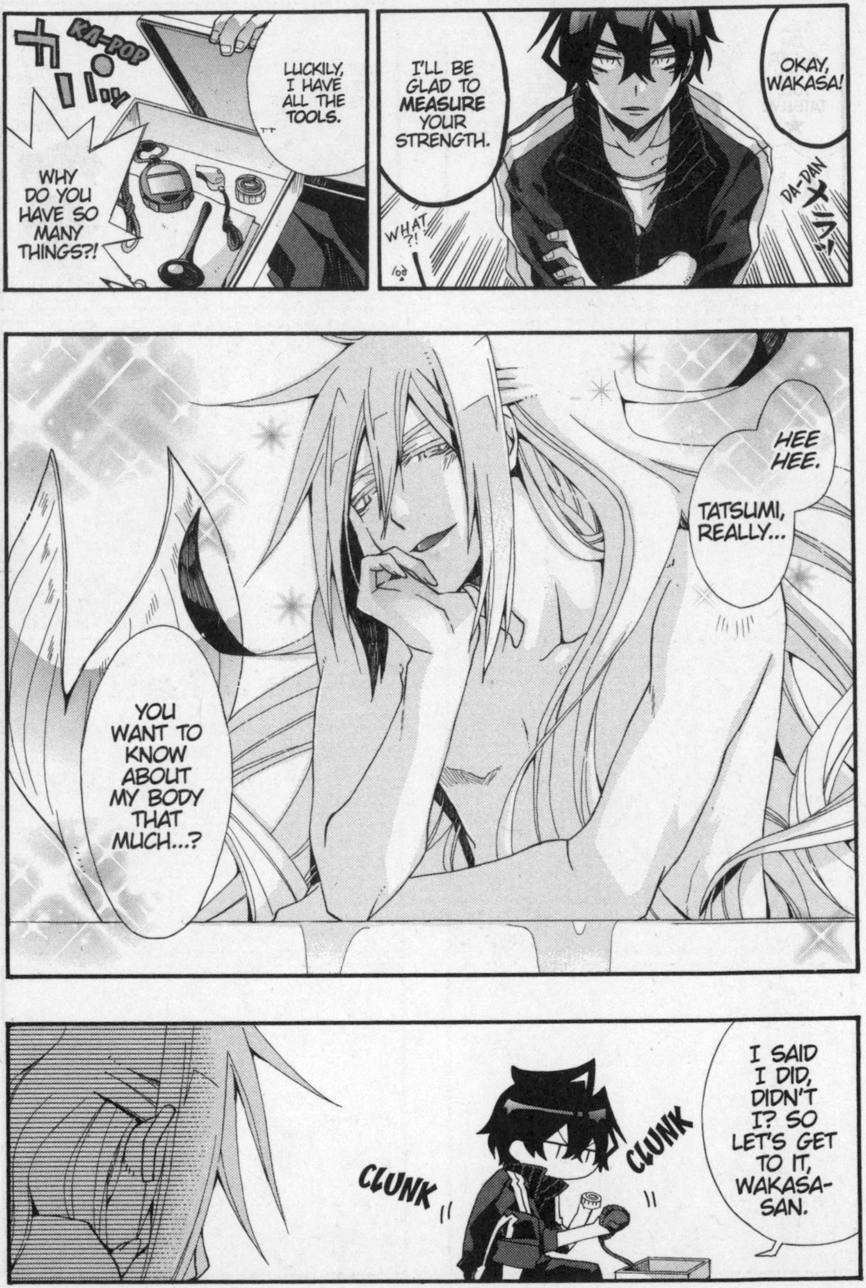
OKAY, WAKASA!
DA-DAN
I'LL BE GLAD TO MEASURE YOUR STRENGTH.
WHAT?!
LUCKILY, I HAVE ALL THE TOOLS.
KA-POP
WHY DO YOU HAVE SO MANY THINGS?!
HEE HEE.
TATSUMI, REALLY...
YOU WANT TO KNOW ABOUT MY BODY THAT MUCH...?
I SAID I DID, DIDN'T I? SO LET'S GET TO IT, WAKASA-SAN.
CLUNK
CLUNK

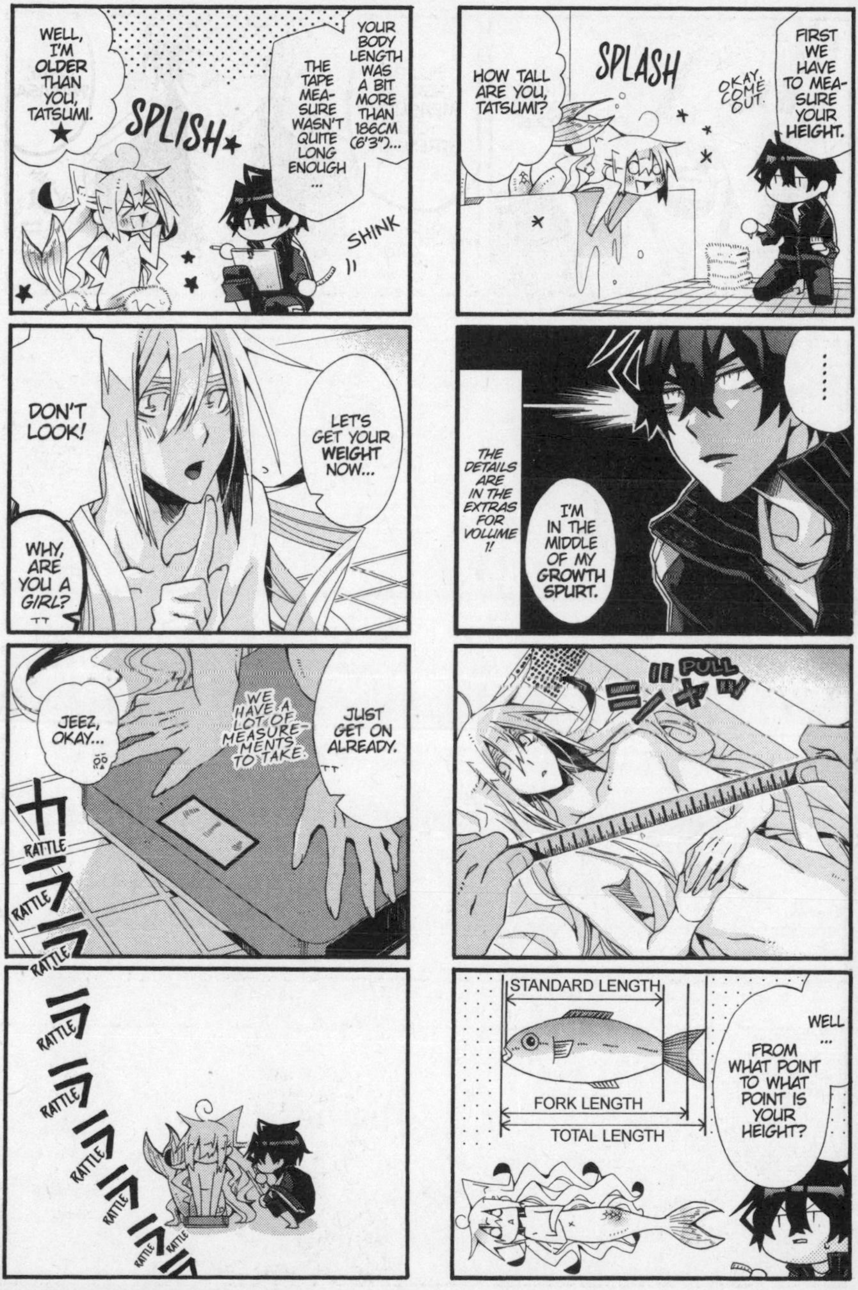
FIRST WE HAVE TO MEA-SURE YOUR HEIGHT.
OKAY, COME OUT.
SPLASH
HOW TALL ARE YOU, TATSUMI?
YOUR BODY LENGTH WAS A BIT MORE THAN 186CM (6'3")...
THE TAPE MEA-SURE WASN'T QUITE LONG ENOUGH...
WELL, I'M OLDER THAN YOU, TATSUMI. ★
SPLISH★
SHINK
......
I'M IN THE MIDDLE OF MY GROWTH SPURT.
THE DETAILS ARE IN THE EXTRAS FOR VOLUME 1!
LET'S GET YOUR WEIGHT NOW...
DON'T LOOK!
WHY, ARE YOU A GIRL?
PULL
JUST GET ON ALREADY.
WE HAVE A LOT OF MEASURE-MENTS TO TAKE.
JEEZ, OKAY...
RATTLE
RATTLE
RATTLE
WELL...
FROM WHAT POINT TO WHAT POINT IS YOUR HEIGHT?
STANDARD LENGTH
FORK LENGTH
TOTAL LENGTH
RATTLE
RATTLE
RATTLE
RATTLE
RATTLE

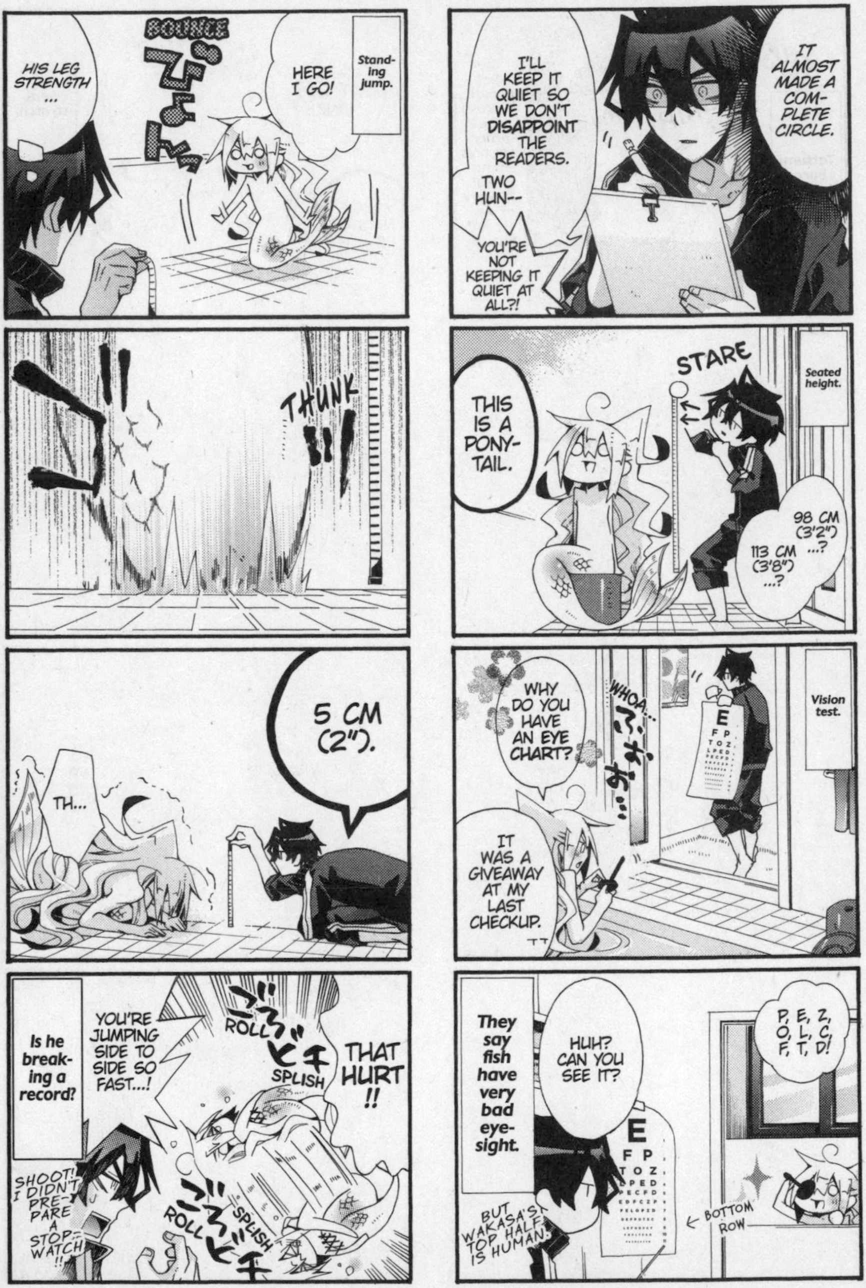
IT ALMOST MADE A COMPLETE CIRCLE.
I'LL KEEP IT QUIET SO WE DON'T DISAPPOINT THE READERS.
TWO HUN--
YOU'RE NOT KEEPING IT QUIET AT ALL?!
Seated height.
STARE
THIS IS A PONYTAIL.
98 CM (3'2") ...?
113 CM (3'8") ...?
Vision test.
WHOA... ふぉぉ...
WHY DO YOU HAVE AN EYE CHART?
IT WAS A GIVEAWAY AT MY LAST CHECKUP.
They say fish have very bad eyesight.
P, E, Z, O, L, C, F, T, D!
HUH? CAN YOU SEE IT?
← BOTTOM ROW
BUT WAKASA'S TOP HALF IS HUMAN!
Standing jump.
HERE I GO!
BOUNCE
ぴょ~ん
HIS LEG STRENGTH...
!!
THUNK
!!
5 CM (2").
TH...
Is he breaking a record?
YOU'RE JUMPING SIDE TO SIDE SO FAST...!
ごろ ROLL
ビチ SPLISH
THAT HURT!!
ごろ ROLL
ビチ SPLISH
SHOOT! I DIDN'T PREPARE A STOPWATCH!!

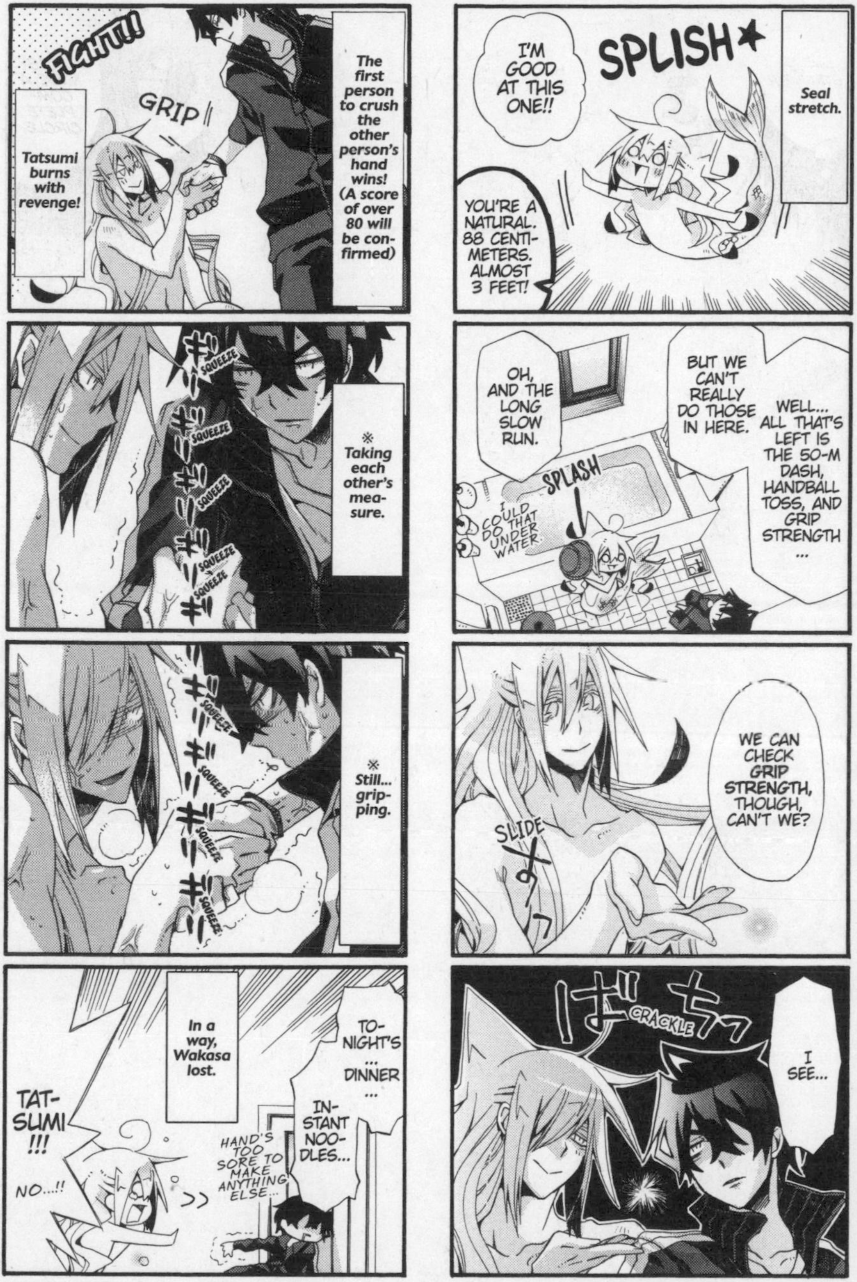
Seal stretch.
SPLISH★
I'M GOOD AT THIS ONE!!
YOU'RE A NATURAL. 88 CENTIMETERS. ALMOST 3 FEET!
WELL... ALL THAT'S LEFT IS THE 50-M DASH, HANDBALL TOSS, AND GRIP STRENGTH...
BUT WE CAN'T REALLY DO THOSE IN HERE.
OH, AND THE LONG SLOW RUN.
SPLASH
I COULD DO THAT UNDER WATER
WE CAN CHECK GRIP STRENGTH, THOUGH, CAN'T WE?
SLIDE
I SEE...
ばちっ
CRACKLE
The first person to crush the other person's hand wins! (A score of over 80 will be confirmed)
FIGHT!!
GRIP
Tatsumi burns with revenge!
※ Taking each other's measure.
SQUEEZE
SQUEEZE
SQUEEZE
SQUEEZE
SQUEEZE
※ Still... grip-ping.
SQUEEZE
SQUEEZE
SQUEEZE
SQUEEZE
SQUEEZE
TO-NIGHT'S ... DINNER ...
In a way, Wakasa lost.
IN-STANT NOO-DLES...
HAND'S TOO SORE TO MAKE ANYTHING ELSE...
TAT-SUMI!!!
NO...!!

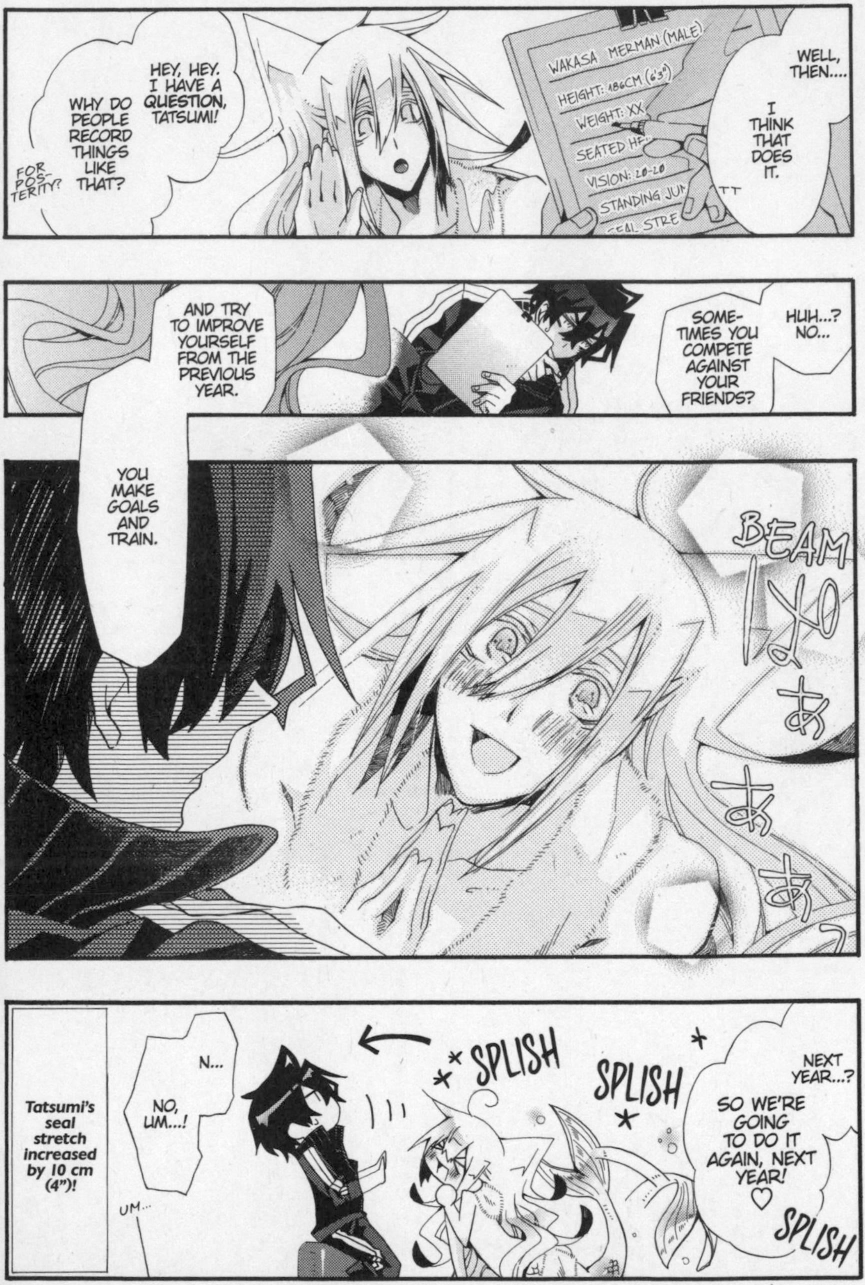
WELL, THEN....
I THINK THAT DOES IT.
WAKASA MERMAN (MALE)
HEIGHT: 186CM (6'3")
WEIGHT: XX
VISION: 20-20
HEY, HEY. I HAVE A QUESTION, TATSUMI!
WHY DO PEOPLE RECORD THINGS LIKE THAT?
FOR POSTERITY?
HUH...? NO...
SOMETIMES YOU COMPETE AGAINST YOUR FRIENDS?
AND TRY TO IMPROVE YOURSELF FROM THE PREVIOUS YEAR.
YOU MAKE GOALS AND TRAIN.
BEAM
ぱあああっ
NEXT YEAR...?
SO WE'RE GOING TO DO IT AGAIN, NEXT YEAR! ♡
SPLISH
SPLISH
SPLISH
N...
NO, UM...!
UM...
Tatsumi's seal stretch increased by 10 cm (4")!

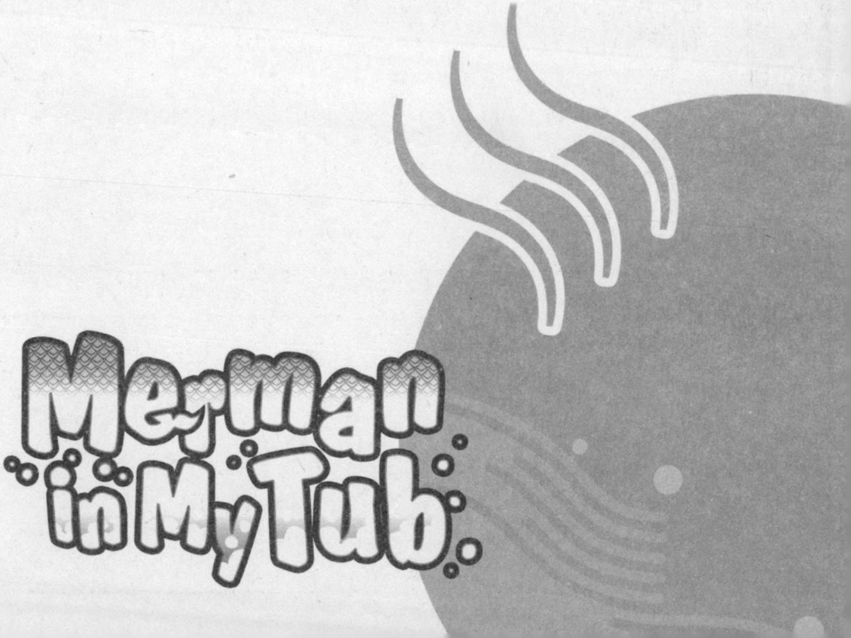

Merman in My Tub

オレん家（ち）のフロ事情

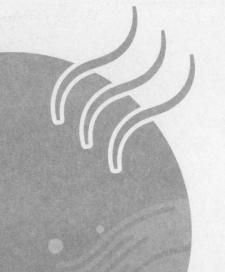

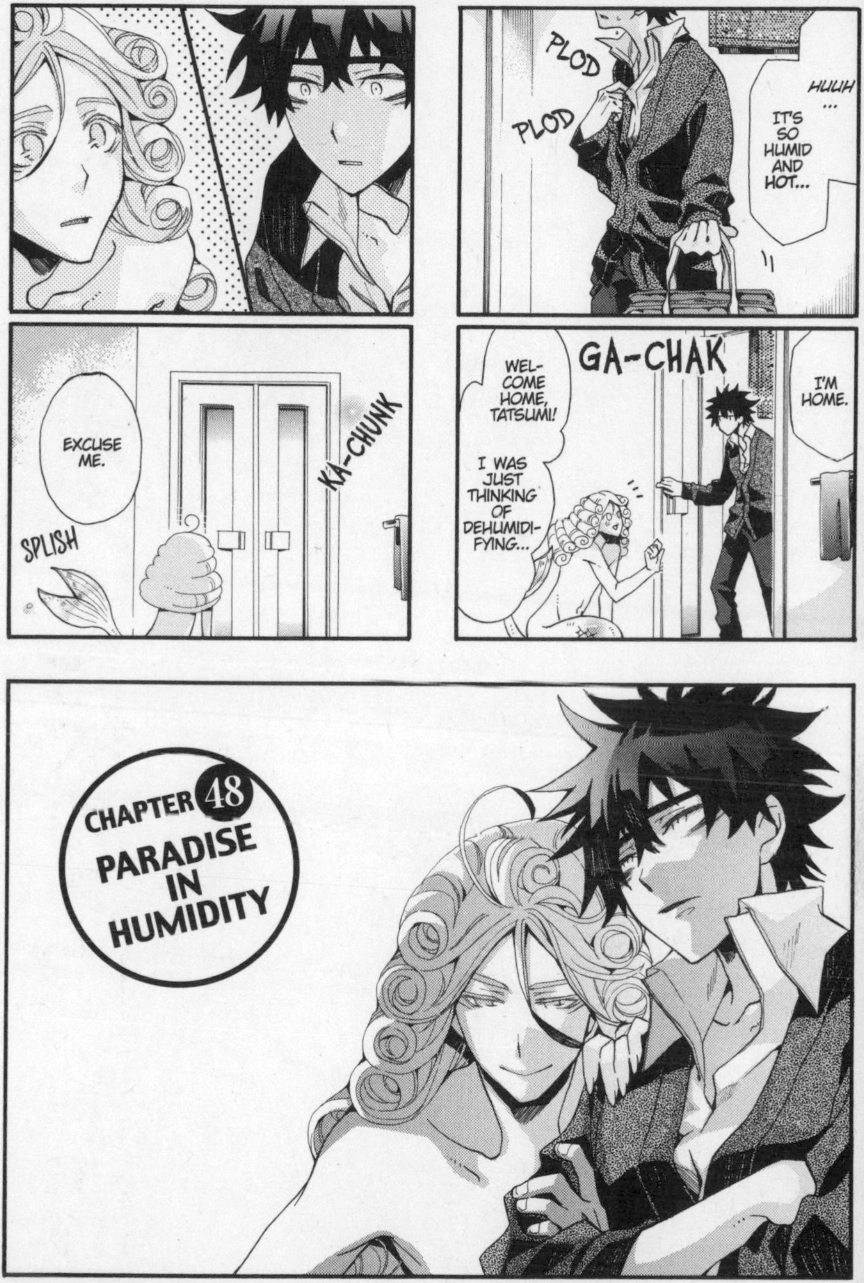
PLOD
PLOD
HUUH... IT'S SO HUMID AND HOT...
I'M HOME.
GA-CHAK
WEL-COME HOME, TATSUMI!
I WAS JUST THINKING OF DEHUMIDI-FYING...
KA-CHUNK
EXCUSE ME.
SPLISH
CHAPTER 48
PARADISE IN HUMIDITY

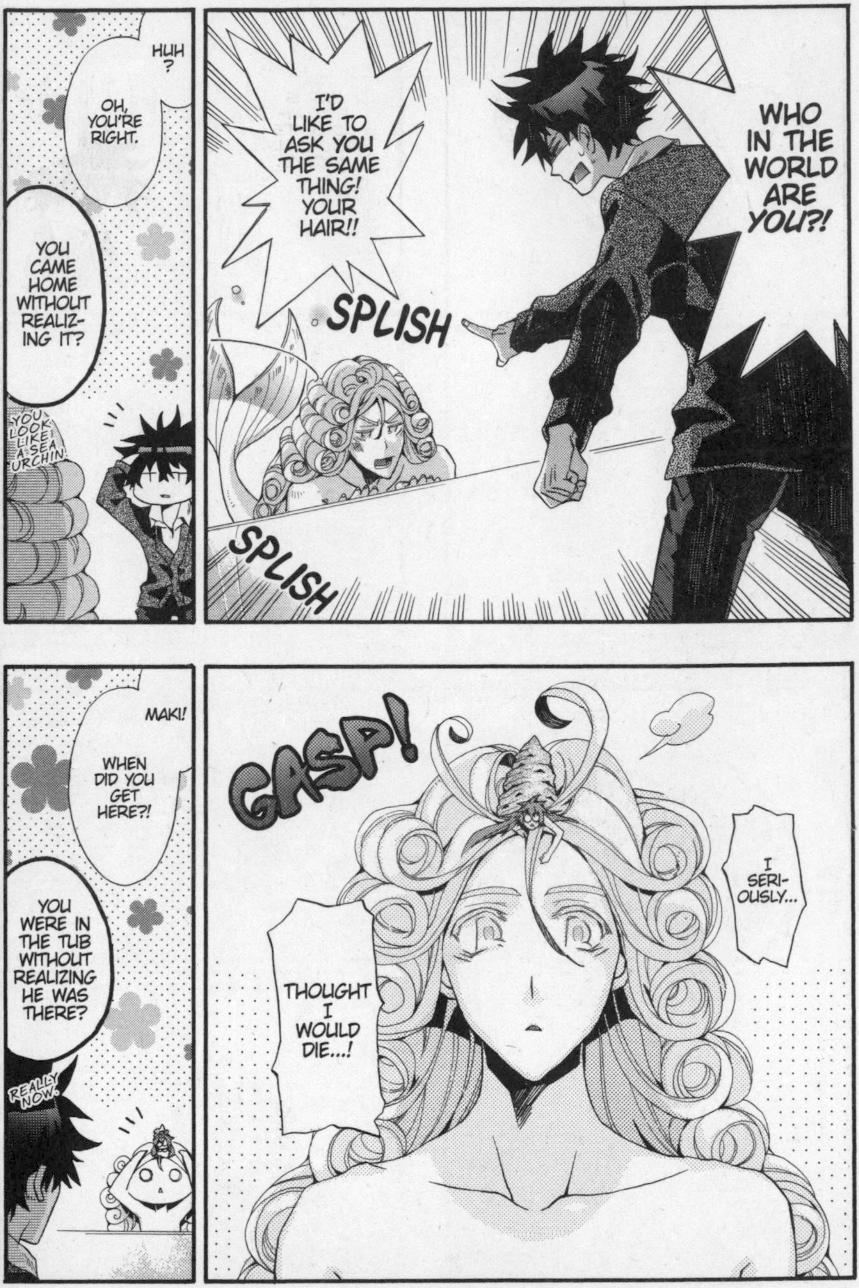
WHO IN THE WORLD ARE YOU?!
I'D LIKE TO ASK YOU THE SAME THING! YOUR HAIR!!
SPLISH
SPLISH
HUH?
OH, YOU'RE RIGHT.
YOU CAME HOME WITHOUT REALIZING IT?
YOU LOOK LIKE A SEA URCHIN.
GASP!
I SERIOUSLY...
THOUGHT I WOULD DIE...!
MAKI!
WHEN DID YOU GET HERE?!
YOU WERE IN THE TUB WITHOUT REALIZING HE WAS THERE?
REALLY NOW.

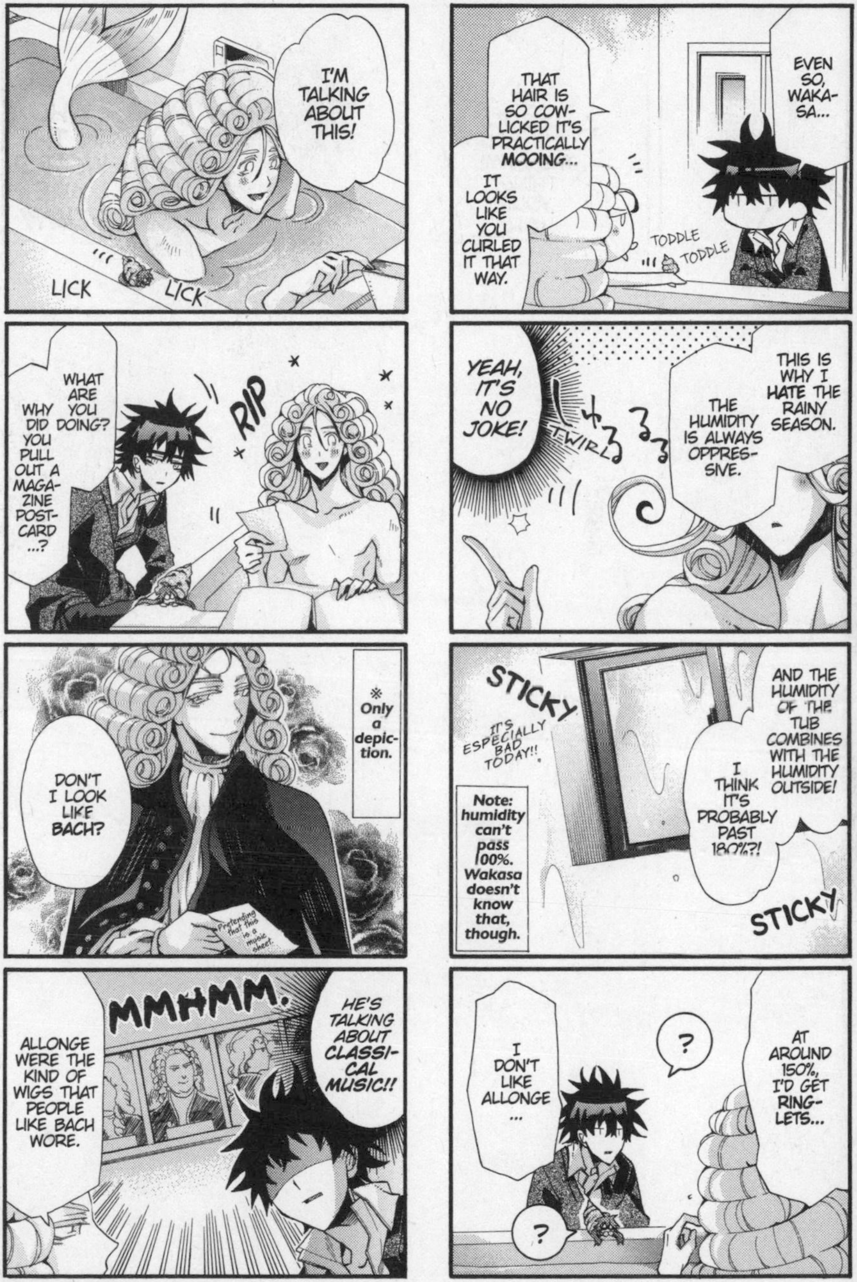
EVEN SO, WAKASA...
THAT HAIR IS SO COWLICKED IT'S PRACTICALLY MOOING...
IT LOOKS LIKE YOU CURLED IT THAT WAY.
TODDLE TODDLE
THIS IS WHY I HATE THE RAINY SEASON.
THE HUMIDITY IS ALWAYS OPPRESSIVE.
YEAH, IT'S NO JOKE!
TWIRL
AND THE HUMIDITY OF THE TUB COMBINES WITH THE HUMIDITY OUTSIDE!
I THINK IT'S PROBABLY PAST 180%?!
STICKY
IT'S ESPECIALLY BAD TODAY!!
Note: humidity can't pass 100%. Wakasa doesn't know that, though.
STICKY
AT AROUND 150%, I'D GET RINGLETS...
?
I DON'T LIKE ALLONGE...
?
I'M TALKING ABOUT THIS!
LICK LICK
WHAT ARE YOU DOING? WHY DID YOU PULL OUT A MAGAZINE POSTCARD...?
RIP
※ Only a depiction.
DON'T I LOOK LIKE BACH?
Pretending that this is a music sheet.
HE'S TALKING ABOUT CLASSICAL MUSIC!!
MMHMM.
ALLONGE WERE THE KIND OF WIGS THAT PEOPLE LIKE BACH WORE.

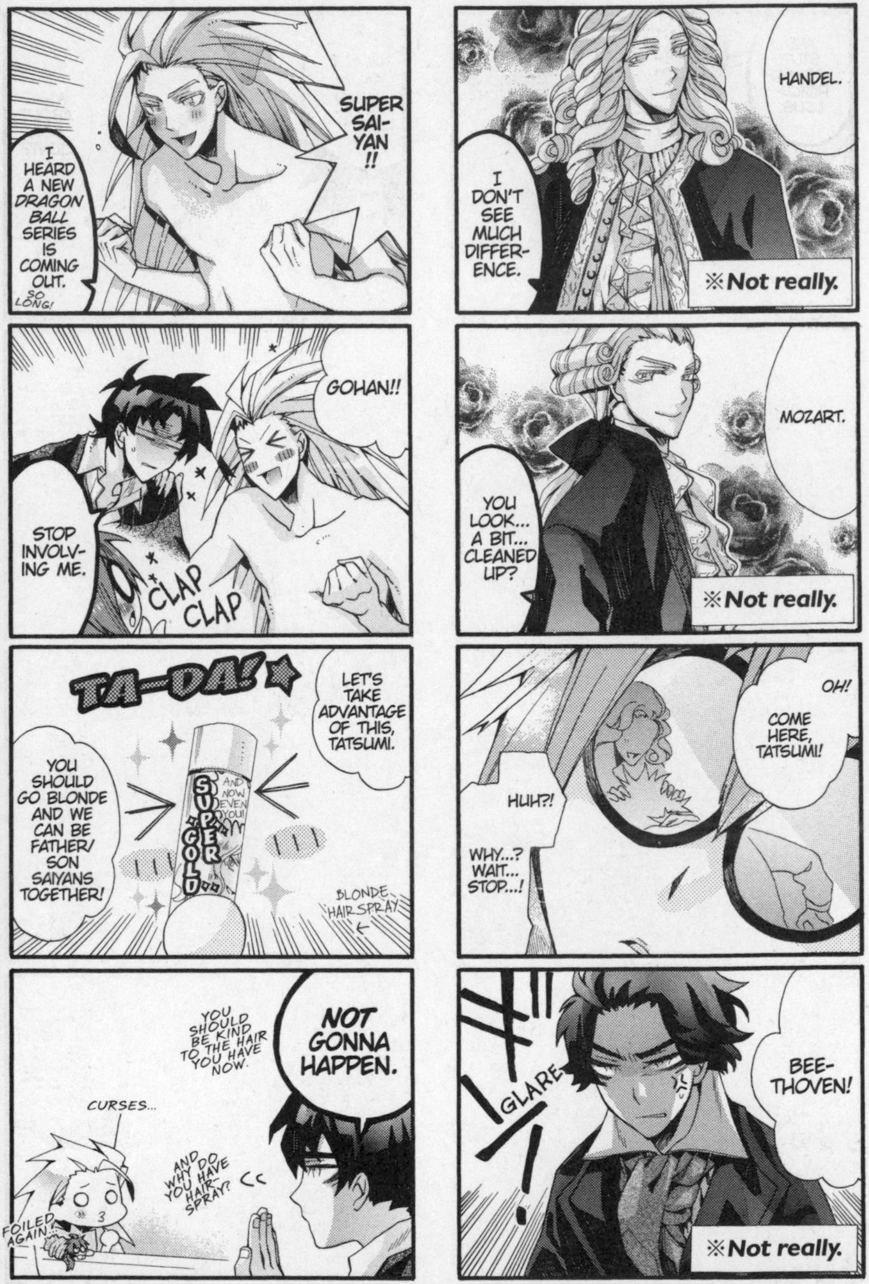
HANDEL.
I DON'T SEE MUCH DIFFERENCE.
※Not really.
MOZART.
YOU LOOK... A BIT... CLEANED UP?
※Not really.
OH!
COME HERE, TATSUMI!
HUH?!
WHY...? WAIT... STOP...!
BEE-THOVEN!
GLARE
※Not really.
SUPER SAI-YAN!!
I HEARD A NEW DRAGON BALL SERIES IS COMING OUT.
SO LONG!
GOHAN!!
STOP INVOLV-ING ME.
CLAP CLAP
TA-DA!
LET'S TAKE ADVANTAGE OF THIS, TATSUMI.
YOU SHOULD GO BLONDE AND WE CAN BE FATHER/SON SAIYANS TOGETHER!
SUPER GOLD
AND NOW EVEN YOU!
BLONDE HAIRSPRAY
NOT GONNA HAPPEN.
YOU SHOULD BE KIND TO THE HAIR YOU HAVE NOW.
CURSES...
AND WHY DO YOU HAVE HAIR-SPRAY?
FOILED AGAIN...

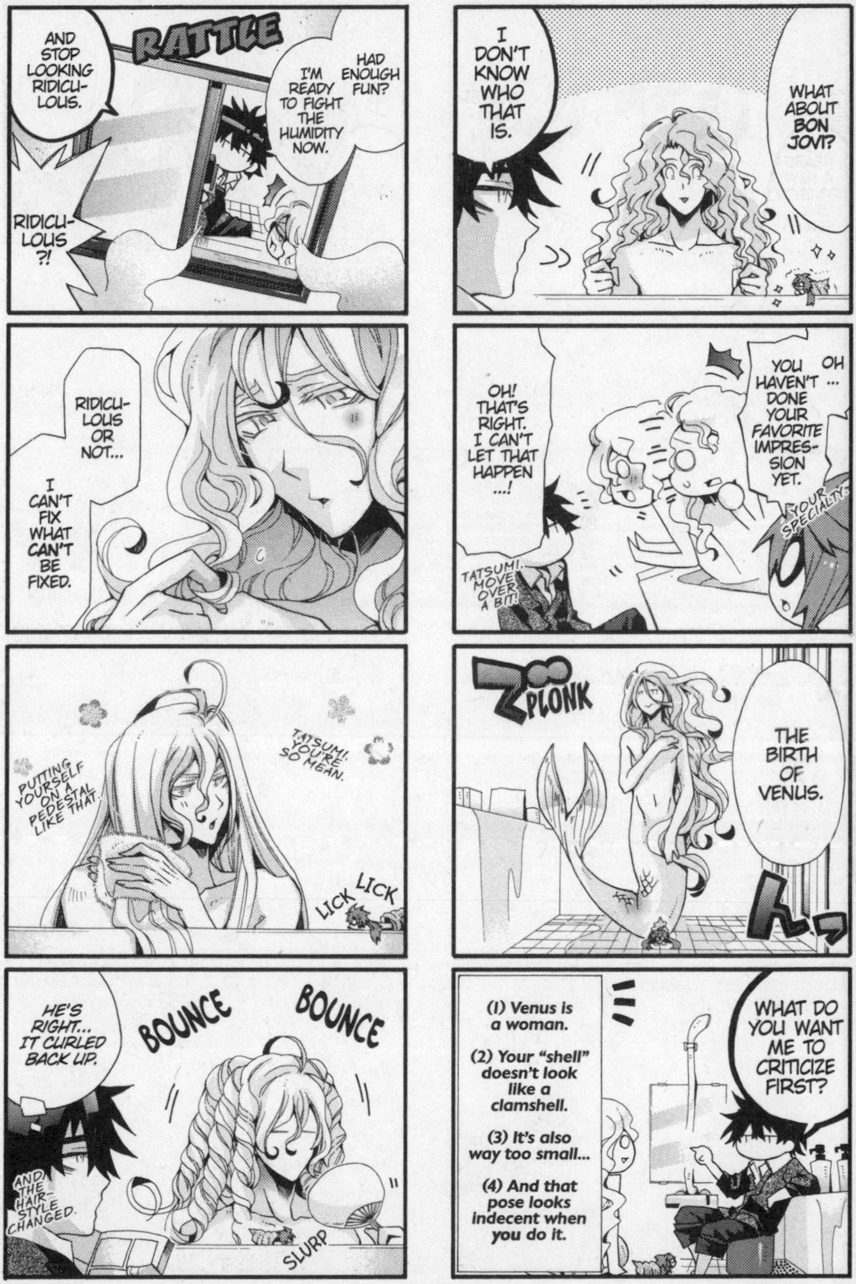
WHAT ABOUT BON JOVI?
I DON'T KNOW WHO THAT IS.
RATTLE
HAD ENOUGH FUN?
I'M READY TO FIGHT THE HUMIDITY NOW.
AND STOP LOOKING RIDICULOUS.
RIDICULOUS ?!
OH ...
YOU HAVEN'T DONE YOUR FAVORITE IMPRESSION YET.
YOUR SPECIALTY.
OH! THAT'S RIGHT. I CAN'T LET THAT HAPPEN ...!
TATSUMI, MOVE OVER A BIT!
RIDICULOUS OR NOT...
I CAN'T FIX WHAT CAN'T BE FIXED.
THE BIRTH OF VENUS.
PLONK
TATSUMI, YOU'RE SO MEAN.
PUTTING YOURSELF ON A PEDESTAL LIKE THAT.
LICK LICK
WHAT DO YOU WANT ME TO CRITICIZE FIRST?
(1) Venus is a woman.
(2) Your "shell" doesn't look like a clamshell.
(3) It's also way too small...
(4) And that pose looks indecent when you do it.
BOUNCE
BOUNCE
HE'S RIGHT... IT CURLED BACK UP.
AND THE HAIRSTYLE CHANGED.
SLURP

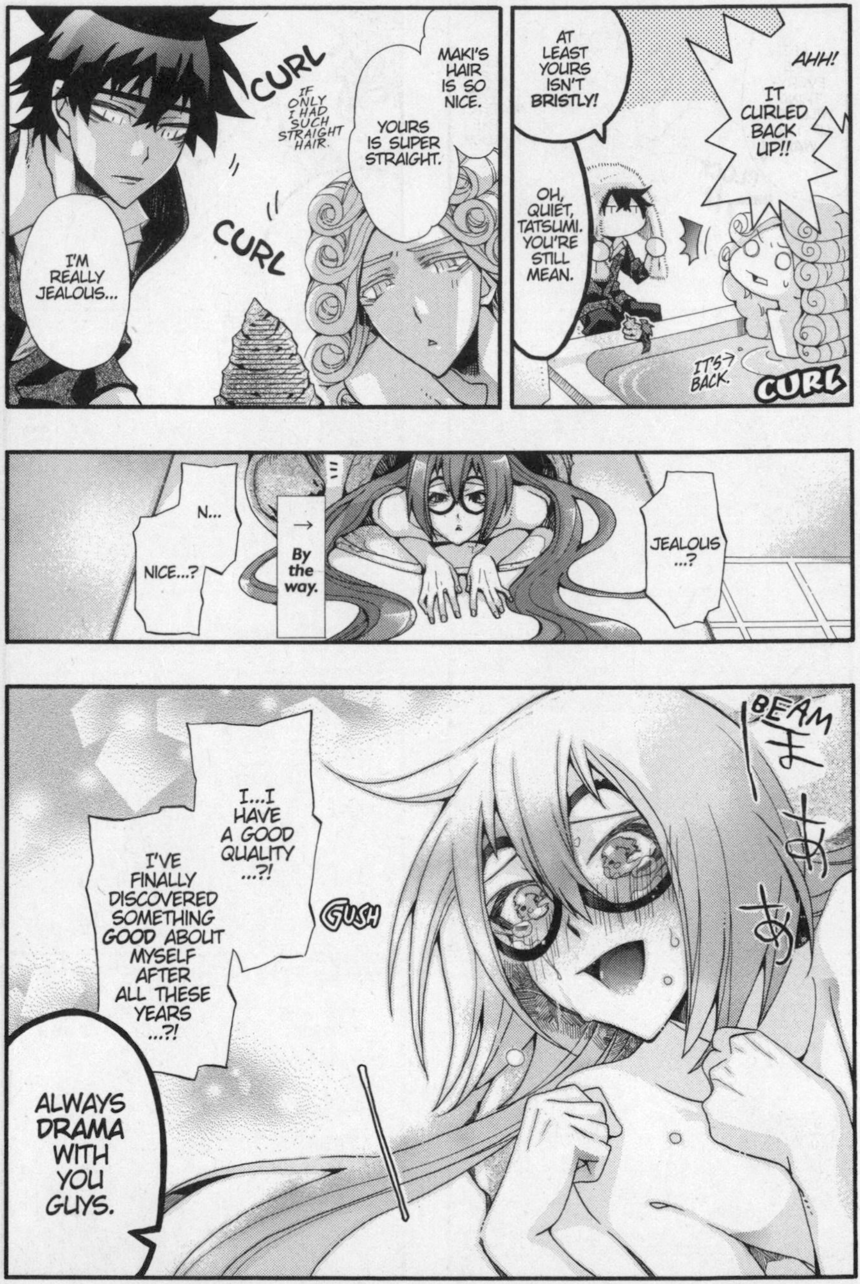
AHH!
IT CURLED BACK UP!!
AT LEAST YOURS ISN'T BRISTLY!
OH, QUIET, TATSUMI. YOU'RE STILL MEAN.
IT'S BACK.
CURL
MAKI'S HAIR IS SO NICE.
YOURS IS SUPER STRAIGHT.
IF ONLY I HAD SUCH STRAIGHT HAIR.
CURL
CURL
I'M REALLY JEALOUS...
JEALOUS...?
By the way.
N...
NICE...?
BEAM
I...I HAVE A GOOD QUALITY...?!
I'VE FINALLY DISCOVERED SOMETHING GOOD ABOUT MYSELF AFTER ALL THESE YEARS...?!
GUSH
ALWAYS DRAMA WITH YOU GUYS.

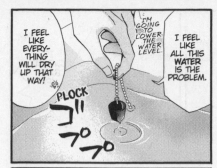

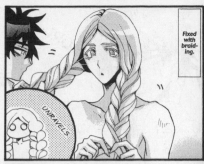

Fixed with braiding.
UNRAVELS
Fixed with a ponytail.
※WITH ADDITIONAL OPTIONS ADDED.
UNRAVELS
Fixed with a beehive.
WE MATCH. ♥
UNRAVELS
?!
WHAT EVEN WAS THAT LAST ONE?!
I FEEL LIKE ALL THIS WATER IS THE PROBLEM.
I'M GOING TO LOWER THE WATER LEVEL.
I FEEL LIKE EVERYTHING WILL DRY UP THAT WAY!
PLOCK
ゴポポ
OH... BUT, YOU'RE RIGHT. IT LOOKS LIKE IT'S SUCKING UP THE WATER...
I SEE.
ARE YOU SEAWEED OR SOMETHING?
SOAKED
SPLISH
One hour later.
TA... TATSUMI...
I NEED WATER...
HIS HAIR IS STRONGER THAN HE IS.
SHRIVEL

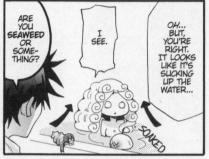

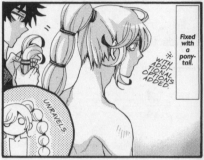

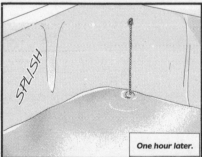

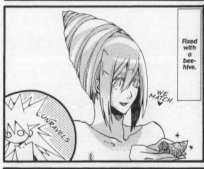

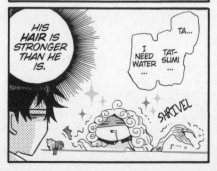

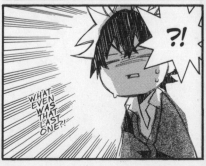

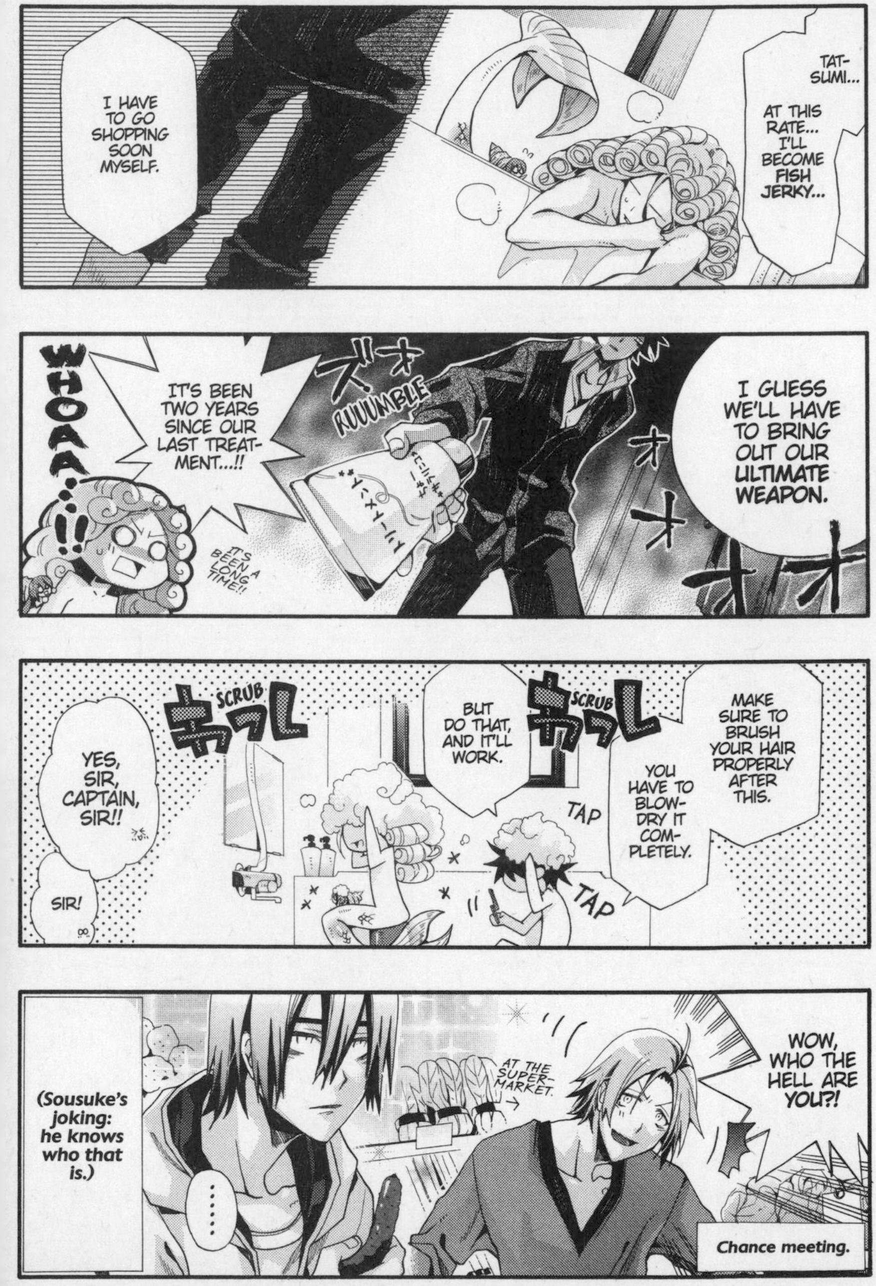
TAT-SUMI... AT THIS RATE... I'LL BECOME FISH JERKY...
I HAVE TO GO SHOPPING SOON MYSELF.
I GUESS WE'LL HAVE TO BRING OUT OUR ULTIMATE WEAPON.
RUUUMBLE
IT'S BEEN TWO YEARS SINCE OUR LAST TREATMENT...!!
WHOAA...!!
IT'S BEEN A LONG TIME!!
MAKE SURE TO BRUSH YOUR HAIR PROPERLY AFTER THIS.
YOU HAVE TO BLOW-DRY IT COMPLETELY.
TAP
TAP
SCRUB
BUT DO THAT, AND IT'LL WORK.
SCRUB
YES, SIR, CAPTAIN, SIR!!
SIR!
WOW, WHO THE HELL ARE YOU?!
AT THE SUPER-MARKET.
......
(Sousuke's joking: he knows who that is.)
Chance meeting.

Merman in My Tub

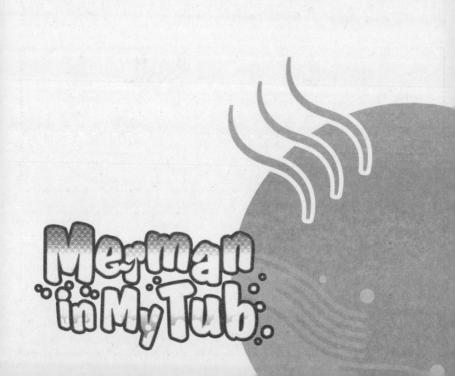

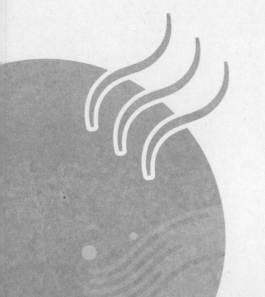

オレん家のフロ事情

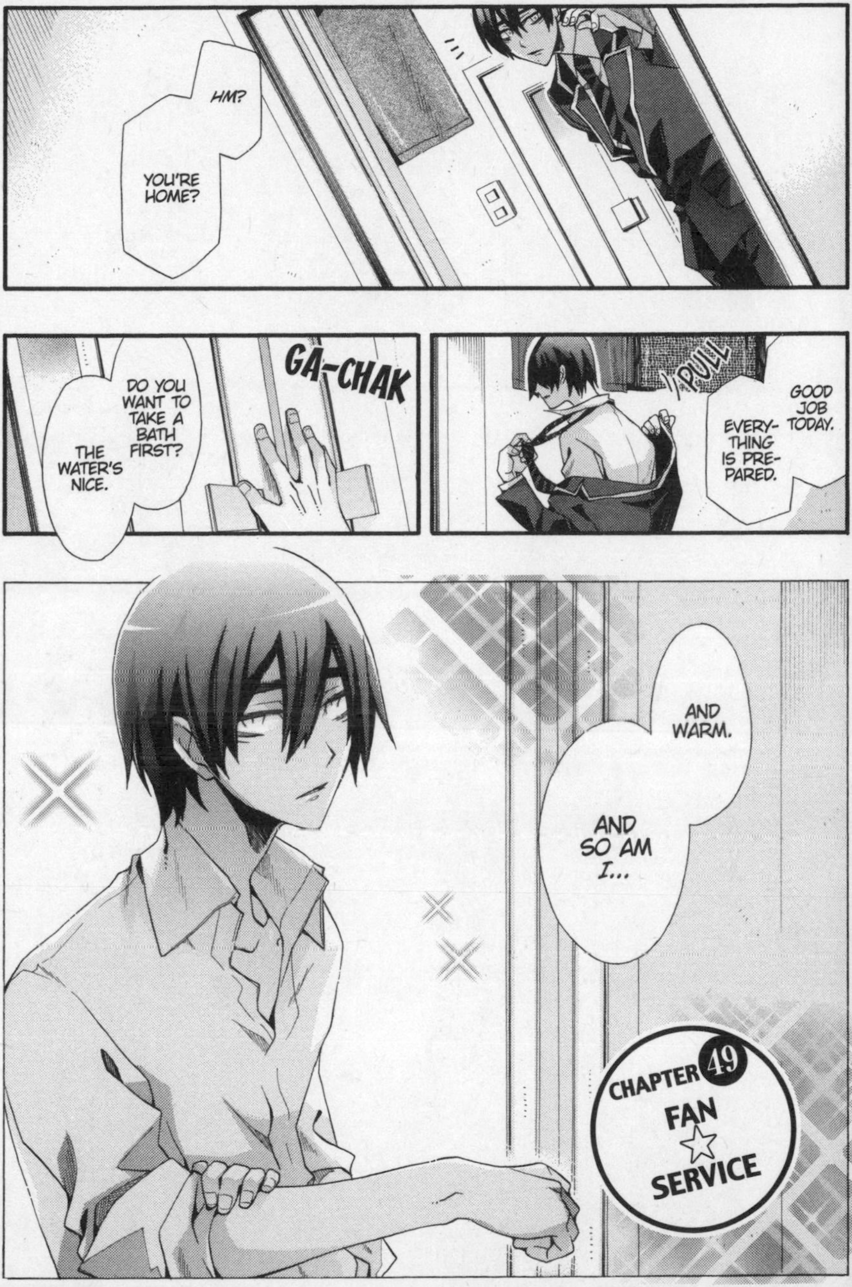
HM?
YOU'RE HOME?
PULL
GOOD JOB TODAY.
EVERY-THING IS PRE-PARED.
GA-CHAK
DO YOU WANT TO TAKE A BATH FIRST?
THE WATER'S NICE.
AND WARM.
AND SO AM I...
CHAPTER 49
FAN ☆ SERVICE

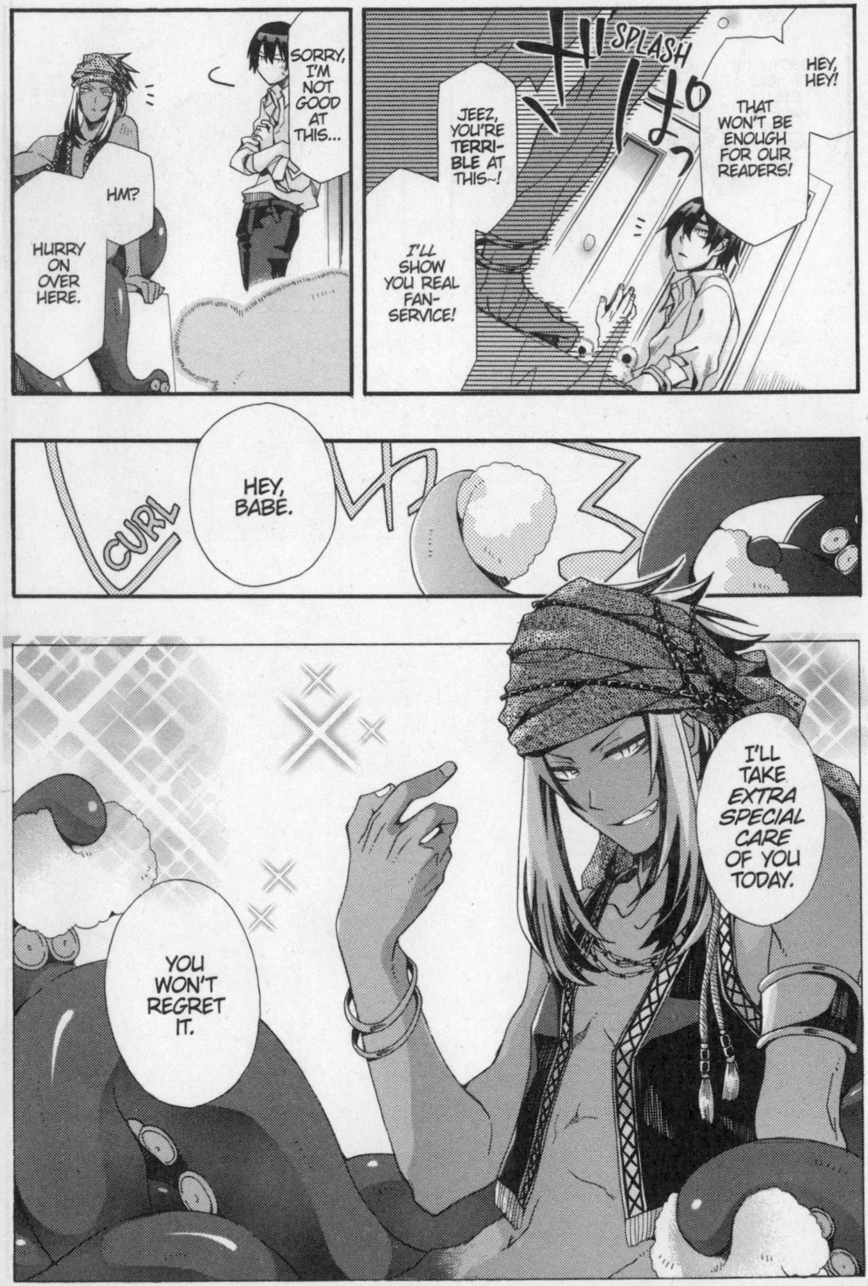
HEY, HEY!
THAT WON'T BE ENOUGH FOR OUR READERS!
SPLASH
JEEZ, YOU'RE TERRIBLE AT THIS~!
I'LL SHOW YOU REAL FAN-SERVICE!
SORRY, I'M NOT GOOD AT THIS...
HM?
HURRY ON OVER HERE.
HEY, BABE.
CURL
I'LL TAKE EXTRA SPECIAL CARE OF YOU TODAY.
YOU WON'T REGRET IT.

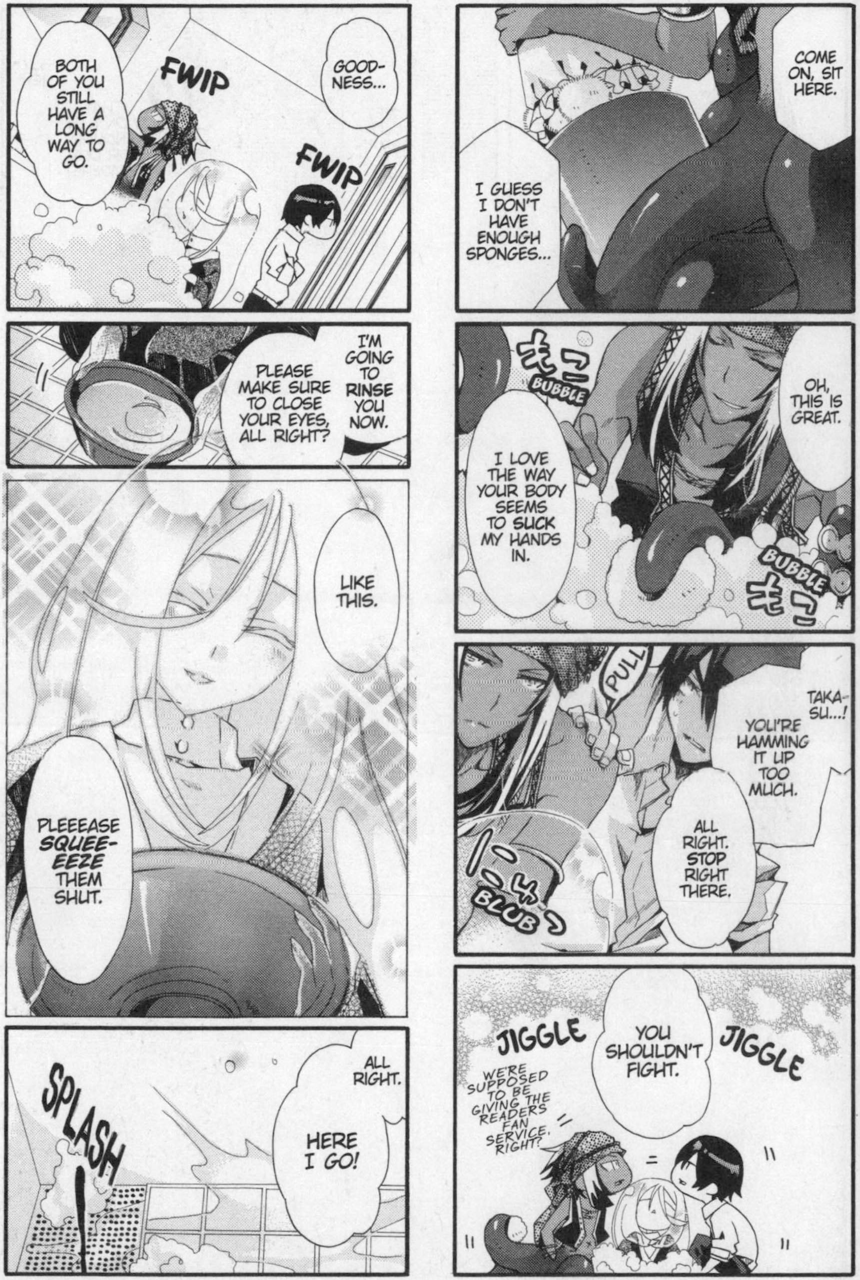
COME ON, SIT HERE.
I GUESS I DON'T HAVE ENOUGH SPONGES...
OH, THIS IS GREAT.
BUBBLE
I LOVE THE WAY YOUR BODY SEEMS TO SUCK MY HANDS IN.
BUBBLE
TAKA-SU...!
YOU'RE HAMMING IT UP TOO MUCH.
PULL
ALL RIGHT. STOP RIGHT THERE.
BLUB
JIGGLE
YOU SHOULDN'T FIGHT.
JIGGLE
WE'RE SUPPOSED TO BE GIVING THE READERS FAN SERVICE, RIGHT?
GOOD-NESS...
FWIP
BOTH OF YOU STILL HAVE A LONG WAY TO GO.
FWIP
I'M GOING TO RINSE YOU NOW.
PLEASE MAKE SURE TO CLOSE YOUR EYES, ALL RIGHT?
LIKE THIS.
PLEEEASE SQUEEE-EEZE THEM SHUT.
ALL RIGHT.
HERE I GO!
SPLASH

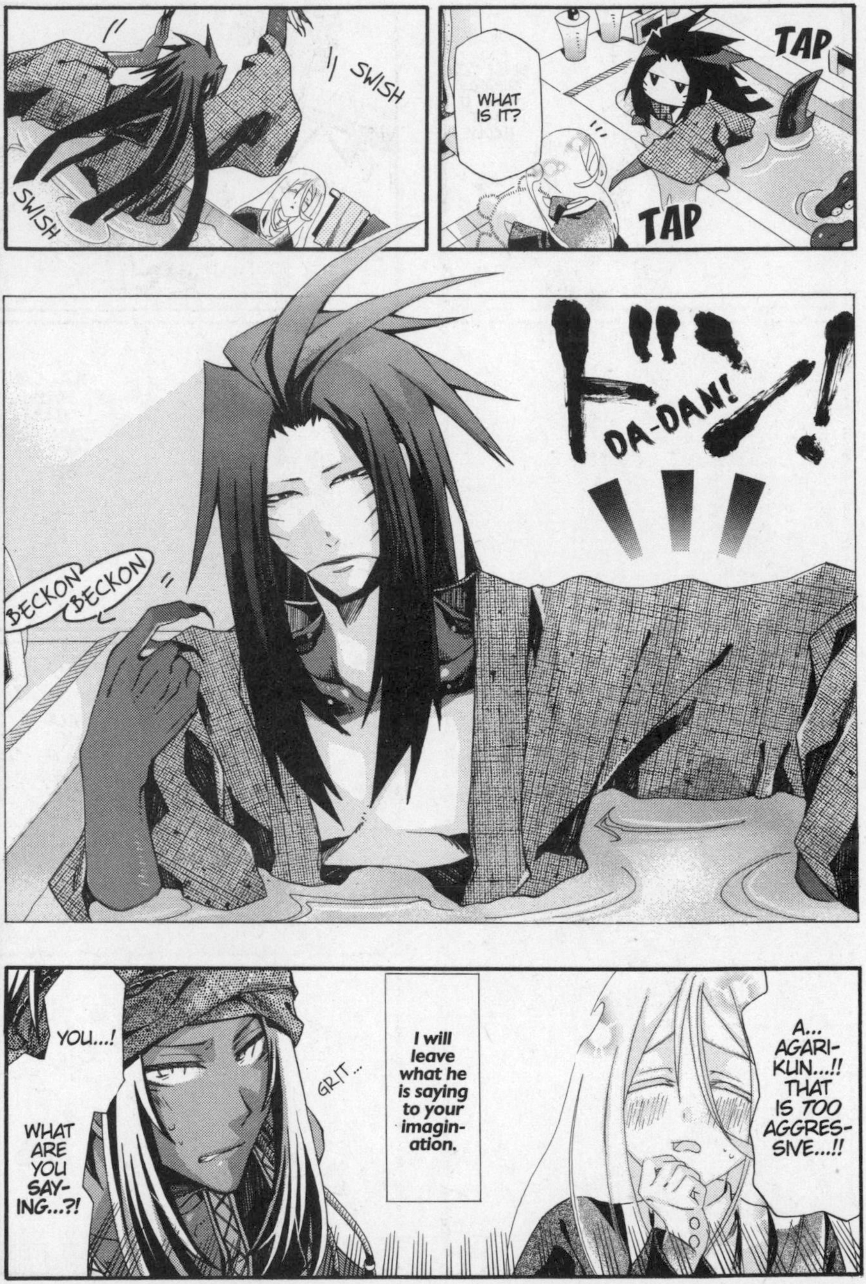
WHAT IS IT?
TAP
TAP
SWISH
SWISH
DA-DAN!
BECKON BECKON
A... AGARI-KUN...!! THAT IS TOO AGGRES-SIVE...!!
I will leave what he is saying to your imagination.
GRIT...
YOU...!
WHAT ARE YOU SAYING...?!

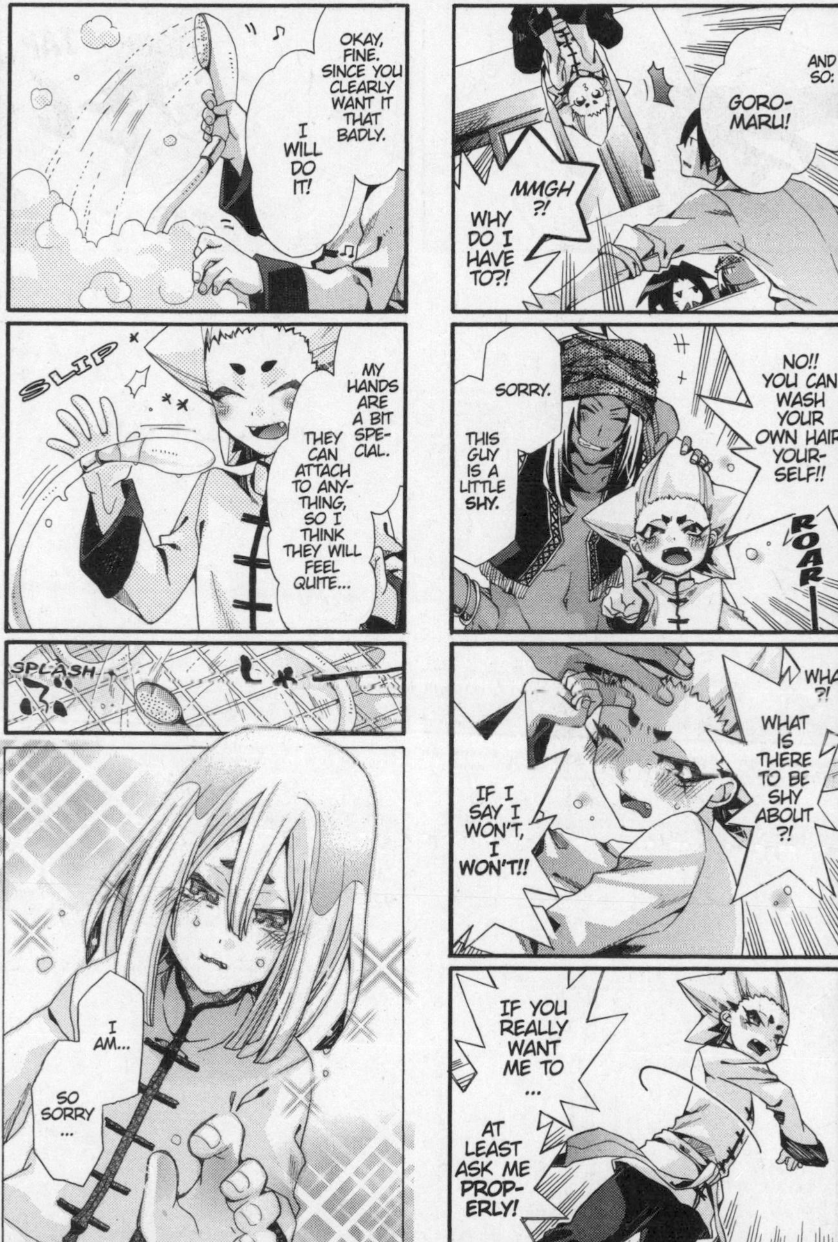
AND SO:
GORO-MARU!
MMGH ?!
WHY DO I HAVE TO?!
NO!! YOU CAN WASH YOUR OWN HAIR YOUR-SELF!!
ROAR
SORRY.
THIS GUY IS A LITTLE SHY.
WHA ?!
WHAT IS THERE TO BE SHY ABOUT ?!
IF I SAY I WON'T, I WON'T!!
IF YOU REALLY WANT ME TO ...
AT LEAST ASK ME PROP-ERLY!
OKAY, FINE. SINCE YOU CLEARLY WANT IT THAT BADLY.
I WILL DO IT!
SLIP
MY HANDS ARE A BIT SPE-CIAL.
THEY CAN ATTACH TO ANY-THING, SO I THINK THEY WILL FEEL QUITE...
SPLASH
I AM...
SO SORRY ...

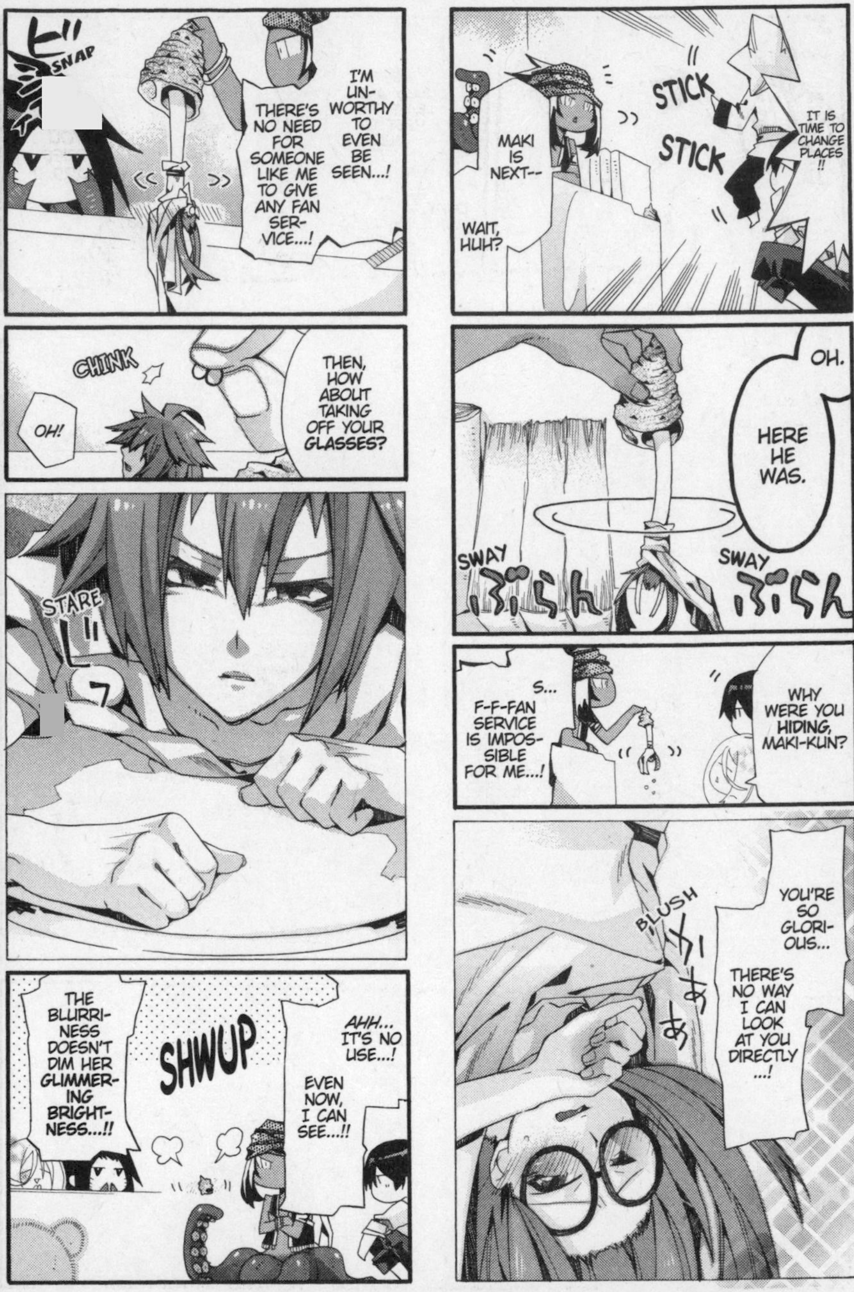

MAKI IS NEXT--
WAIT, HUH?
STICK
STICK
IT IS TIME TO CHANGE PLACES!!
OH.
HERE HE WAS.
SWAY ぶらん
SWAY ぶらん
WHY WERE YOU HIDING, MAKI-KUN?
S... F-F-FAN SERVICE IS IMPOSSIBLE FOR ME...!
BLUSH かあああ
YOU'RE SO GLORIOUS...
THERE'S NO WAY I CAN LOOK AT YOU DIRECTLY...!
ビッ SNAP
I'M UN-WORTHY TO EVEN BE SEEN...!
THERE'S NO NEED FOR SOMEONE LIKE ME TO GIVE ANY FAN SERVICE...!
CHINK
THEN, HOW ABOUT TAKING OFF YOUR GLASSES?
OH!
STARE じーっ
SHWUP
AHH... IT'S NO USE...!
EVEN NOW, I CAN SEE...!!
THE BLURRINESS DOESN'T DIM HER GLIMMERING BRIGHTNESS...!!

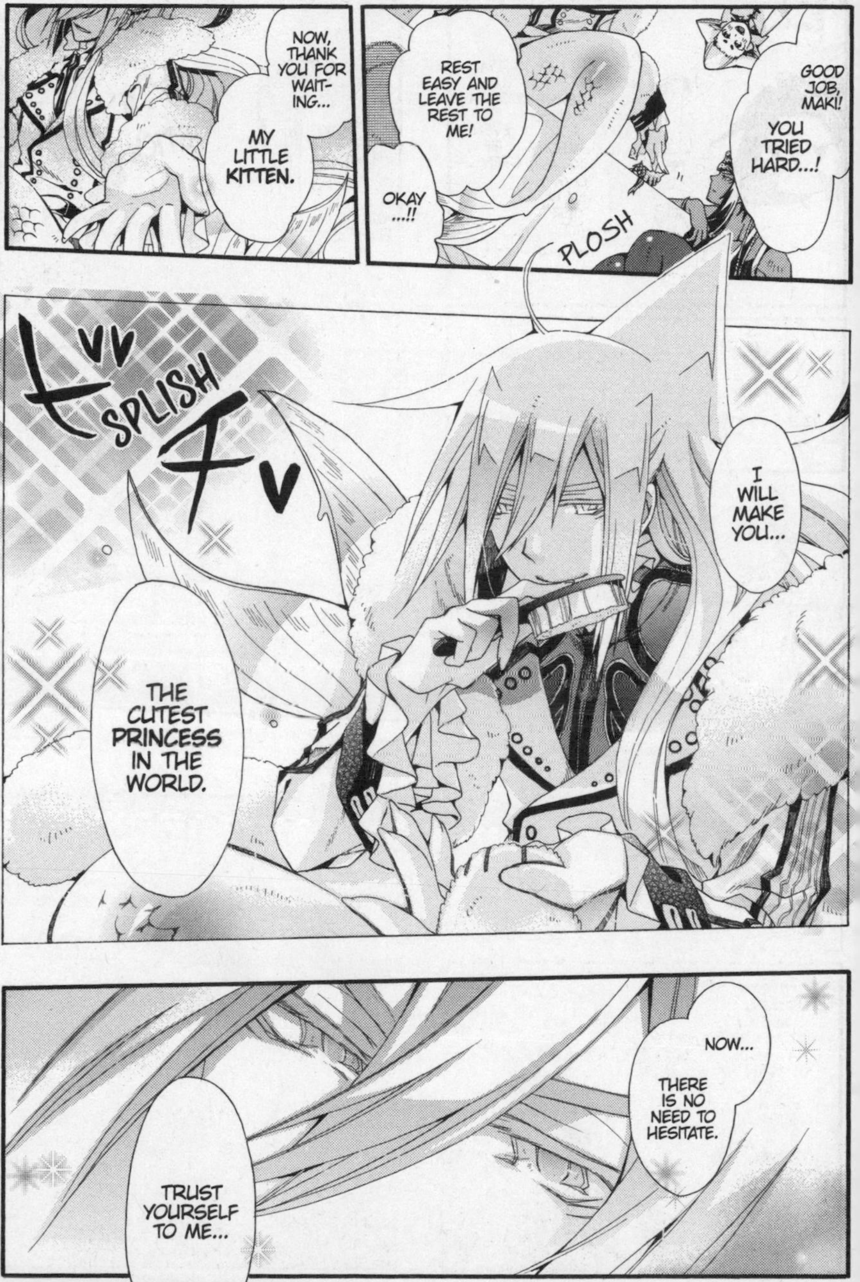
GOOD JOB, MAKI!
YOU TRIED HARD...!
REST EASY AND LEAVE THE REST TO ME!
OKAY ...!!
PLOSH
NOW, THANK YOU FOR WAIT-ING...
MY LITTLE KITTEN.
SPLISH
I WILL MAKE YOU...
THE CUTEST PRINCESS IN THE WORLD.
NOW...
THERE IS NO NEED TO HESITATE.
TRUST YOURSELF TO ME...

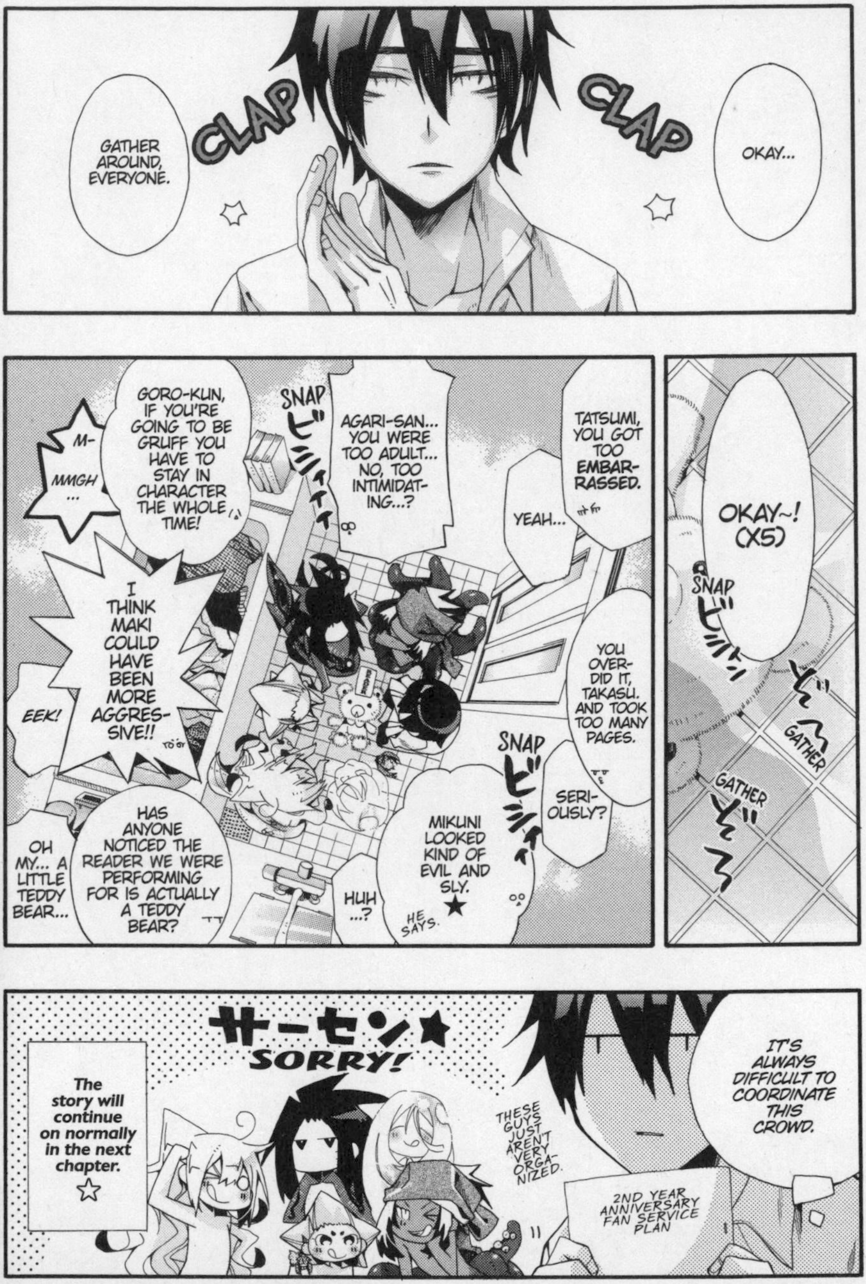
OKAY...
CLAP
CLAP
GATHER AROUND, EVERYONE.
OKAY~! (X5)
SNAP
GATHER
GATHER
TATSUMI, YOU GOT TOO EMBARRASSED.
YEAH...
SNAP
AGARI-SAN... YOU WERE TOO ADULT... NO, TOO INTIMIDATING...?
GORO-KUN, IF YOU'RE GOING TO BE GRUFF YOU HAVE TO STAY IN CHARACTER THE WHOLE TIME!
M-MMGH...
YOU OVERDID IT, TAKASU. AND TOOK TOO MANY PAGES.
SNAP
SERIOUSLY?
I THINK MAKI COULD HAVE BEEN MORE AGGRESSIVE!!
EEK!
MIKUNI LOOKED KIND OF EVIL AND SLY. ★
HE SAYS.
HUH...?
HAS ANYONE NOTICED THE READER WE WERE PERFORMING FOR IS ACTUALLY A TEDDY BEAR?
OH MY... A LITTLE TEDDY BEAR...
IT'S ALWAYS DIFFICULT TO COORDINATE THIS CROWD.
2ND YEAR ANNIVERSARY FAN SERVICE PLAN
サーセン★
SORRY!
THESE GUYS JUST AREN'T VERY ORGANIZED.
The story will continue on normally in the next chapter. ☆

Merman in My Tub

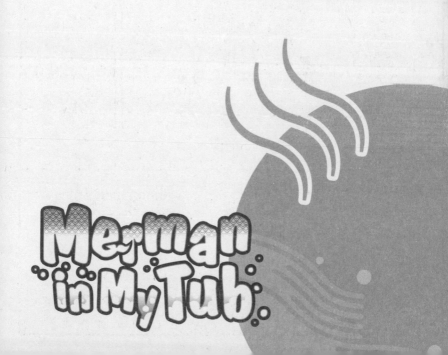

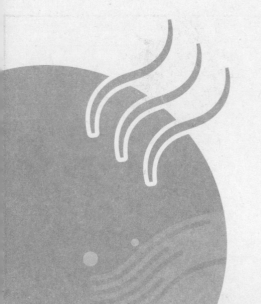

オレん家のフロ事情

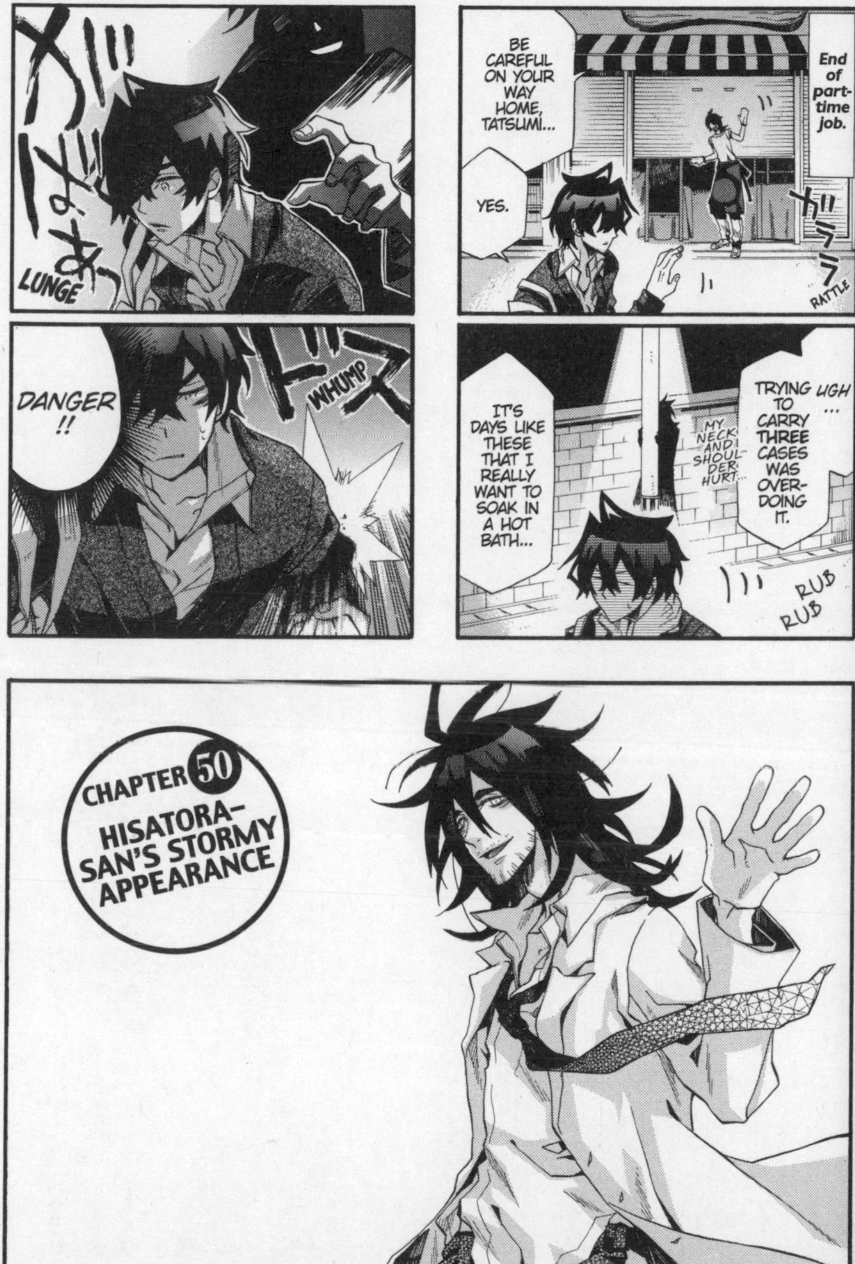
End of part-time job.
BE CAREFUL ON YOUR WAY HOME, TATSUMI...
YES.
RATTLE
LUNGE
UGH...
TRYING TO CARRY THREE CASES WAS OVER-DOING IT.
MY NECK AND SHOUL-DER HURT...
IT'S DAYS LIKE THESE THAT I REALLY WANT TO SOAK IN A HOT BATH...
RUB RUB
WHUMP
DANGER!!
CHAPTER 50
HISATORA-SAN'S STORMY APPEARANCE

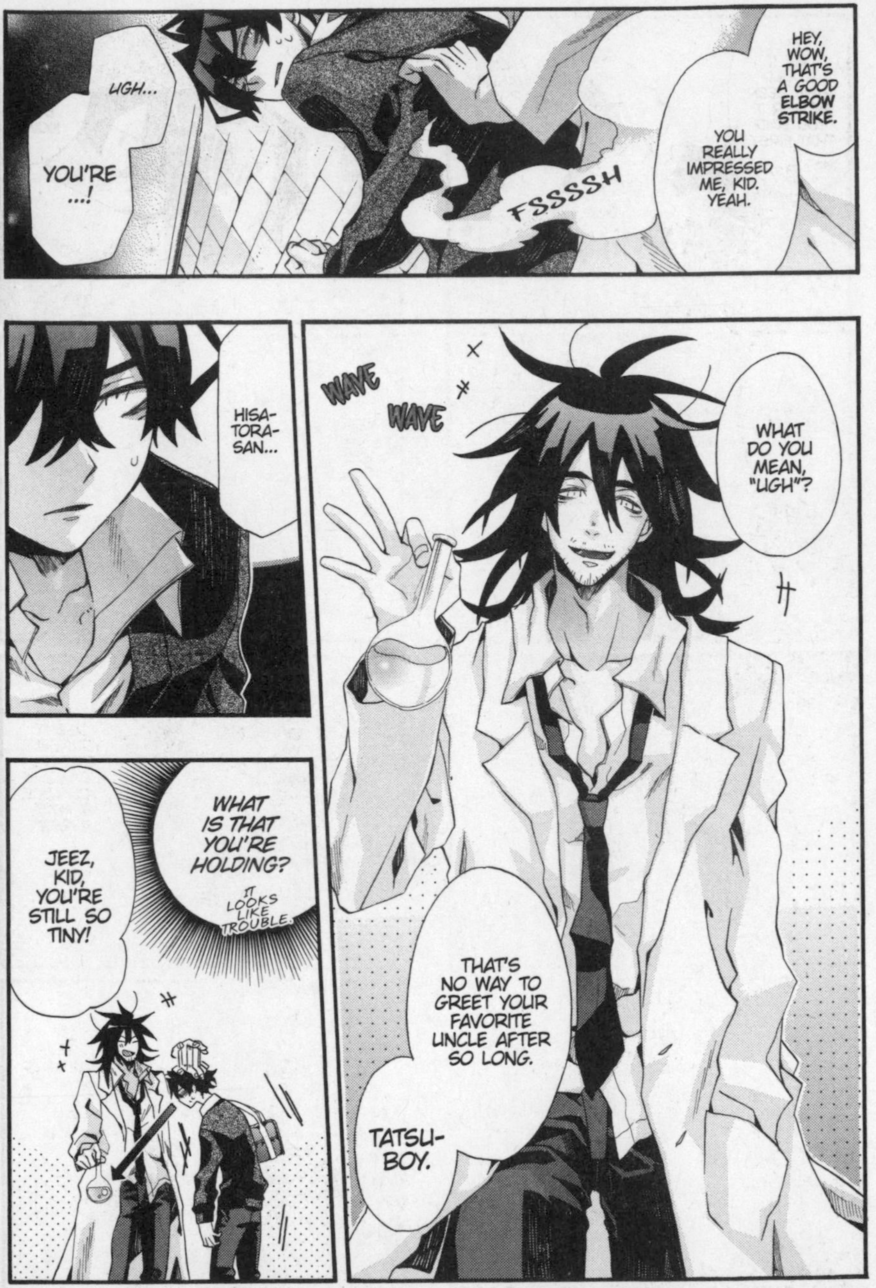
HEY, WOW, THAT'S A GOOD ELBOW STRIKE.
YOU REALLY IMPRESSED ME, KID. YEAH.
FSSSSH
UGH...
YOU'RE ...!
WHAT DO YOU MEAN, "UGH"?
WAVE
WAVE
THAT'S NO WAY TO GREET YOUR FAVORITE UNCLE AFTER SO LONG.
TATSU-BOY.
HISATORA-SAN...
WHAT IS THAT YOU'RE HOLDING?
IT LOOKS LIKE TROUBLE.
JEEZ, KID, YOU'RE STILL SO TINY!

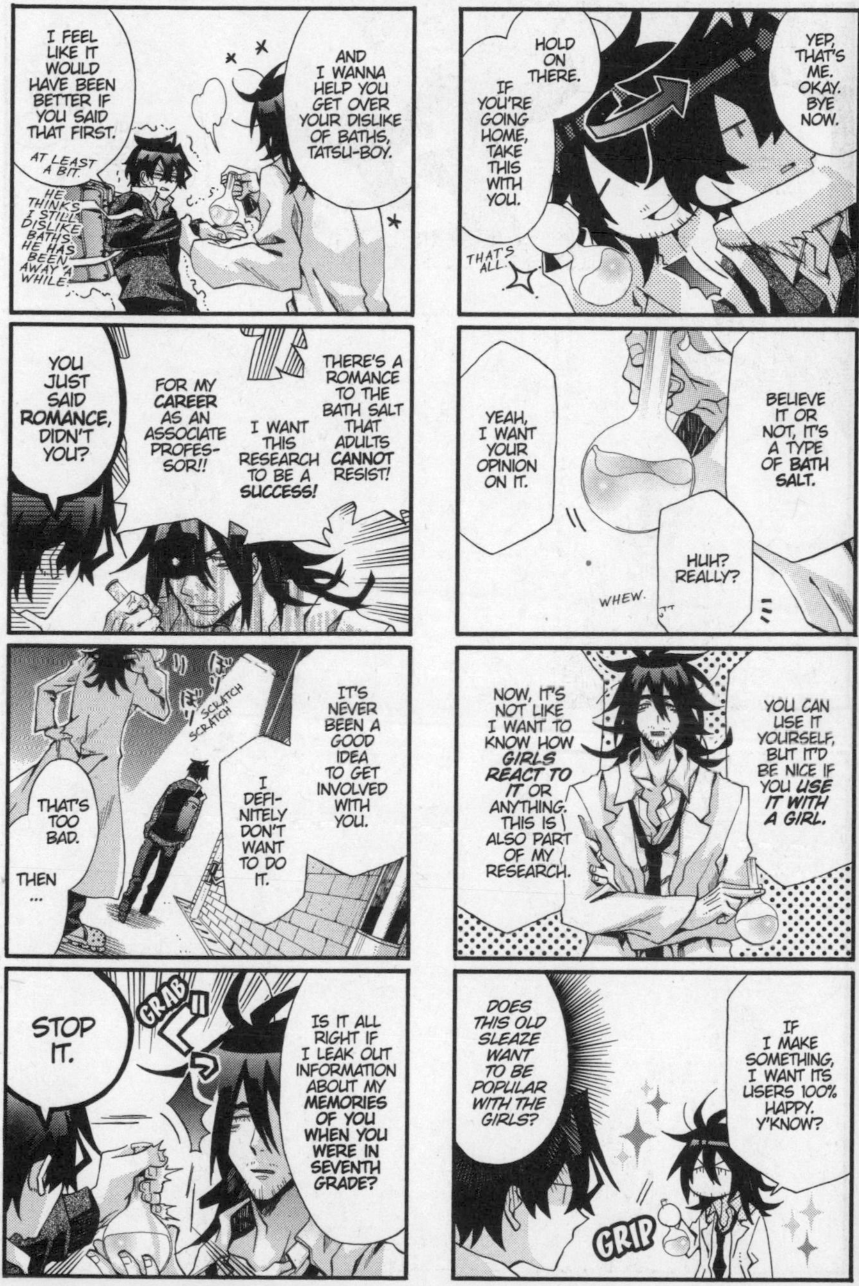
YEP, THAT'S ME. OKAY. BYE NOW.
HOLD ON THERE.
IF YOU'RE GOING HOME, TAKE THIS WITH YOU.
THAT'S ALL.
AND I WANNA HELP YOU GET OVER YOUR DISLIKE OF BATHS, TATSU-BOY.
I FEEL LIKE IT WOULD HAVE BEEN BETTER IF YOU SAID THAT FIRST.
AT LEAST A BIT.
HE THINKS I STILL DISLIKE BATHS. HE HAS BEEN AWAY A WHILE.
BELIEVE IT OR NOT, IT'S A TYPE OF BATH SALT.
YEAH, I WANT YOUR OPINION ON IT.
HUH? REALLY?
WHEW.
THERE'S A ROMANCE TO THE BATH SALT THAT ADULTS CANNOT RESIST!
I WANT THIS RESEARCH TO BE A SUCCESS!
FOR MY CAREER AS AN ASSOCIATE PROFES-SOR!!
YOU JUST SAID ROMANCE, DIDN'T YOU?
YOU CAN USE IT YOURSELF, BUT IT'D BE NICE IF YOU USE IT WITH A GIRL.
NOW, IT'S NOT LIKE I WANT TO KNOW HOW GIRLS REACT TO IT OR ANYTHING. THIS IS ALSO PART OF MY RESEARCH.
IT'S NEVER BEEN A GOOD IDEA TO GET INVOLVED WITH YOU.
I DEFINITELY DON'T WANT TO DO IT.
SCRATCH SCRATCH
THAT'S TOO BAD.
THEN ...
IF I MAKE SOMETHING, I WANT ITS USERS 100% HAPPY. Y'KNOW?
DOES THIS OLD SLEAZE WANT TO BE POPULAR WITH THE GIRLS?
GRIP
IS IT ALL RIGHT IF I LEAK OUT INFORMATION ABOUT MY MEMORIES OF YOU WHEN YOU WERE IN SEVENTH GRADE?
GRAB
STOP IT.

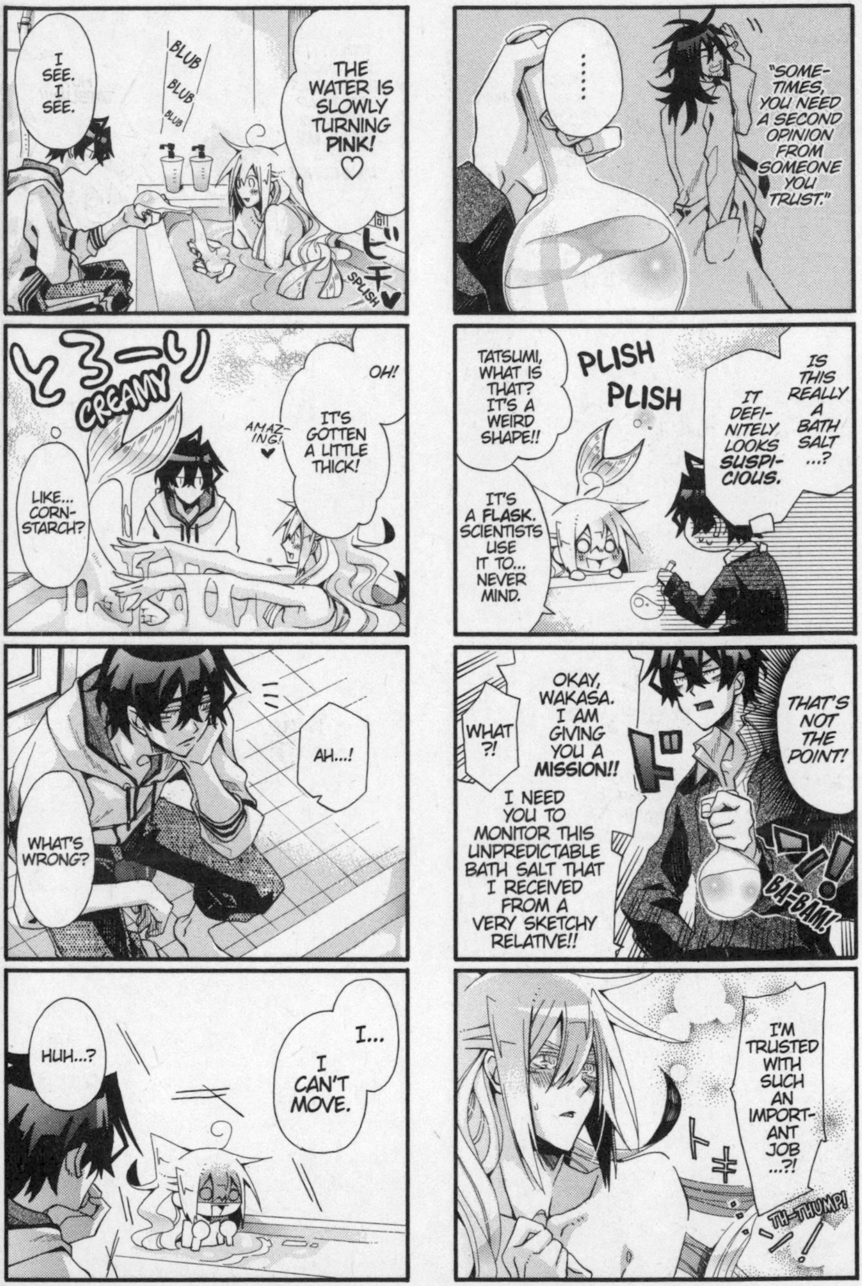
"SOMETIMES, YOU NEED A SECOND OPINION FROM SOMEONE YOU TRUST."
......
IS THIS REALLY A BATH SALT ...?
IT DEFINITELY LOOKS SUSPICIOUS.
PLISH PLISH
TATSUMI, WHAT IS THAT? IT'S A WEIRD SHAPE!!
IT'S A FLASK. SCIENTISTS USE IT TO... NEVER MIND.
THAT'S NOT THE POINT!
OKAY, WAKASA. I AM GIVING YOU A MISSION!!
WHAT?!
ド
I NEED YOU TO MONITOR THIS UNPREDICTABLE BATH SALT THAT I RECEIVED FROM A VERY SKETCHY RELATIVE!!
BA-BAM!
I'M TRUSTED WITH SUCH AN IMPORTANT JOB ...?!
ドキ
TH-THUMP!
THE WATER IS SLOWLY TURNING PINK! ♡
BLUB BLUB BLUB
I SEE. I SEE.
ピチ
SPLISH ♥
OH!
IT'S GOTTEN A LITTLE THICK!
AMAZING! ♥
とろ〜ん
CREAMY
LIKE... CORNSTARCH?
AH...!
WHAT'S WRONG?
I... I CAN'T MOVE.
HUH...?

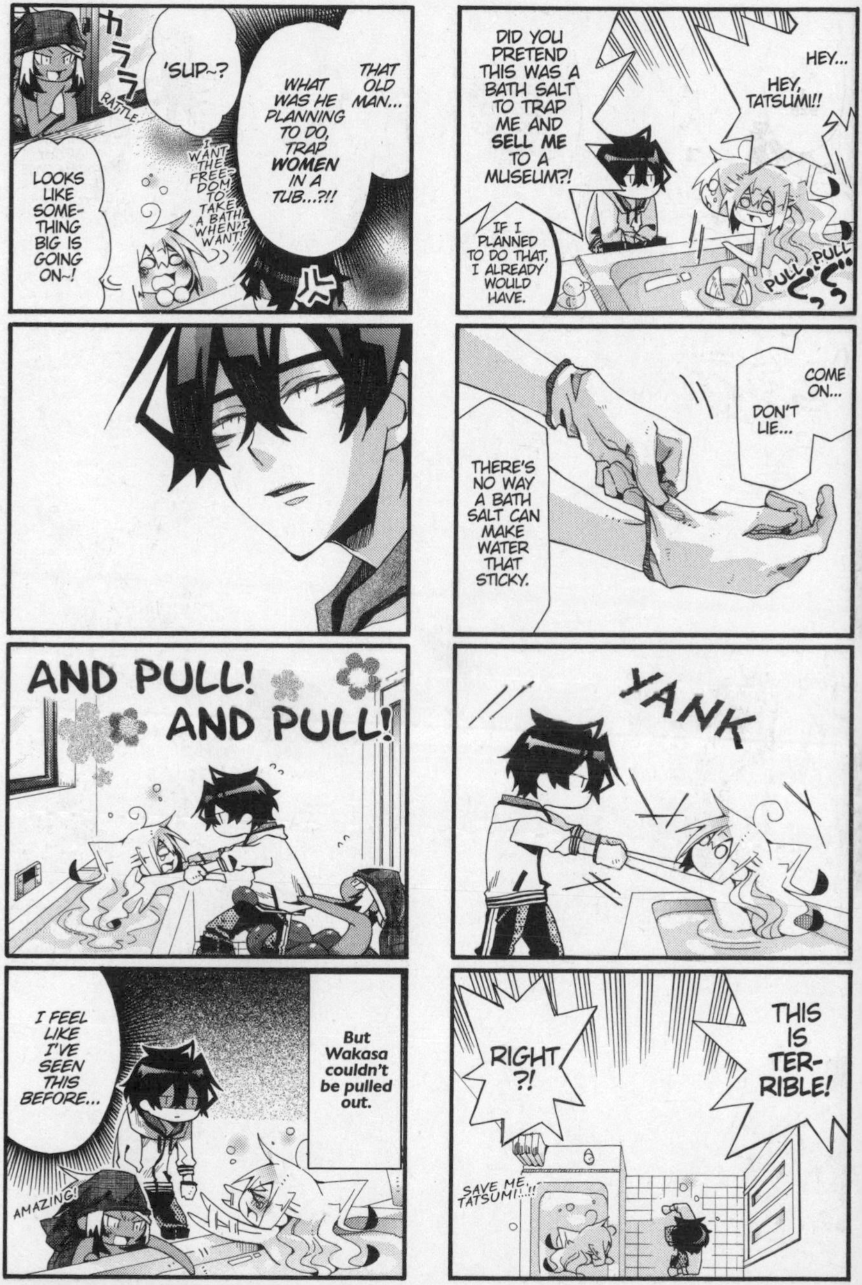
HEY...
HEY, TATSUMI!!
DID YOU PRETEND THIS WAS A BATH SALT TO TRAP ME AND SELL ME TO A MUSEUM?!
IF I PLANNED TO DO THAT, I ALREADY WOULD HAVE.
PULL PULL
THAT OLD MAN...
WHAT WAS HE PLANNING TO DO, TRAP WOMEN IN A TUB...?!!
I WANT THE FREEDOM TO TAKE A BATH WHEN I WANT!
'SUP~?
カララ
RATTLE
LOOKS LIKE SOMETHING BIG IS GOING ON~!
COME ON...
DON'T LIE...
THERE'S NO WAY A BATH SALT CAN MAKE WATER THAT STICKY.
YANK
AND PULL!
AND PULL!
THIS IS TERRIBLE!
RIGHT?!
SAVE ME, TATSUMI...!!
But Wakasa couldn't be pulled out.
I FEEL LIKE I'VE SEEN THIS BEFORE...
AMAZING!

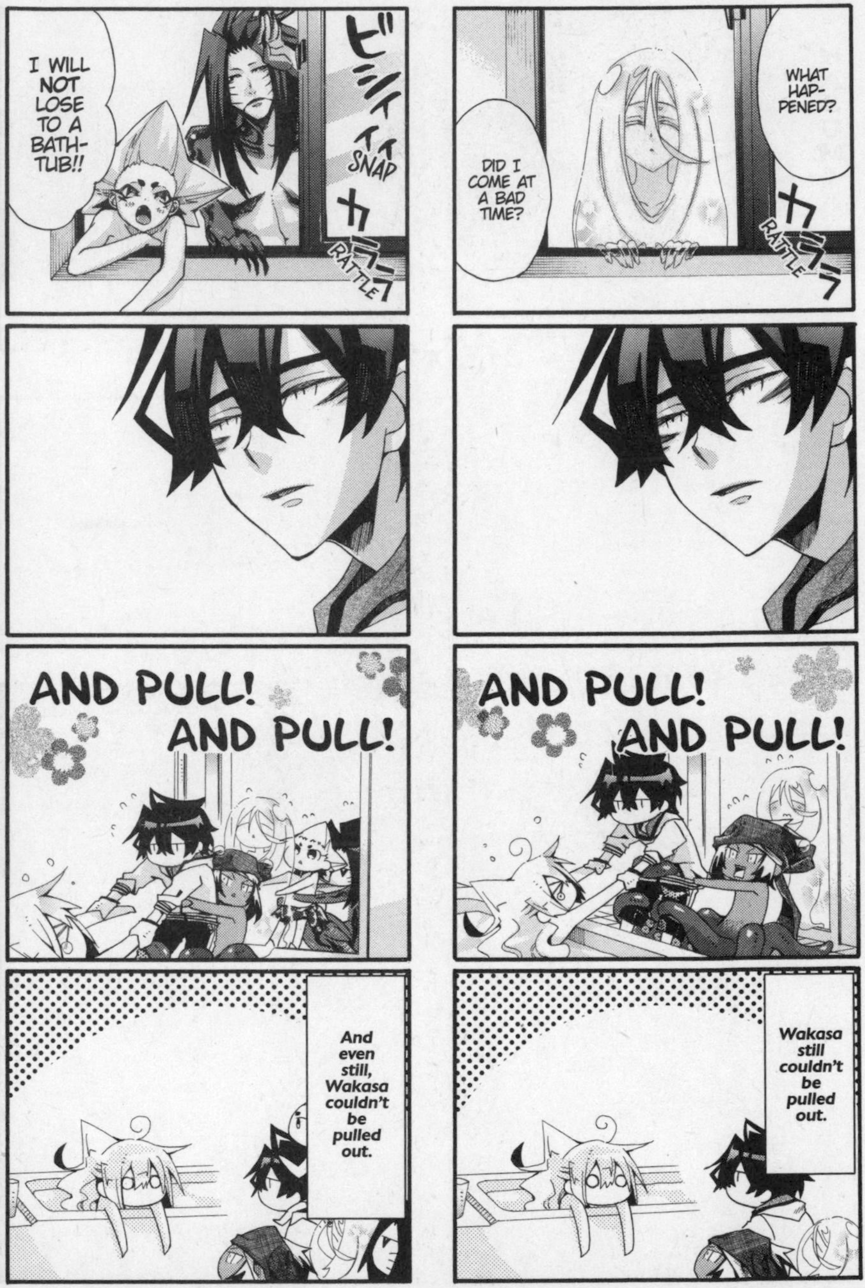
WHAT HAP-PENED?
DID I COME AT A BAD TIME?
カラララ
RATTLE
AND PULL!
AND PULL!
Wakasa still couldn't be pulled out.
I WILL NOT LOSE TO A BATH-TUB!!
ビシィィ
SNAP
カララー
RATTLE
AND PULL!
AND PULL!
And even still, Wakasa couldn't be pulled out.

I'M SORRY FOR BARGING INTO SUCH A BATTLE-FIELD...!!

'((

WH... WHAT HAP-PENED HERE ...?!

RATTLE RATTLE RATTLE

AND PULL!

AND PULL!

And finally, Wakasa was free.

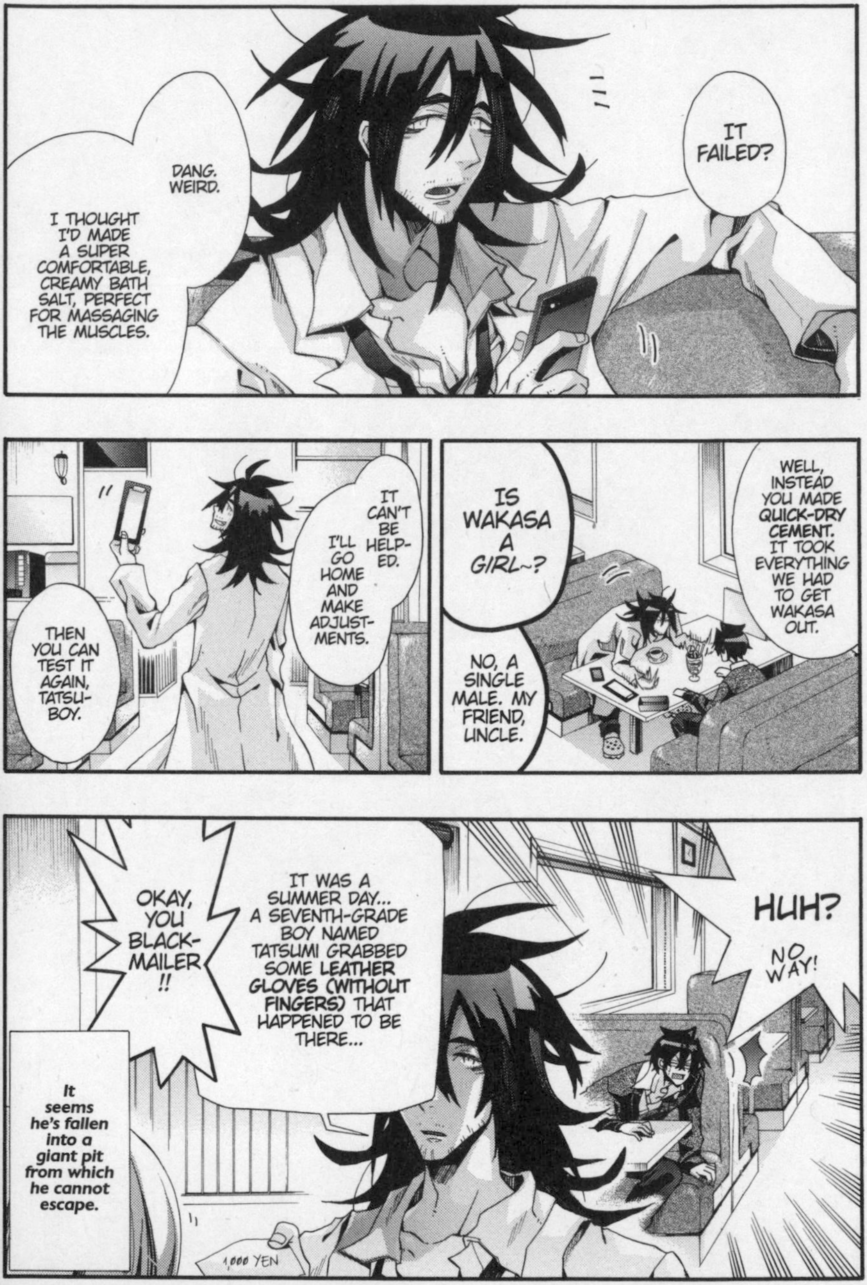
IT FAILED?
DANG. WEIRD.
I THOUGHT I'D MADE A SUPER COMFORTABLE, CREAMY BATH SALT, PERFECT FOR MASSAGING THE MUSCLES.
WELL, INSTEAD YOU MADE QUICK-DRY CEMENT. IT TOOK EVERYTHING WE HAD TO GET WAKASA OUT.
IS WAKASA A GIRL~?
NO, A SINGLE MALE. MY FRIEND, UNCLE.
IT CAN'T BE HELPED.
I'LL GO HOME AND MAKE ADJUSTMENTS.
THEN YOU CAN TEST IT AGAIN, TATSU-BOY.
HUH?
NO WAY!
IT WAS A SUMMER DAY... A SEVENTH-GRADE BOY NAMED TATSUMI GRABBED SOME LEATHER GLOVES (WITHOUT FINGERS) THAT HAPPENED TO BE THERE...
OKAY, YOU BLACKMAILER!!
It seems he's fallen into a giant pit from which he cannot escape.
1,000 YEN

Merman in My Tub

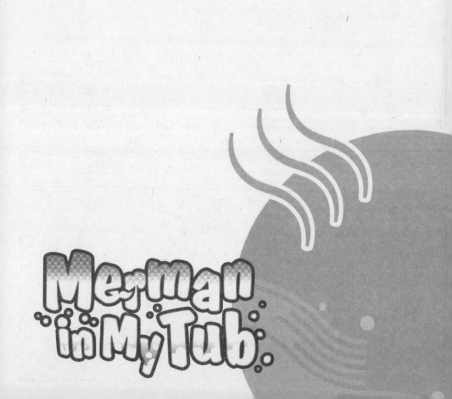

オレん家（ち）のフロ事情

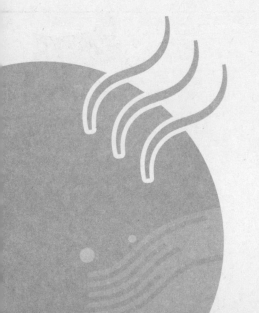

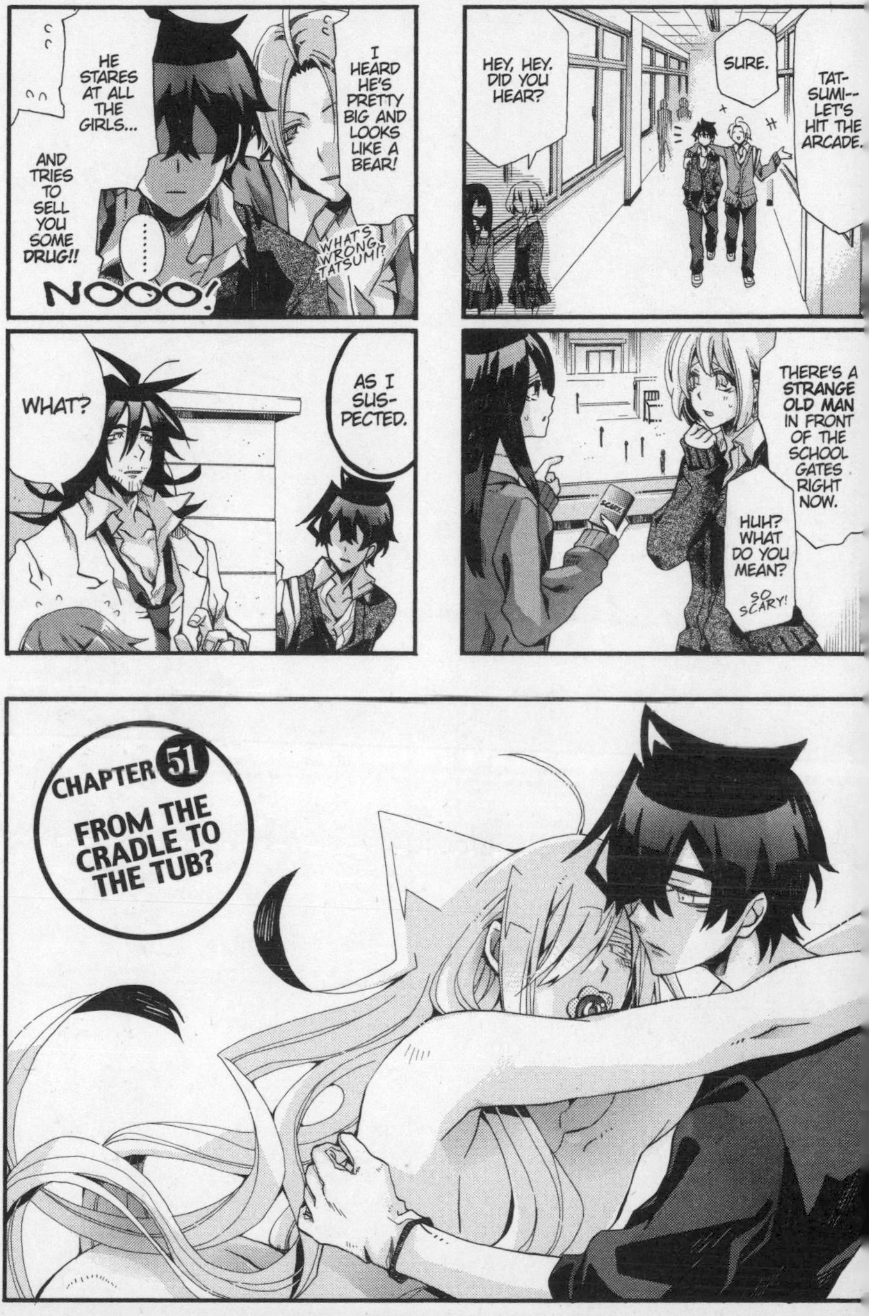
TAT-SUMI-- LET'S HIT THE ARCADE.
SURE.
HEY, HEY. DID YOU HEAR?
I HEARD HE'S PRETTY BIG AND LOOKS LIKE A BEAR!
HE STARES AT ALL THE GIRLS...
AND TRIES TO SELL YOU SOME DRUG!!
WHAT'S WRONG, TATSUMI?
......
NOOO!
THERE'S A STRANGE OLD MAN IN FRONT OF THE SCHOOL GATES RIGHT NOW.
HUH? WHAT DO YOU MEAN?
SO SCARY!
AS I SUS-PECTED.
WHAT?
CHAPTER 51
FROM THE CRADLE TO THE TUB?

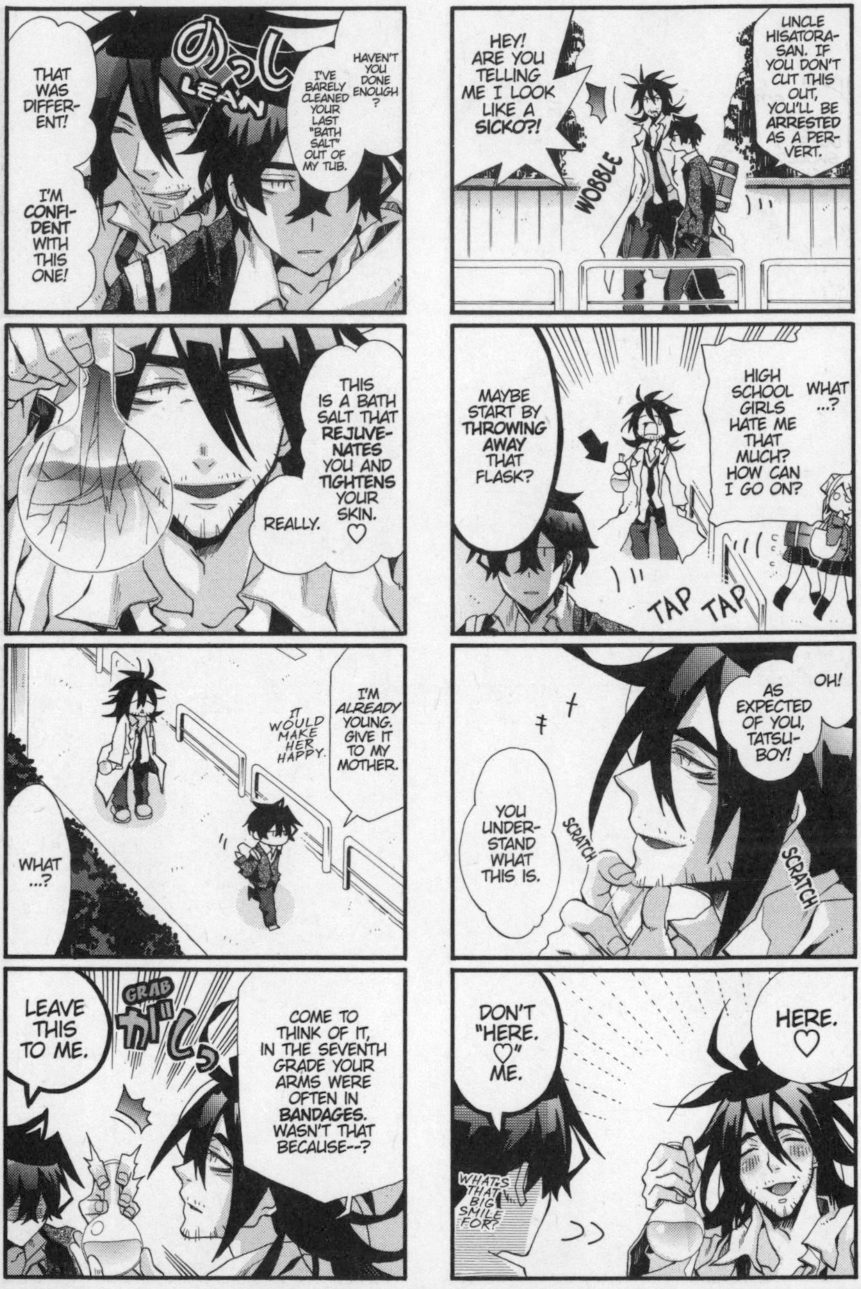

UNCLE HISATORA-SAN. IF YOU DON'T CUT THIS OUT, YOU'LL BE ARRESTED AS A PERVERT.
HEY! ARE YOU TELLING ME I LOOK LIKE A SICKO?!
WOBBLE
HAVEN'T YOU DONE ENOUGH?
I'VE BARELY CLEANED YOUR LAST "BATH SALT" OUT OF MY TUB.
のっし
LEAN
THAT WAS DIFFERENT!
I'M CONFIDENT WITH THIS ONE!
WHAT ...?
HIGH SCHOOL GIRLS HATE ME THAT MUCH? HOW CAN I GO ON?
MAYBE START BY THROWING AWAY THAT FLASK?
TAP TAP
THIS IS A BATH SALT THAT REJUVENATES YOU AND TIGHTENS YOUR SKIN. ♡
REALLY.
OH!
AS EXPECTED OF YOU, TATSU-BOY!
YOU UNDERSTAND WHAT THIS IS.
SCRATCH
SCRATCH
I'M ALREADY YOUNG. GIVE IT TO MY MOTHER.
IT WOULD MAKE HER HAPPY.
WHAT ...?
HERE. ♡
DON'T "HERE. ♡" ME.
WHAT'S THAT BIG SMILE FOR?
COME TO THINK OF IT, IN THE SEVENTH GRADE YOUR ARMS WERE OFTEN IN BANDAGES. WASN'T THAT BECAUSE--?
GRAB
がしっ
LEAVE THIS TO ME.

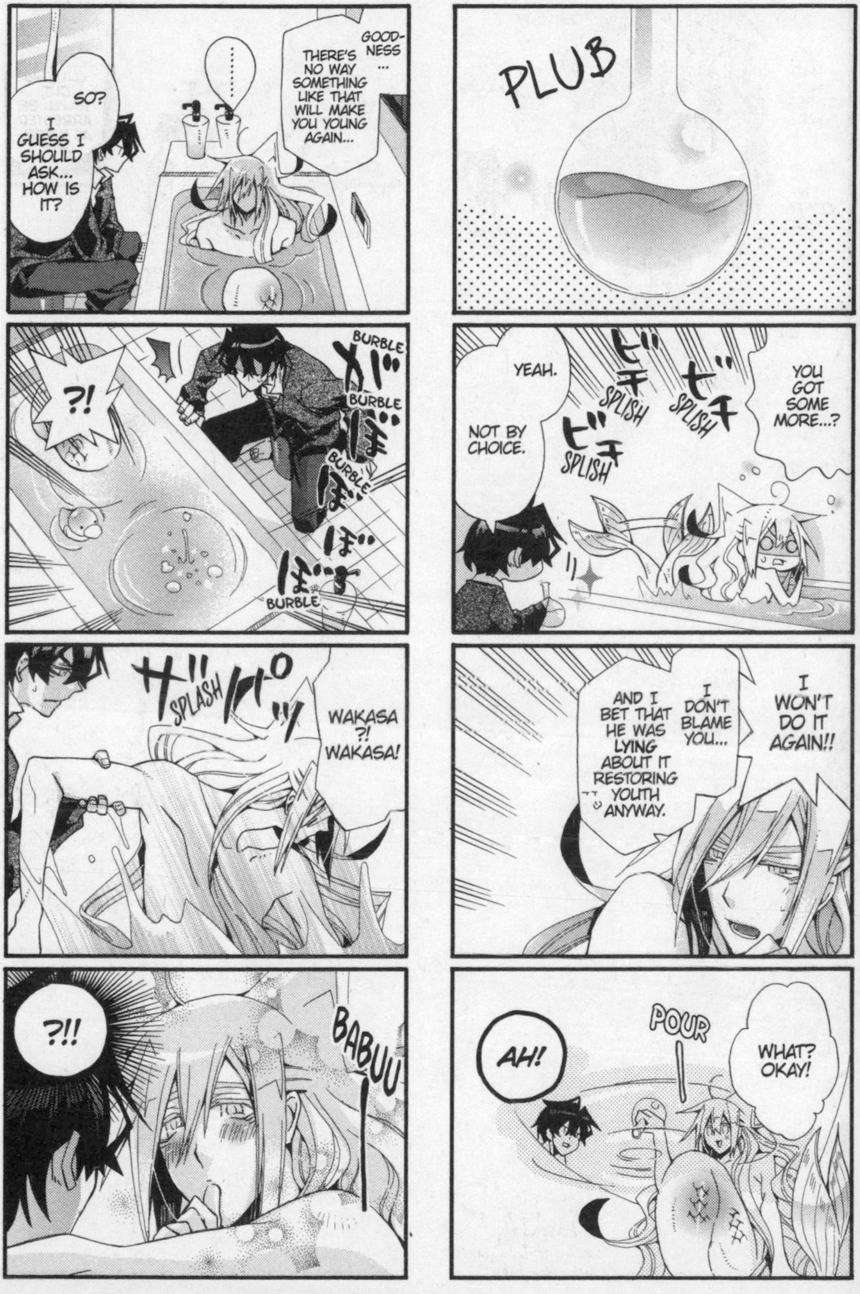
PLUB
YOU GOT SOME MORE...?
SPLISH
SPLISH
SPLISH
YEAH.
NOT BY CHOICE.
I WON'T DO IT AGAIN!!
I DON'T BLAME YOU...
AND I BET THAT HE WAS LYING ABOUT IT RESTORING YOUTH ANYWAY.
WHAT? OKAY!
POUR
AH!
GOODNESS...
THERE'S NO WAY SOMETHING LIKE THAT WILL MAKE YOU YOUNG AGAIN...
......
SO?
I GUESS I SHOULD ASK... HOW IS IT?
BURBLE
BURBLE
BURBLE
BURBLE
?!
WAKASA?! WAKASA!
SPLASH
BABUU
?!!

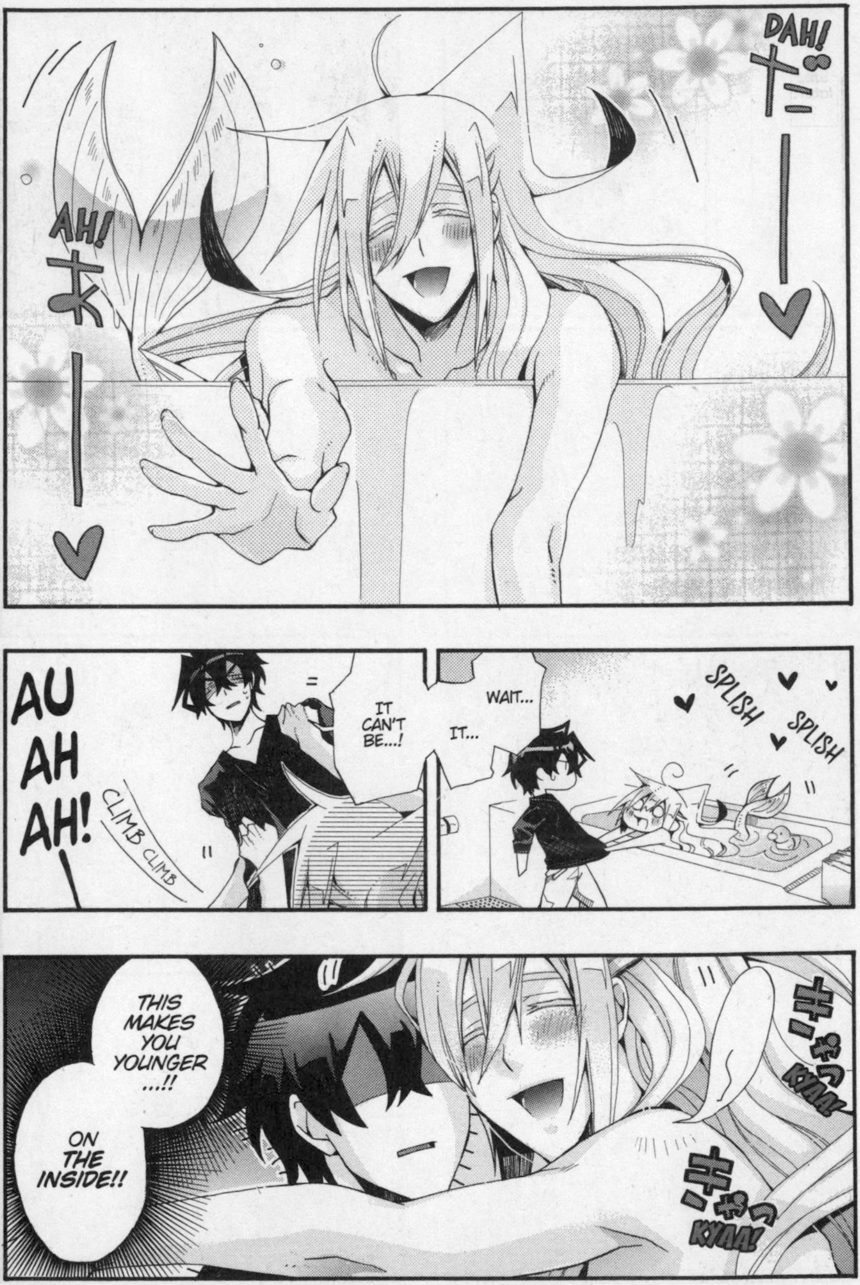
DAH!
だー
AH!
あー
SPLISH SPLISH
WAIT...
IT...
IT CAN'T BE...!
AU AH AH!
CLIMB CLIMB
きゃっ
KYAA!
きゃっ
KYAA!
THIS MAKES YOU YOUNGER...!!
ON THE INSIDE!!

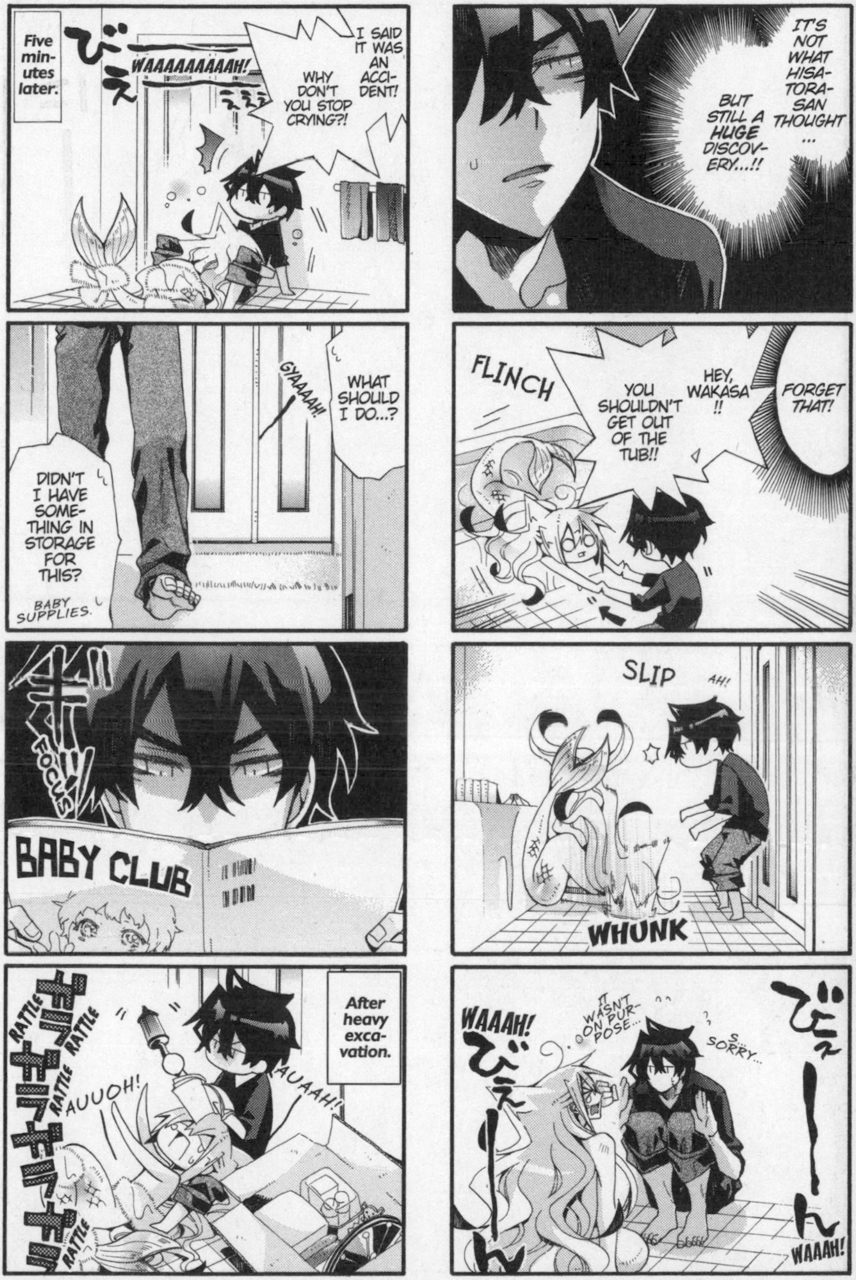
IT'S NOT WHAT HISATORA-SAN THOUGHT...
BUT STILL A HUGE DISCOVERY...!!
FORGET THAT!
HEY, WAKASA!!
YOU SHOULDN'T GET OUT OF THE TUB!!
FLINCH
AH!
SLIP
WHUNK
びえーーーん
WAAAH!
S... SORRY...
IT WASN'T ON PURPOSE...
WAAAH!
びえーーん
I SAID IT WAS AN ACCIDENT!
WHY DON'T YOU STOP CRYING?!
びえーーーーえええ
WAAAAAAAAAH!
Five minutes later.
WHAT SHOULD I DO...?
GYAAAAH!
DIDN'T I HAVE SOMETHING IN STORAGE FOR THIS?
BABY SUPPLIES.
FOCUS
BABY CLUB
After heavy excavation.
AUAAAH!
AUUOH!
RATTLE RATTLE
RATTLE
RATTLE

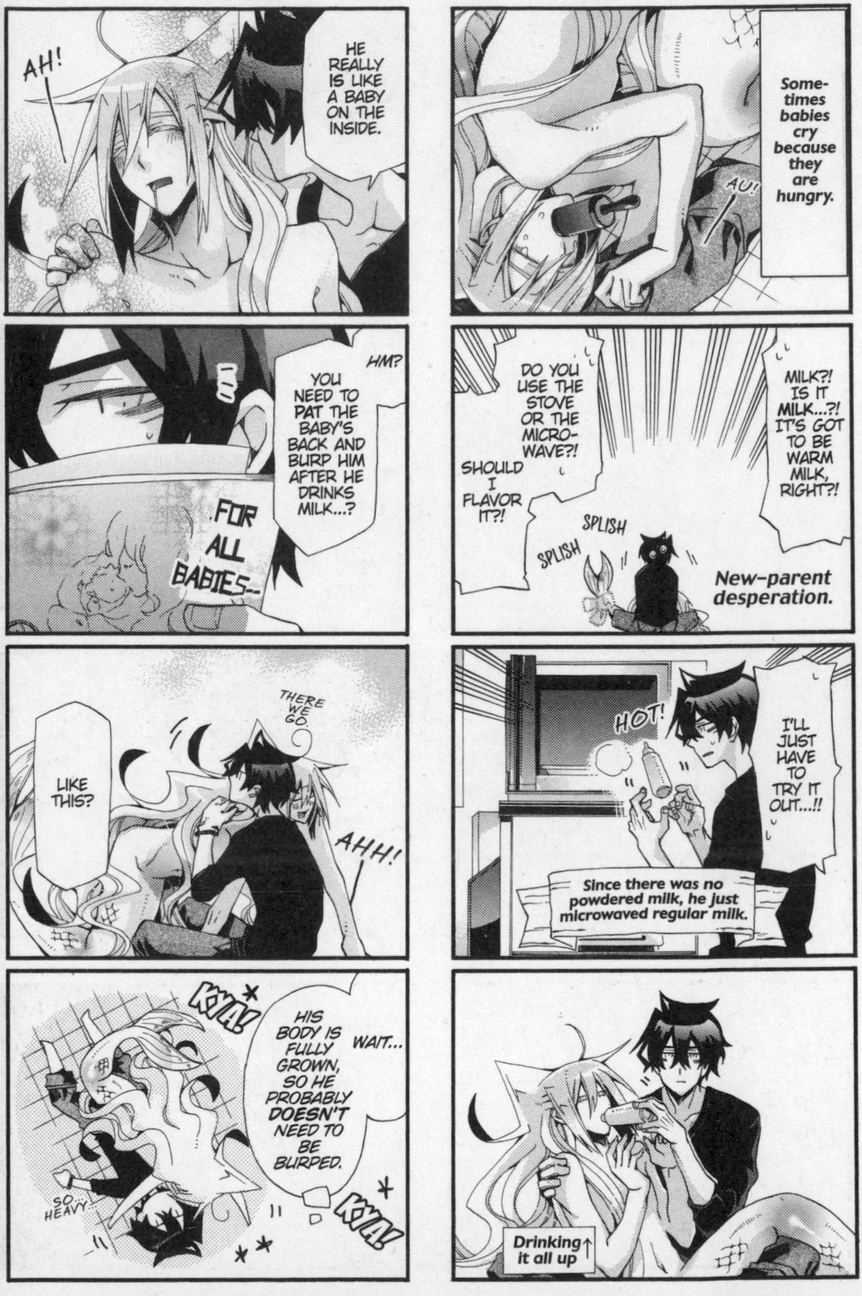
Some-times babies cry because they are hungry.
AU!
MILK?! IS IT MILK...?! IT'S GOT TO BE WARM MILK, RIGHT?!
DO YOU USE THE STOVE OR THE MICRO-WAVE?!
SHOULD I FLAVOR IT?!
SPLISH
SPLISH
New-parent desperation.
I'LL JUST HAVE TO TRY IT OUT...!!
HOT!
Since there was no powdered milk, he just microwaved regular milk.
Drinking it all up
HE REALLY IS LIKE A BABY ON THE INSIDE.
AH!
HM?
YOU NEED TO PAT THE BABY'S BACK AND BURP HIM AFTER HE DRINKS MILK...?
FOR ALL BABIES--
THERE WE GO.
LIKE THIS?
AHH!
WAIT...
HIS BODY IS FULLY GROWN, SO HE PROBABLY DOESN'T NEED TO BE BURPED.
KYA!
SO... HEAVY...
KYA!

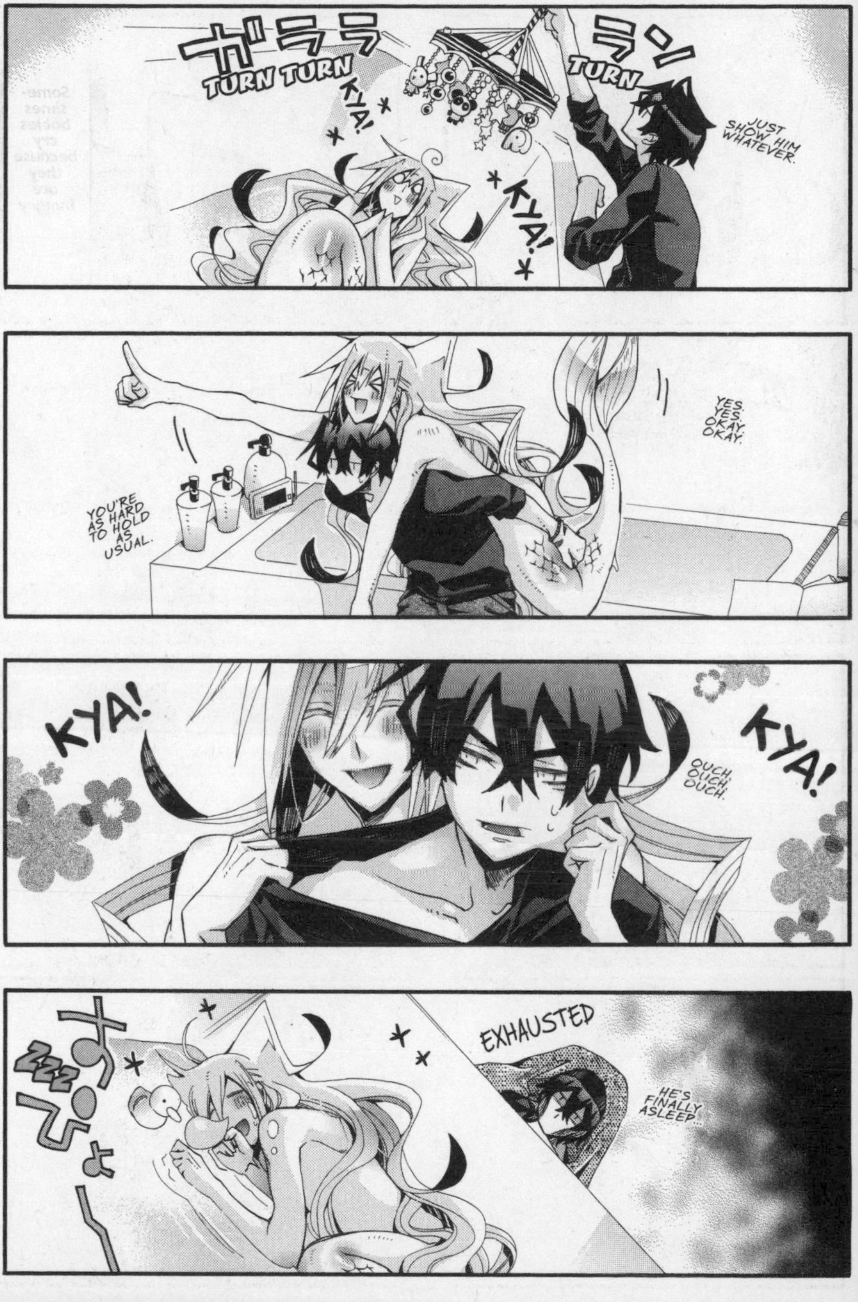
ラ〜
TURN
JUST SHOW HIM WHATEVER.
KYA!
ガララ
TURN TURN
KYA!
YES. YES. OKAY. OKAY.
YOU'RE AS HARD TO HOLD AS USUAL.
KYA!
OUCH. OUCH. OUCH.
KYA!
EXHAUSTED
HE'S FINALLY ASLEEP...
ZZZ
すぴょ〜

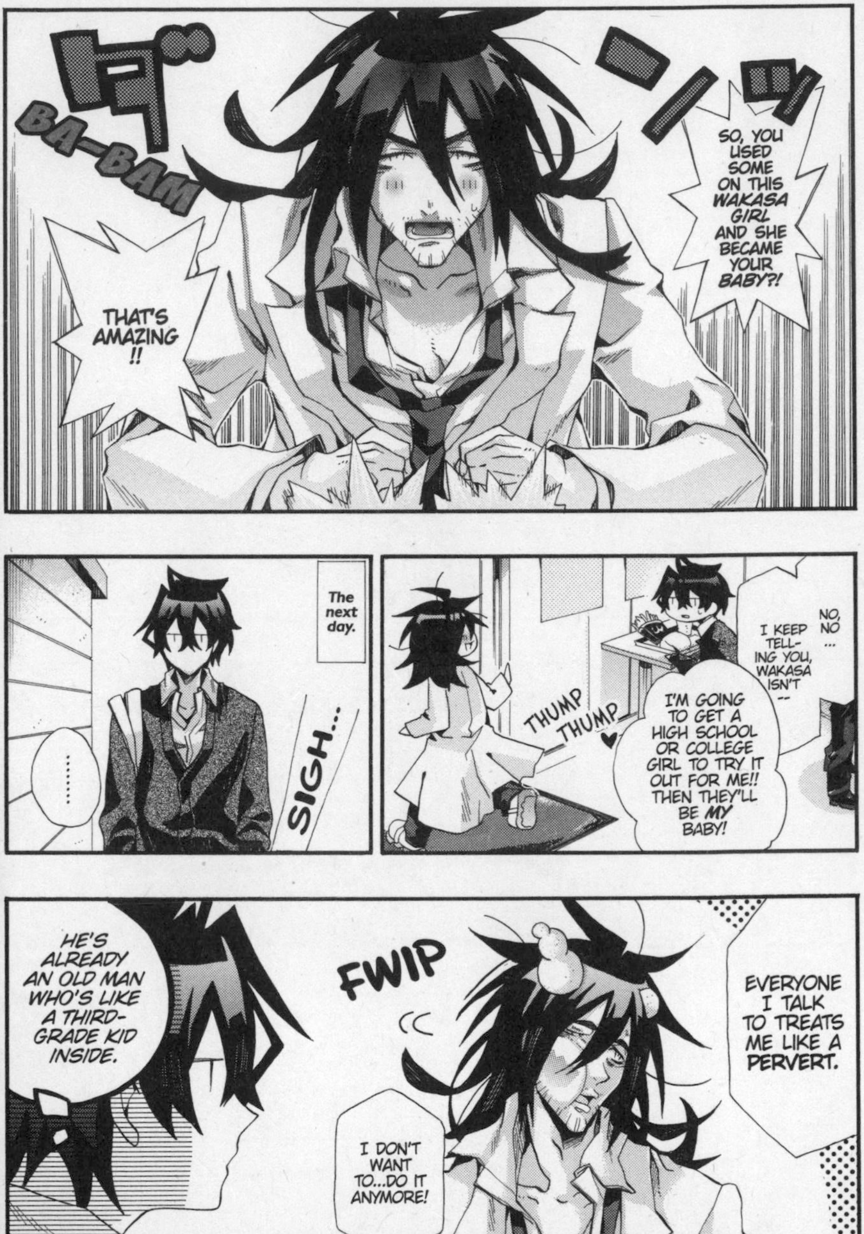
SO, YOU USED SOME ON THIS WAKASA GIRL AND SHE BECAME YOUR BABY?!
BA-BAM
THAT'S AMAZING!!
NO, NO ...
I KEEP TELLING YOU, WAKASA ISN'T --
I'M GOING TO GET A HIGH SCHOOL OR COLLEGE GIRL TO TRY IT OUT FOR ME!! THEN THEY'LL BE MY BABY!
THUMP THUMP
The next day.
SIGH...
......
EVERYONE I TALK TO TREATS ME LIKE A PERVERT.
FWIP
I DON'T WANT TO...DO IT ANYMORE!
HE'S ALREADY AN OLD MAN WHO'S LIKE A THIRD-GRADE KID INSIDE.

Merman in My Tub

オレん家(ち)のフロ事情

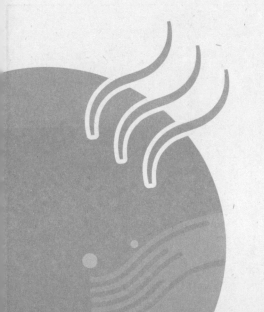

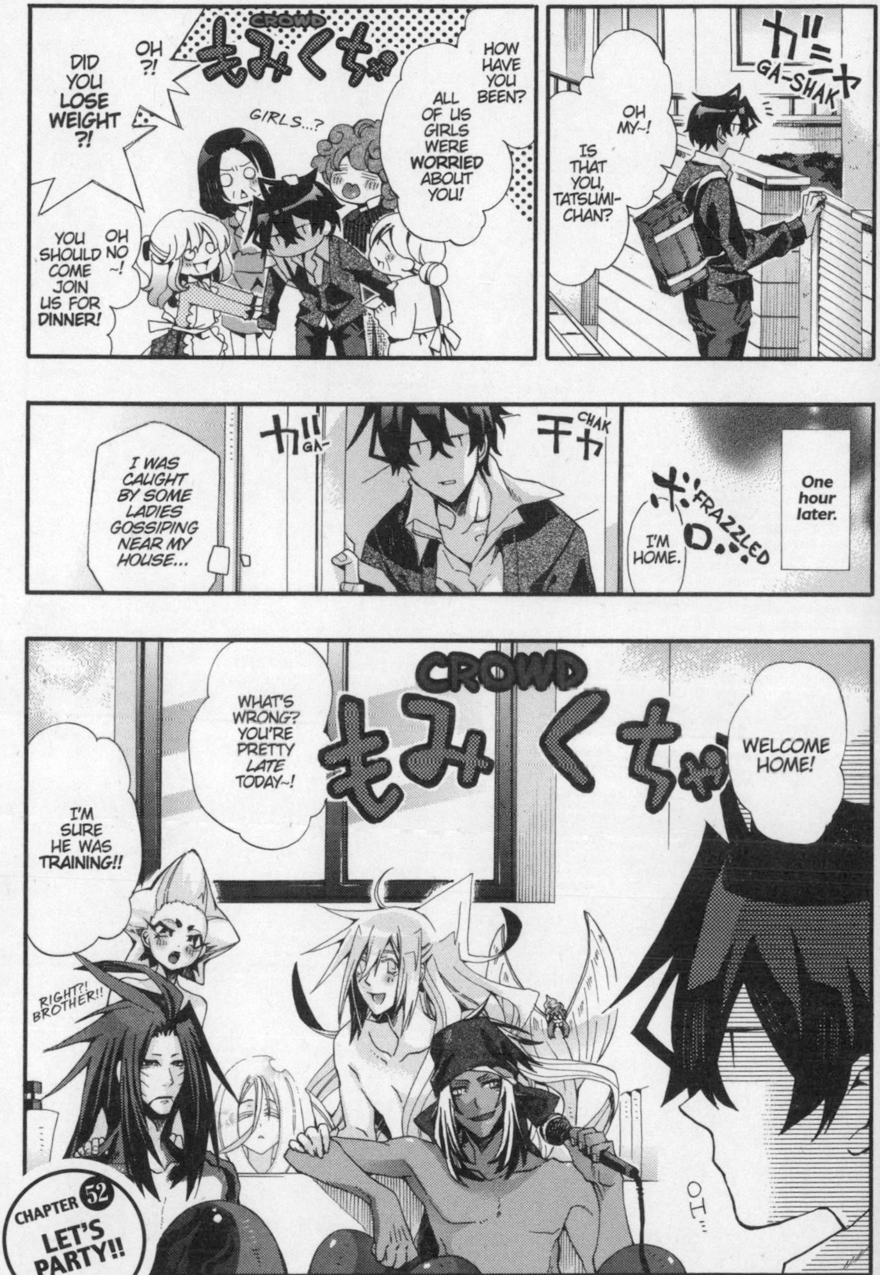

ガシャ
GA-SHAK
OH MY~!
IS THAT YOU, TATSUMI-CHAN?
CROWD
もみくちゃ
HOW HAVE YOU BEEN?
ALL OF US GIRLS WERE WORRIED ABOUT YOU!
GIRLS...?
OH ?!
DID YOU LOSE WEIGHT ?!
OH NO ~!
YOU SHOULD COME JOIN US FOR DINNER!
One hour later.
FRAZZLED
I'M HOME.
CHAK
GA-
I WAS CAUGHT BY SOME LADIES GOSSIPING NEAR MY HOUSE...
WELCOME HOME!
CROWD
もみくちゃ
WHAT'S WRONG? YOU'RE PRETTY LATE TODAY~!
I'M SURE HE WAS TRAINING!!
RIGHT?! BROTHER!!
OH...
CHAPTER 52
LET'S PARTY!!

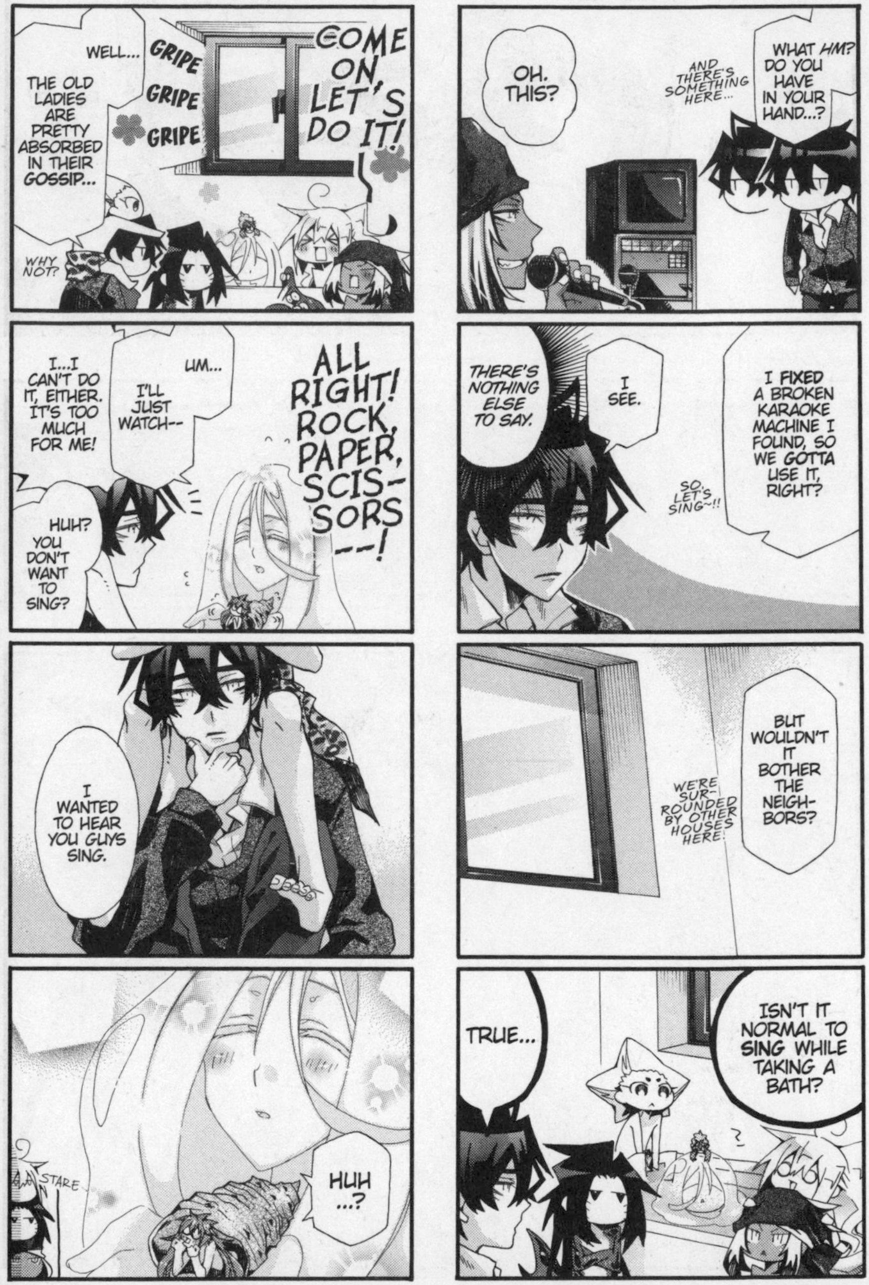
WHAT HM? DO YOU HAVE IN YOUR HAND...?
AND THERE'S SOMETHING HERE...
OH. THIS?
I FIXED A BROKEN KARAOKE MACHINE I FOUND, SO WE GOTTA USE IT, RIGHT?
SO, LET'S SING~!!
I SEE.
THERE'S NOTHING ELSE TO SAY.
BUT WOULDN'T IT BOTHER THE NEIGHBORS?
WE'RE SURROUNDED BY OTHER HOUSES HERE.
ISN'T IT NORMAL TO SING WHILE TAKING A BATH?
TRUE...
COME ON, LET'S DO IT!
GRIPE
GRIPE
GRIPE
WELL... THE OLD LADIES ARE PRETTY ABSORBED IN THEIR GOSSIP...
WHY NOT?
ALL RIGHT! ROCK, PAPER, SCISSORS--!
UM... I'LL JUST WATCH--
I...I CAN'T DO IT, EITHER. IT'S TOO MUCH FOR ME!
HUH? YOU DON'T WANT TO SING?
I WANTED TO HEAR YOU GUYS SING.
HUH ...?
STARE

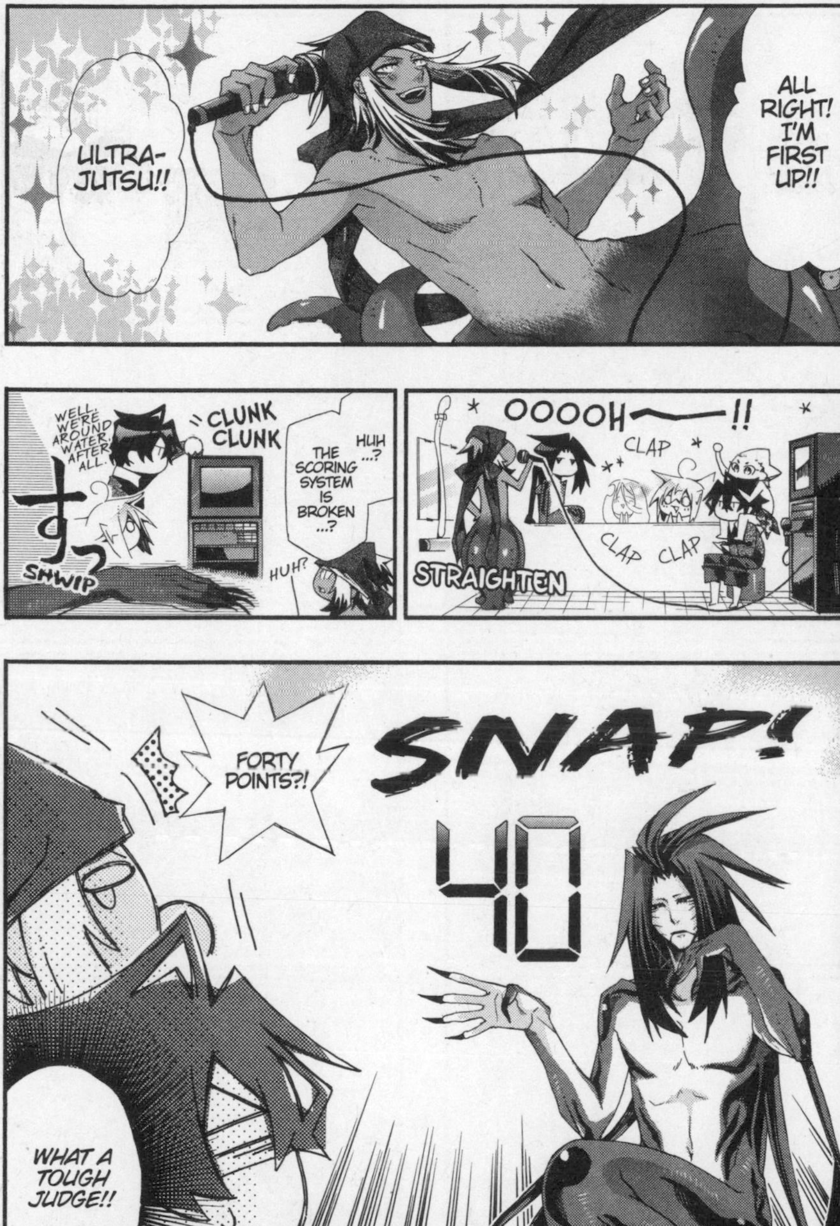
ALL RIGHT! I'M FIRST UP!!
ULTRA-JUTSU!!
OOOOH—!!
CLAP
CLAP CLAP
STRAIGHTEN
HUH ...?
THE SCORING SYSTEM IS BROKEN ...?
HUH?
CLUNK CLUNK
WELL, WE'RE AROUND WATER, AFTER ALL.
すっ
SHWIP
SNAP!
40
FORTY POINTS?!
WHAT A TOUGH JUDGE!!

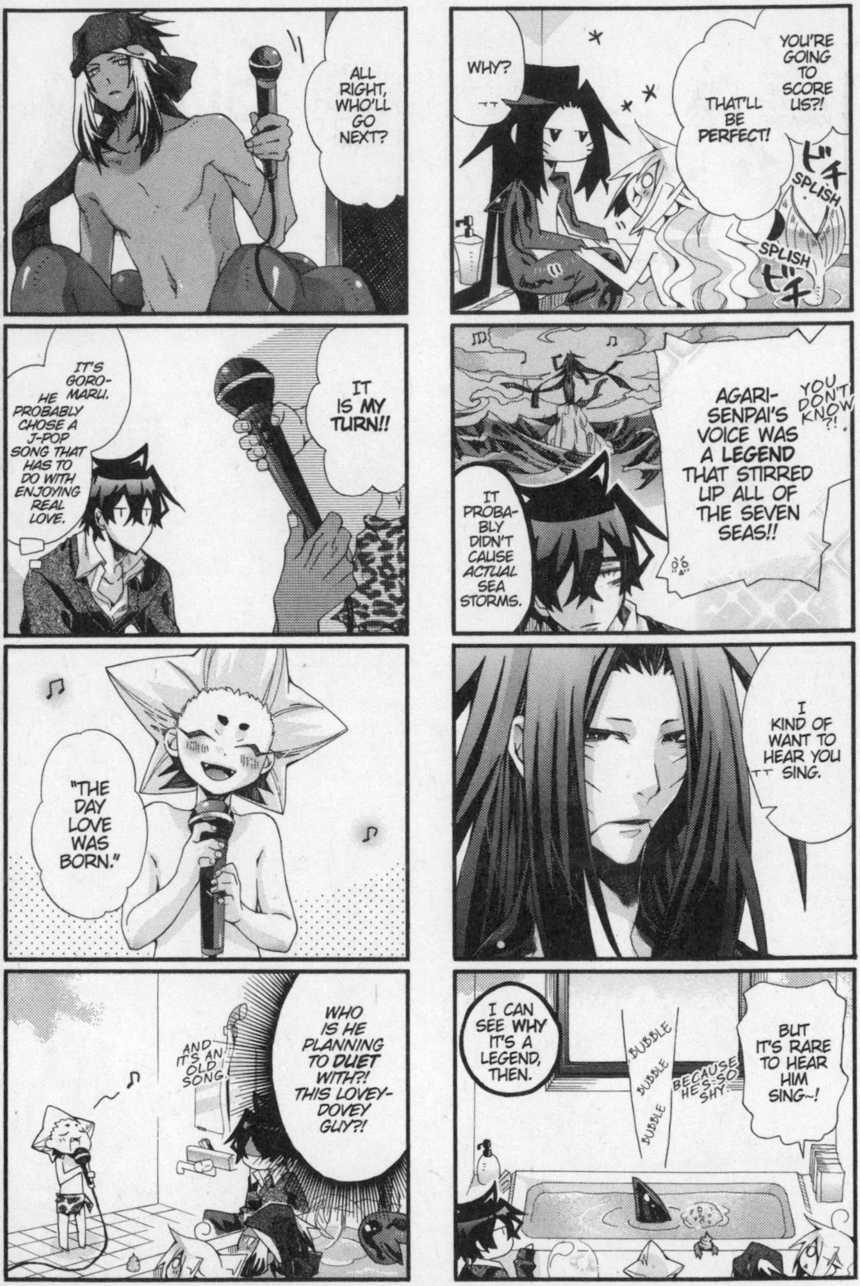
YOU'RE GOING TO SCORE US?!
THAT'LL BE PERFECT!
WHY?
ビチ
SPLISH
SPLISH
ビチ
YOU DON'T KNOW?!
AGARI-SENPAI'S VOICE WAS A LEGEND THAT STIRRED UP ALL OF THE SEVEN SEAS!!
IT PROBABLY DIDN'T CAUSE ACTUAL SEA STORMS.
I KIND OF WANT TO HEAR YOU SING.
BUT IT'S RARE TO HEAR HIM SING~!
BECAUSE HE'S SO SHY.
BUBBLE
BUBBLE
BUBBLE
I CAN SEE WHY IT'S A LEGEND, THEN.
ALL RIGHT, WHO'LL GO NEXT?
IT IS MY TURN!!
IT'S GOROMARU. HE PROBABLY CHOSE A J-POP SONG THAT HAS TO DO WITH ENJOYING REAL LOVE.
"THE DAY LOVE WAS BORN."
WHO IS HE PLANNING TO DUET WITH?! THIS LOVEY-DOVEY GUY?!
AND IT'S AN OLD SONG.

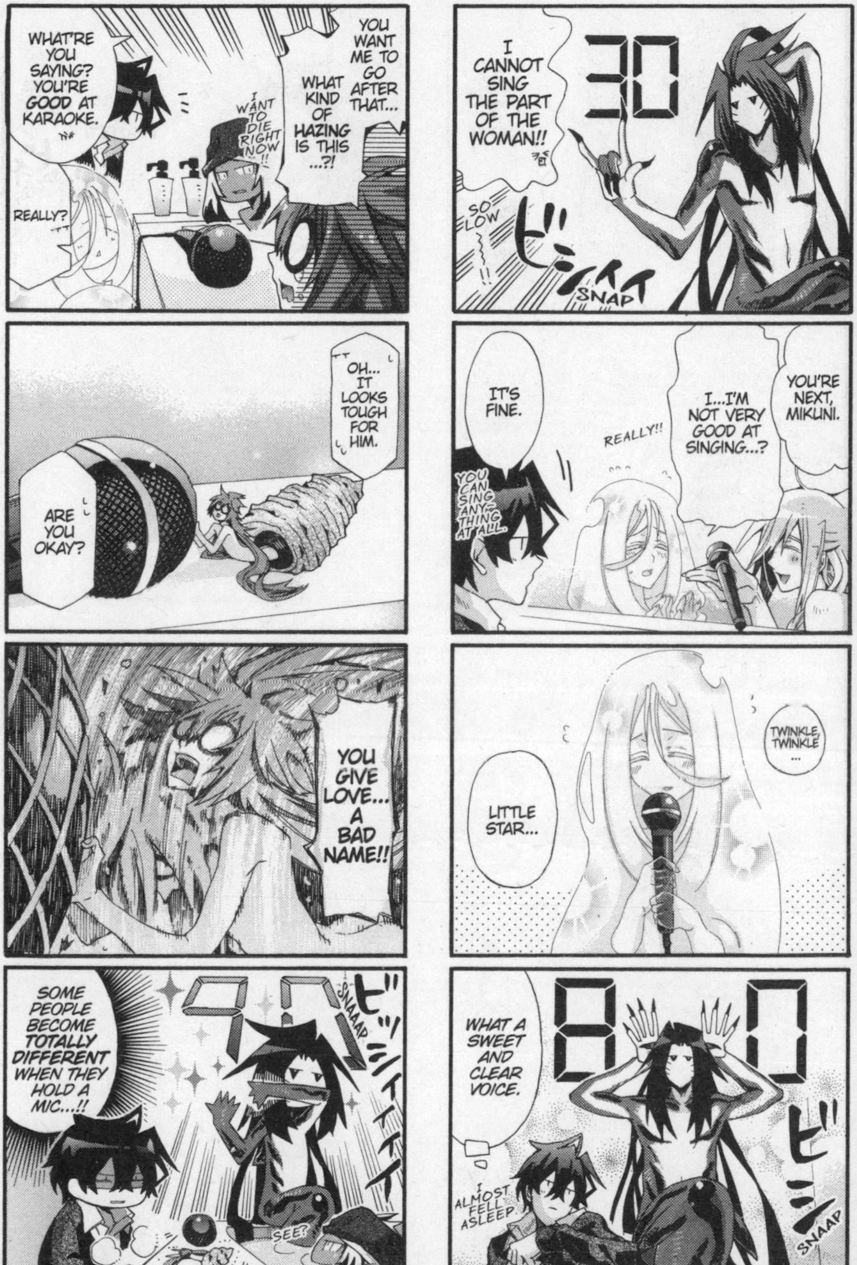
I CANNOT SING THE PART OF THE WOMAN!!
30
SO LOW ~~!!
SNAP
YOU'RE NEXT, MIKUNI.
I...I'M NOT VERY GOOD AT SINGING...?
REALLY!!
IT'S FINE.
YOU CAN SING ANYTHING AT ALL.
TWINKLE, TWINKLE ...
LITTLE STAR...
80
WHAT A SWEET AND CLEAR VOICE.
I ALMOST FELL ASLEEP.
SNAAP
YOU WANT ME TO GO AFTER THAT...
WHAT KIND OF HAZING IS THIS ...?!
I WANT TO DIE RIGHT NOW!!
WHAT'RE YOU SAYING? YOU'RE GOOD AT KARAOKE.
REALLY?
OH... IT LOOKS TOUGH FOR HIM.
ARE YOU OKAY?
YOU GIVE LOVE... A BAD NAME!!
97
SNAAAP
SOME PEOPLE BECOME TOTALLY DIFFERENT WHEN THEY HOLD A MIC...!!
SEE?

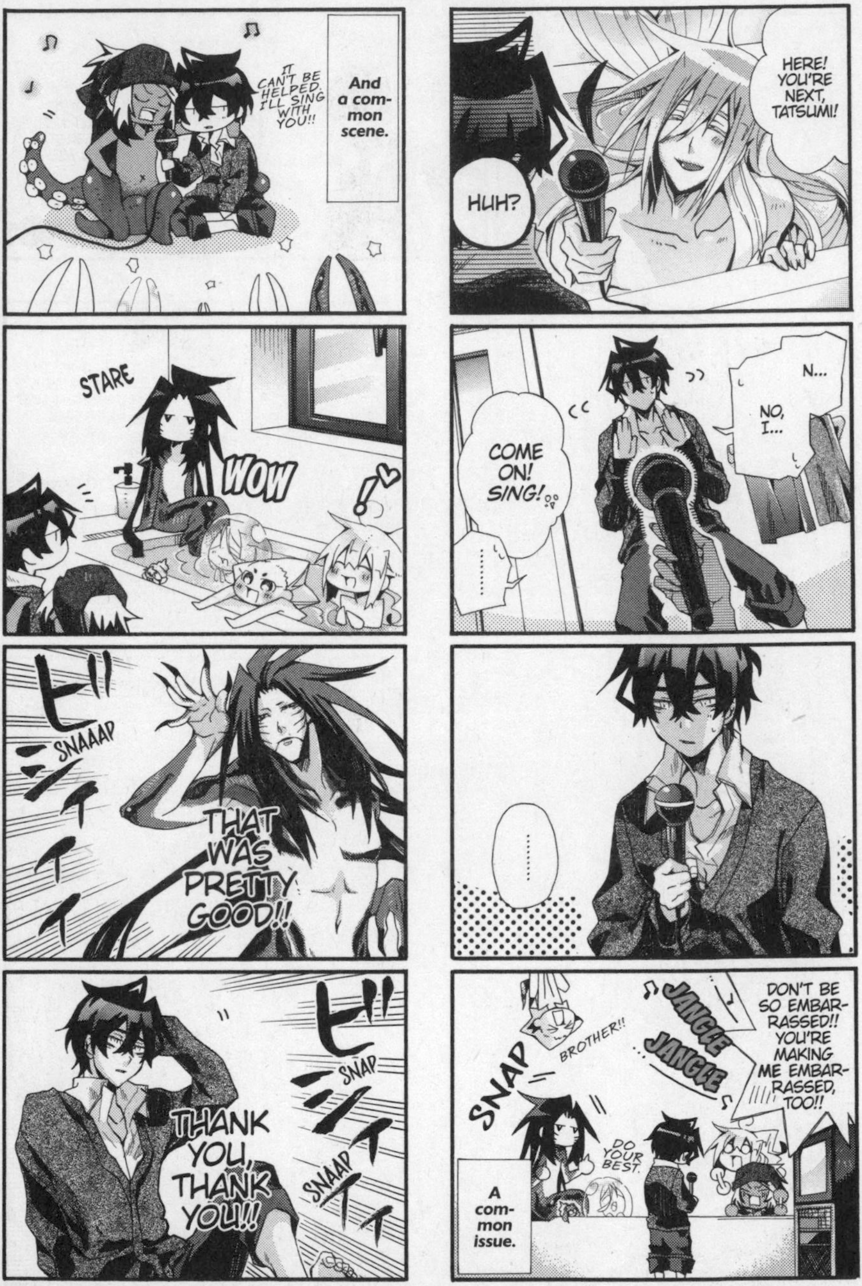
HERE! YOU'RE NEXT, TATSUMI!
HUH?
N... NO, I...
COME ON! SING!
......
......
DON'T BE SO EMBARRASSED!! YOU'RE MAKING ME EMBARRASSED, TOO!!
JANGLE JANGLE
BROTHER!!
SNAP
DO YOUR BEST.
A common issue.
And a common scene.
IT CAN'T BE HELPED. I'LL SING WITH YOU!!
STARE
WOW
SNAAAP
THAT WAS PRETTY GOOD!!
SNAP
SNAAP
THANK YOU, THANK YOU!!

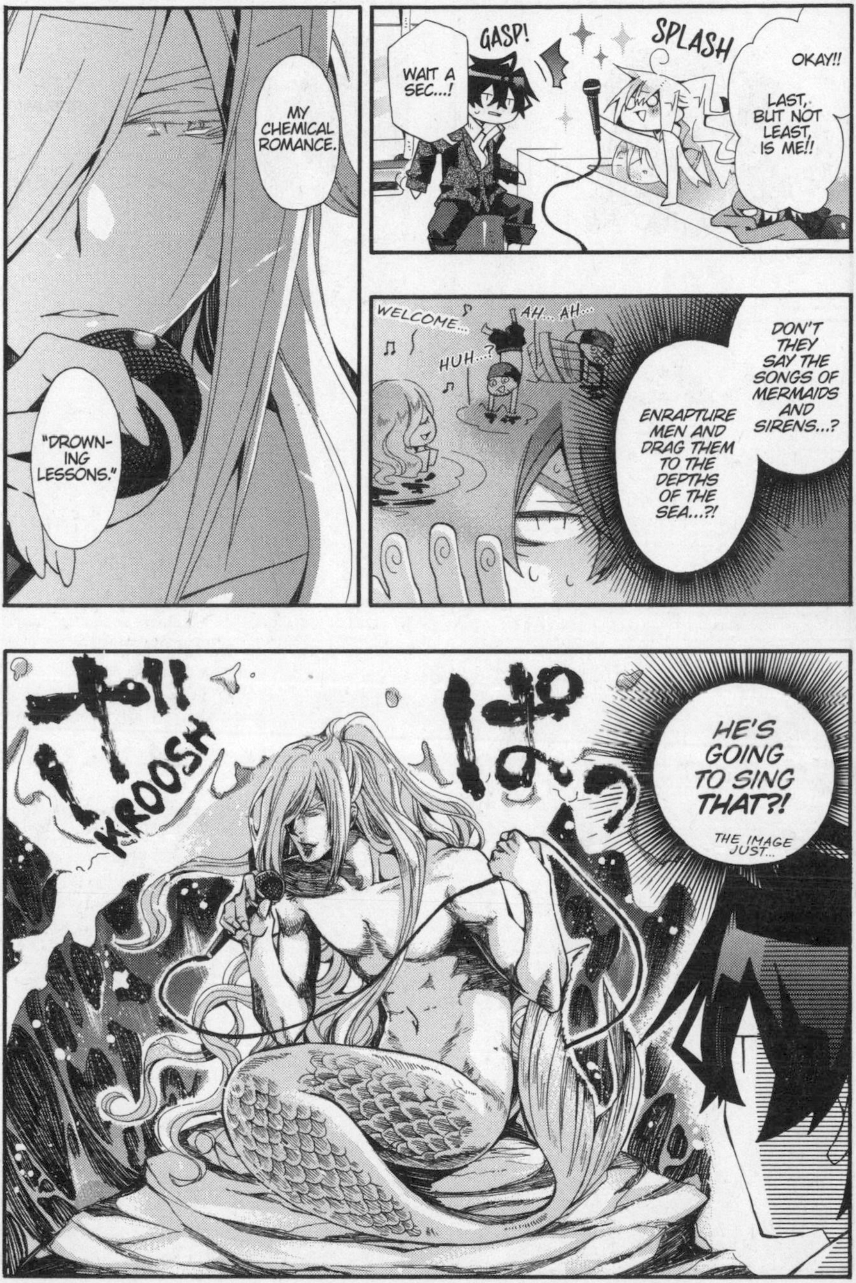
OKAY!!
LAST, BUT NOT LEAST, IS ME!!
SPLASH
GASP!
WAIT A SEC...!
DON'T THEY SAY THE SONGS OF MERMAIDS AND SIRENS...?
ENRAPTURE MEN AND DRAG THEM TO THE DEPTHS OF THE SEA...?!
AH... AH...
WELCOME...
HUH...?
MY CHEMICAL ROMANCE.
"DROWNING-ING LESSONS."
HE'S GOING TO SING THAT?!
THE IMAGE JUST...
KROOSH

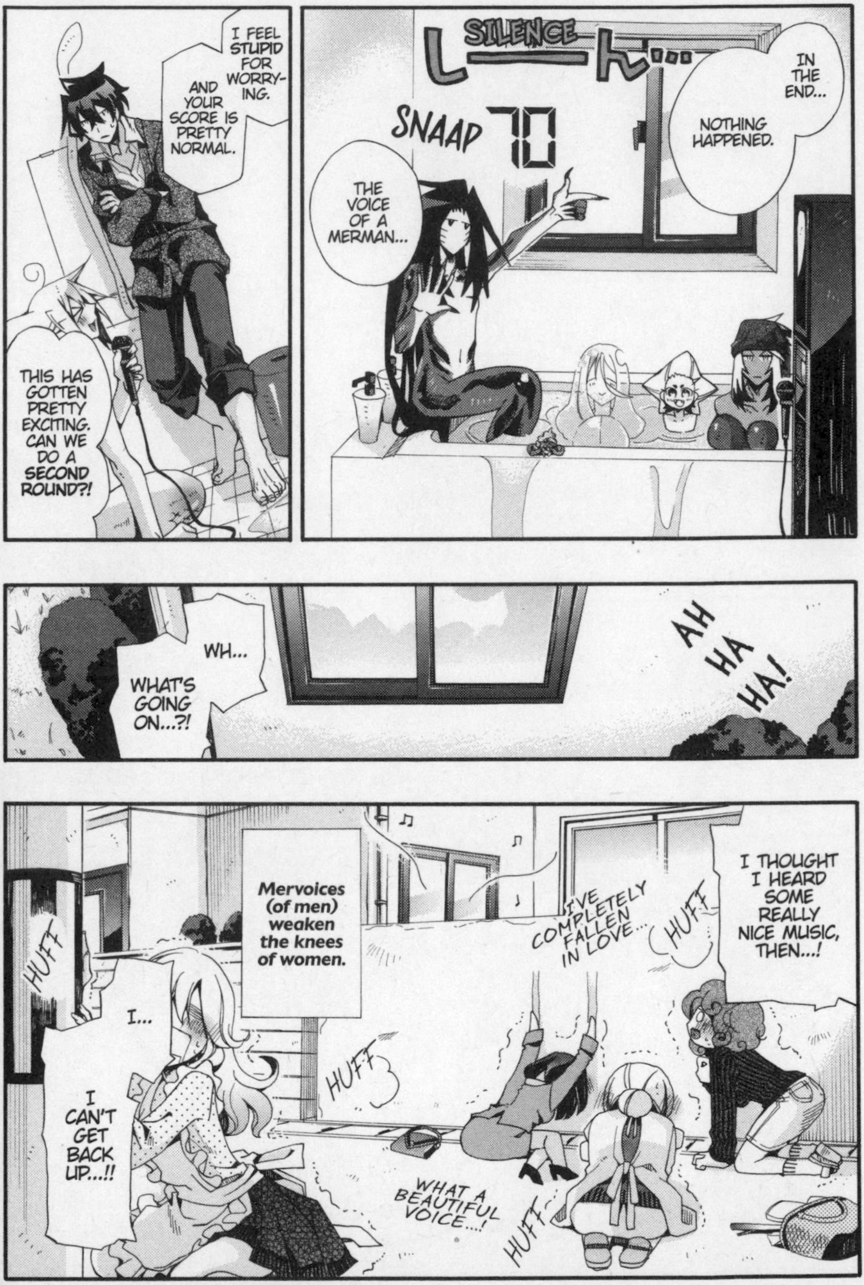
IN THE END... NOTHING HAPPENED.
SILENCE
SNAAP
70
THE VOICE OF A MERMAN...
I FEEL STUPID FOR WORRY-ING.
AND YOUR SCORE IS PRETTY NORMAL.
THIS HAS GOTTEN PRETTY EXCITING. CAN WE DO A SECOND ROUND?!
AH HA HA!
WH...
WHAT'S GOING ON...?!
I THOUGHT I HEARD SOME REALLY NICE MUSIC, THEN...!
HUFF
I'VE COMPLETELY FALLEN IN LOVE...
Mervoices (of men) weaken the knees of women.
HUFF
WHAT A BEAUTIFUL VOICE...!
HUFF
HUFF
I...
I CAN'T GET BACK UP...!!

Merman in My Tub

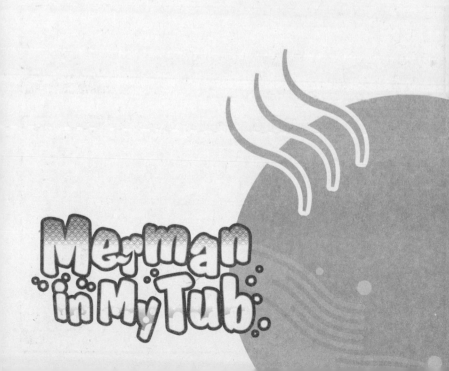

オレん家（ち）のフロ事情

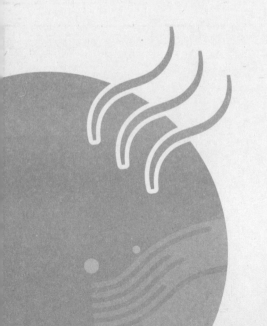

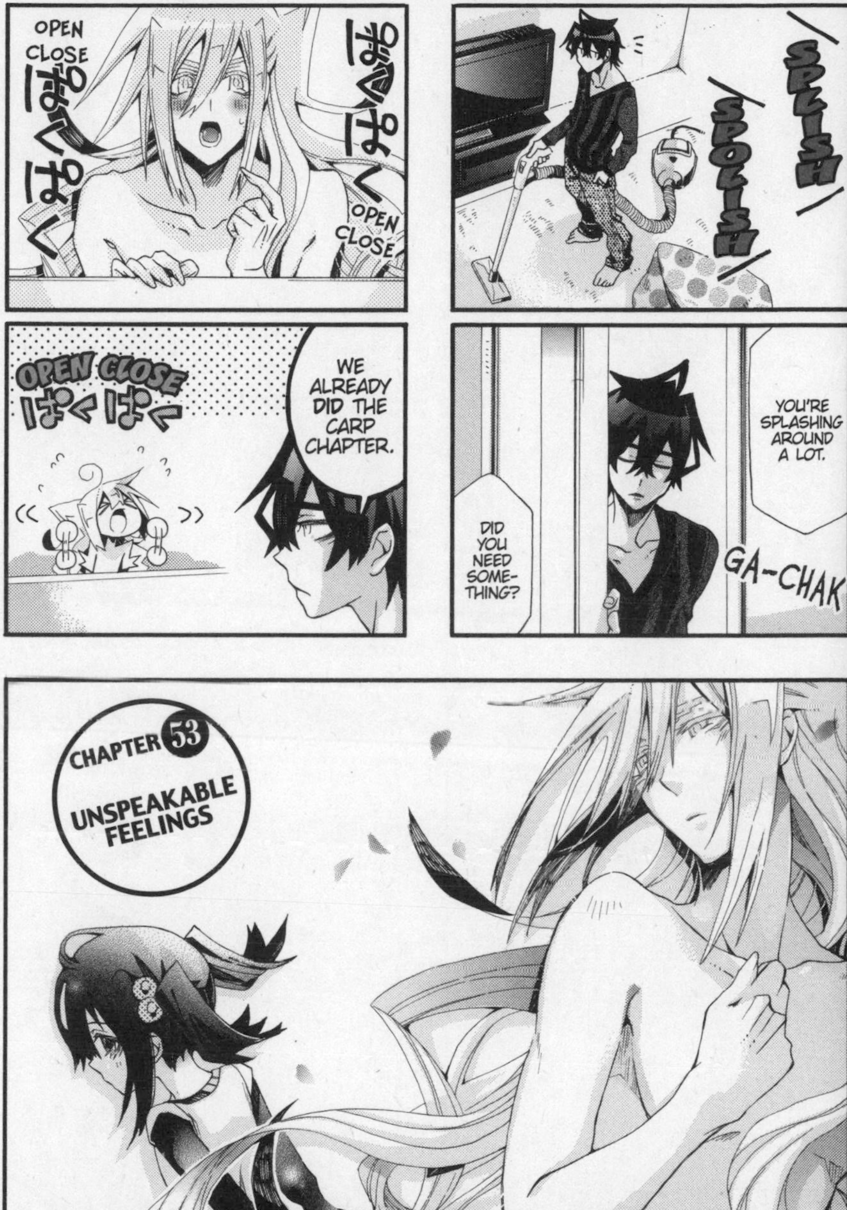
SPLISH
SPLISH
ぱくぱく
OPEN CLOSE
OPEN CLOSE
ぱくぱく
YOU'RE SPLASHING AROUND A LOT.
GA-CHAK
DID YOU NEED SOMETHING?
WE ALREADY DID THE CARP CHAPTER.
OPEN CLOSE
ぱくぱく
CHAPTER 53
UNSPEAKABLE FEELINGS

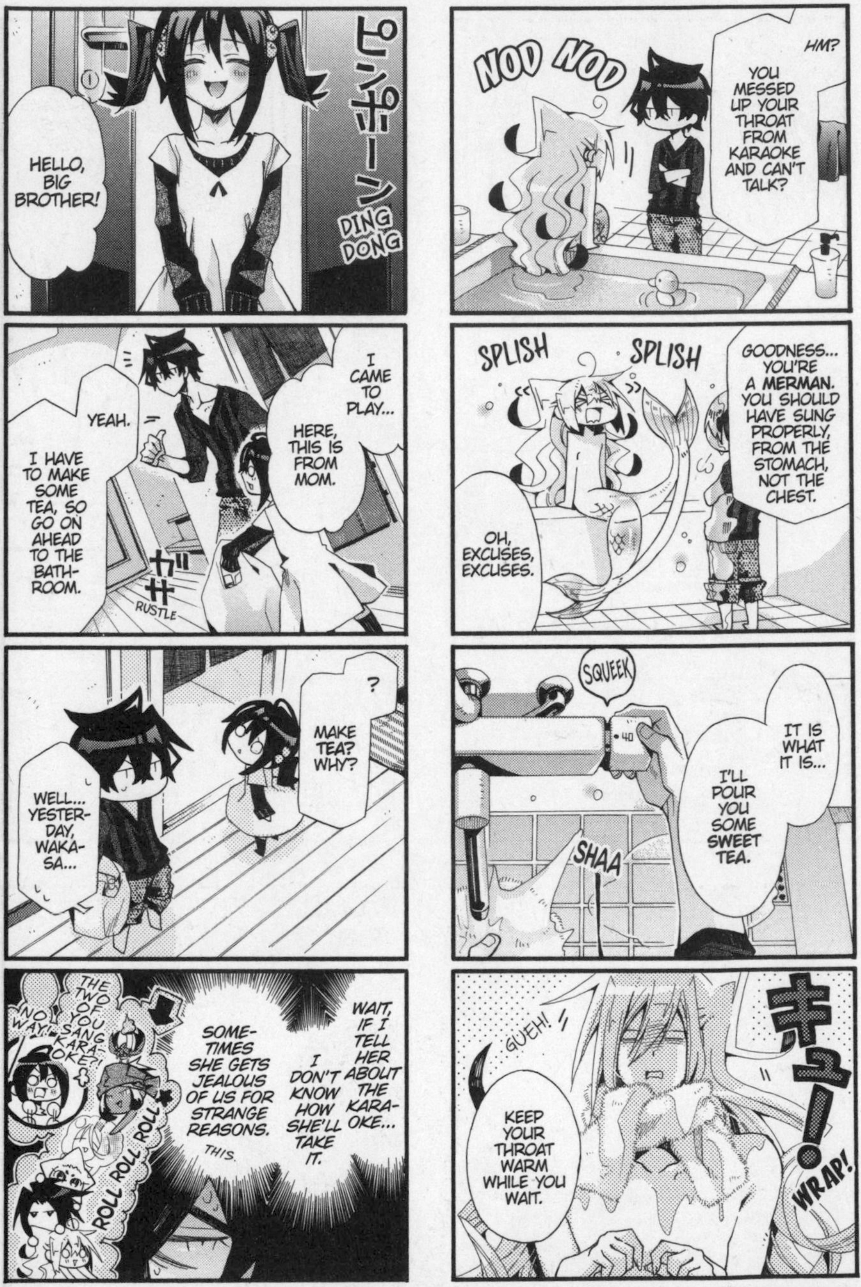
NOD NOD
HM?
YOU MESSED UP YOUR THROAT FROM KARAOKE AND CAN'T TALK?
SPLISH SPLISH
GOODNESS... YOU'RE A MERMAN. YOU SHOULD HAVE SUNG PROPERLY, FROM THE STOMACH, NOT THE CHEST.
OH, EXCUSES, EXCUSES.
SQUEEK
IT IS WHAT IT IS...
I'LL POUR YOU SOME SWEET TEA.
SHAA
キュ!
WRAP!
GUEH!
KEEP YOUR THROAT WARM WHILE YOU WAIT.
ピンポーン
DING DONG
HELLO, BIG BROTHER!
I CAME TO PLAY...
HERE, THIS IS FROM MOM.
YEAH.
I HAVE TO MAKE SOME TEA, SO GO ON AHEAD TO THE BATH-ROOM.
ガサ
RUSTLE
?
MAKE TEA? WHY?
WELL... YESTER-DAY, WAKA-SA...
WAIT, IF I TELL HER ABOUT THE KARA-OKE...
I DON'T KNOW HOW SHE'LL TAKE IT.
SOME-TIMES SHE GETS JEALOUS OF US FOR STRANGE REASONS.
THIS.
THE TWO OF YOU SANG KARA-OKE?!
NO WAY!
ROLL ROLL ROLL

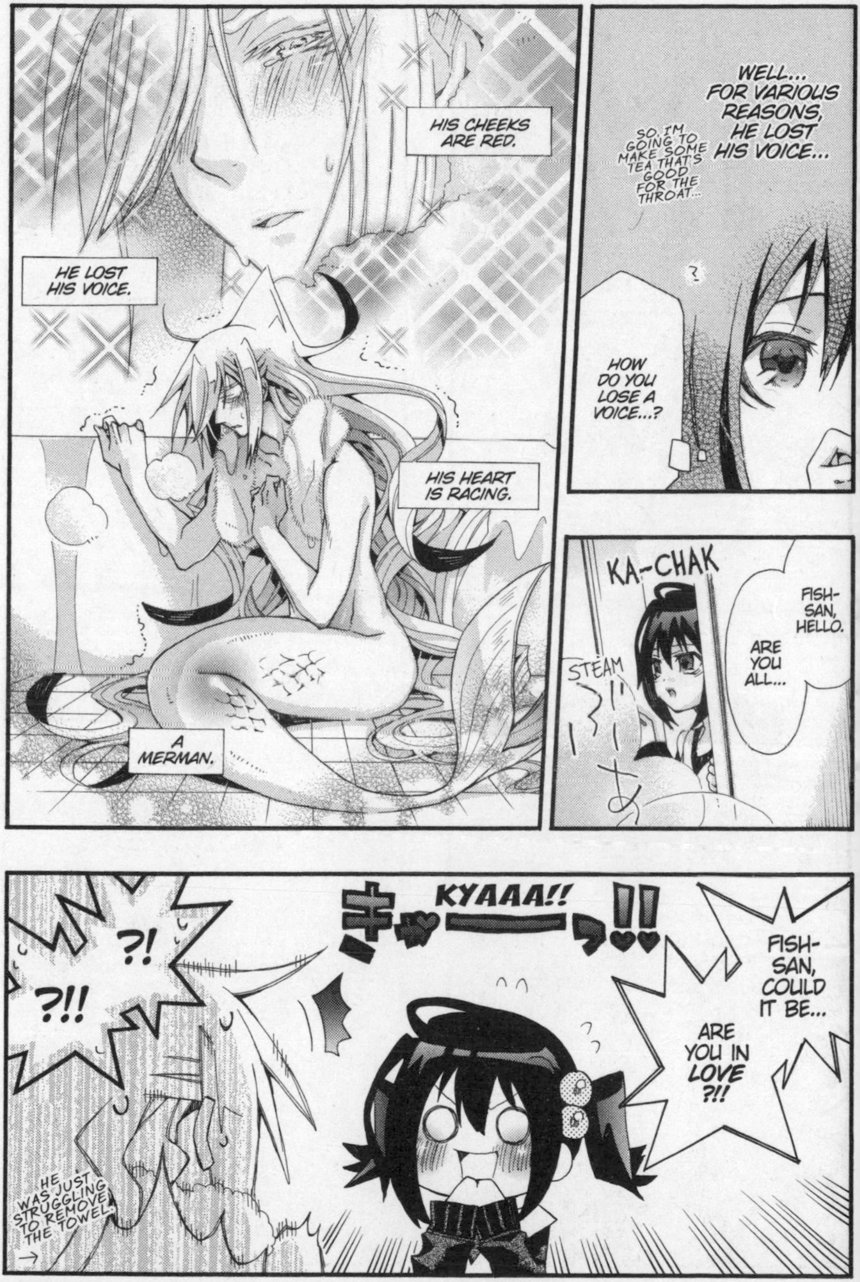
WELL... FOR VARIOUS REASONS, HE LOST HIS VOICE...
SO, I'M GOING TO MAKE SOME TEA THAT'S GOOD FOR THE THROAT...
?
HOW DO YOU LOSE A VOICE...?
KA-CHAK
FISH-SAN, HELLO.
ARE YOU ALL...
STEAM
HIS CHEEKS ARE RED.
HE LOST HIS VOICE.
HIS HEART IS RACING.
A MERMAN.
KYAAA!!
FISH-SAN, COULD IT BE...
ARE YOU IN LOVE ?!!
?!
?!!
HE WAS JUST STRUGGLING TO REMOVE THE TOWEL.

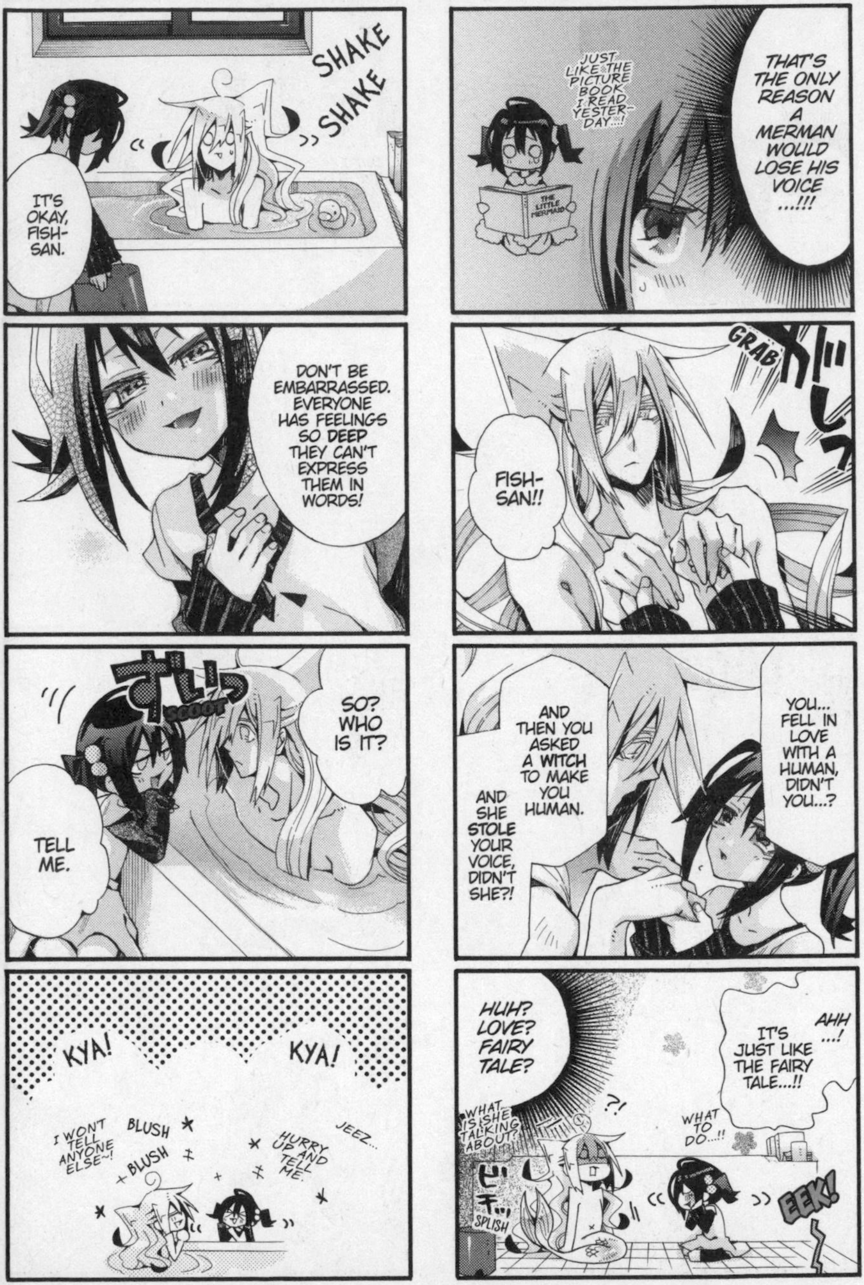
THAT'S THE ONLY REASON A MERMAN WOULD LOSE HIS VOICE ...!!!
JUST LIKE THE PICTURE BOOK I READ YESTERDAY...!
THE LITTLE MERMAID
SHAKE
SHAKE
IT'S OKAY, FISH-SAN.
GRAB
FISH-SAN!!
DON'T BE EMBARRASSED. EVERYONE HAS FEELINGS SO DEEP THEY CAN'T EXPRESS THEM IN WORDS!
YOU... FELL IN LOVE WITH A HUMAN, DIDN'T YOU...?
AND THEN YOU ASKED A WITCH TO MAKE YOU HUMAN.
AND SHE STOLE YOUR VOICE, DIDN'T SHE?!
SO? WHO IS IT?
SCOOT
TELL ME.
AHH ...!
IT'S JUST LIKE THE FAIRY TALE...!!
HUH? LOVE? FAIRY TALE?
?!
WHAT TO DO...!!
WHAT IS SHE TALKING ABOUT?
EEK!
SPLISH
KYA!
KYA!
JEEZ...
HURRY UP AND TELL ME.
BLUSH
I WON'T TELL ANYONE ELSE~!
BLUSH

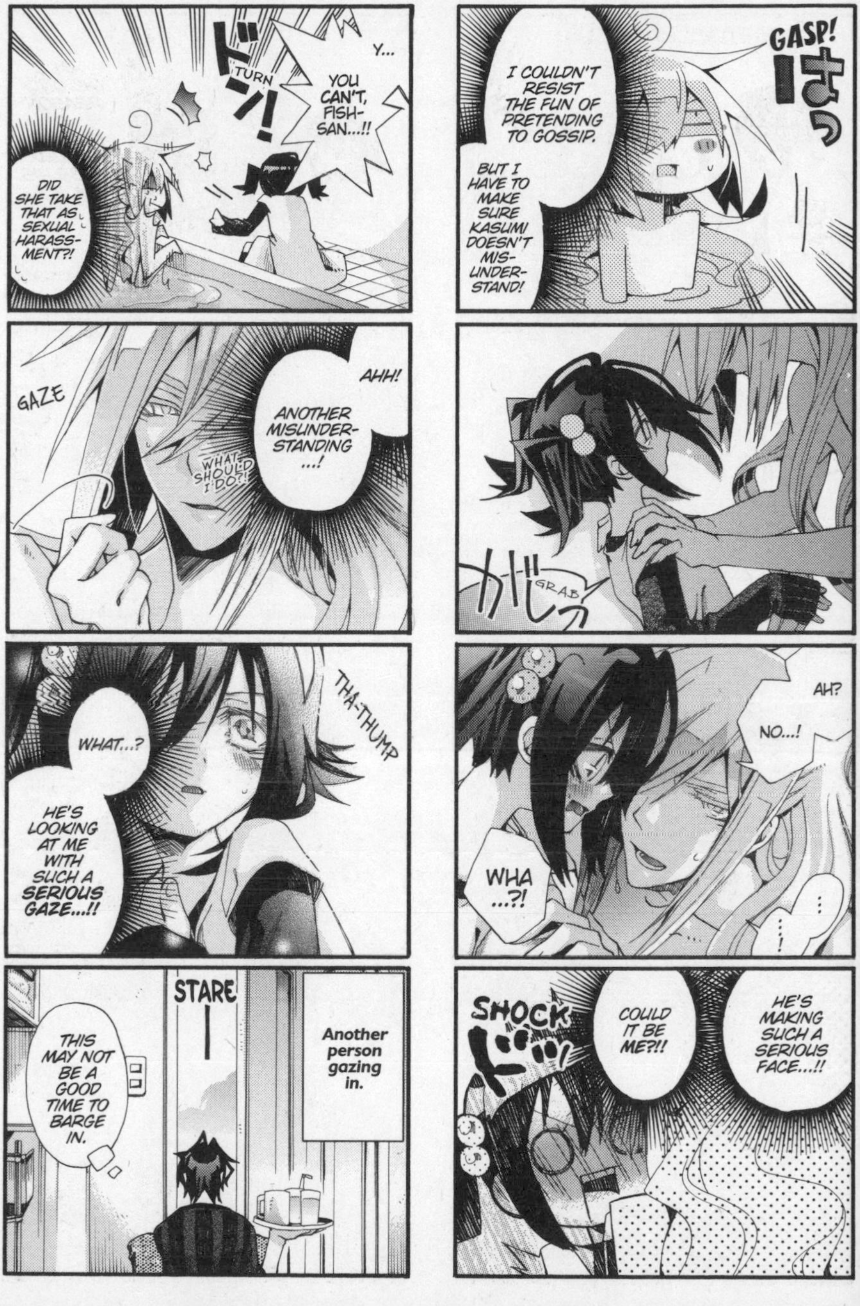
GASP!
はっ
I COULDN'T RESIST THE FUN OF PRETENDING TO GOSSIP.
BUT I HAVE TO MAKE SURE KASUMI DOESN'T MIS-UNDER-STAND!
かじっ
GRAB
AH?
NO...!
WHA ...?!
...!
...!
HE'S MAKING SUCH A SERIOUS FACE...!!
COULD IT BE ME?!!
SHOCK
Y...
YOU CAN'T, FISH-SAN...!!
ドン!
TURN
DID SHE TAKE THAT AS SEXUAL HARASS-MENT?!
AHH!
ANOTHER MISUNDER-STANDING ...!
WHAT SHOULD I DO?!
GAZE
THA-THUMP
WHAT...?
HE'S LOOKING AT ME WITH SUCH A SERIOUS GAZE...!!
STARE
Another person gazing in.
THIS MAY NOT BE A GOOD TIME TO BARGE IN.

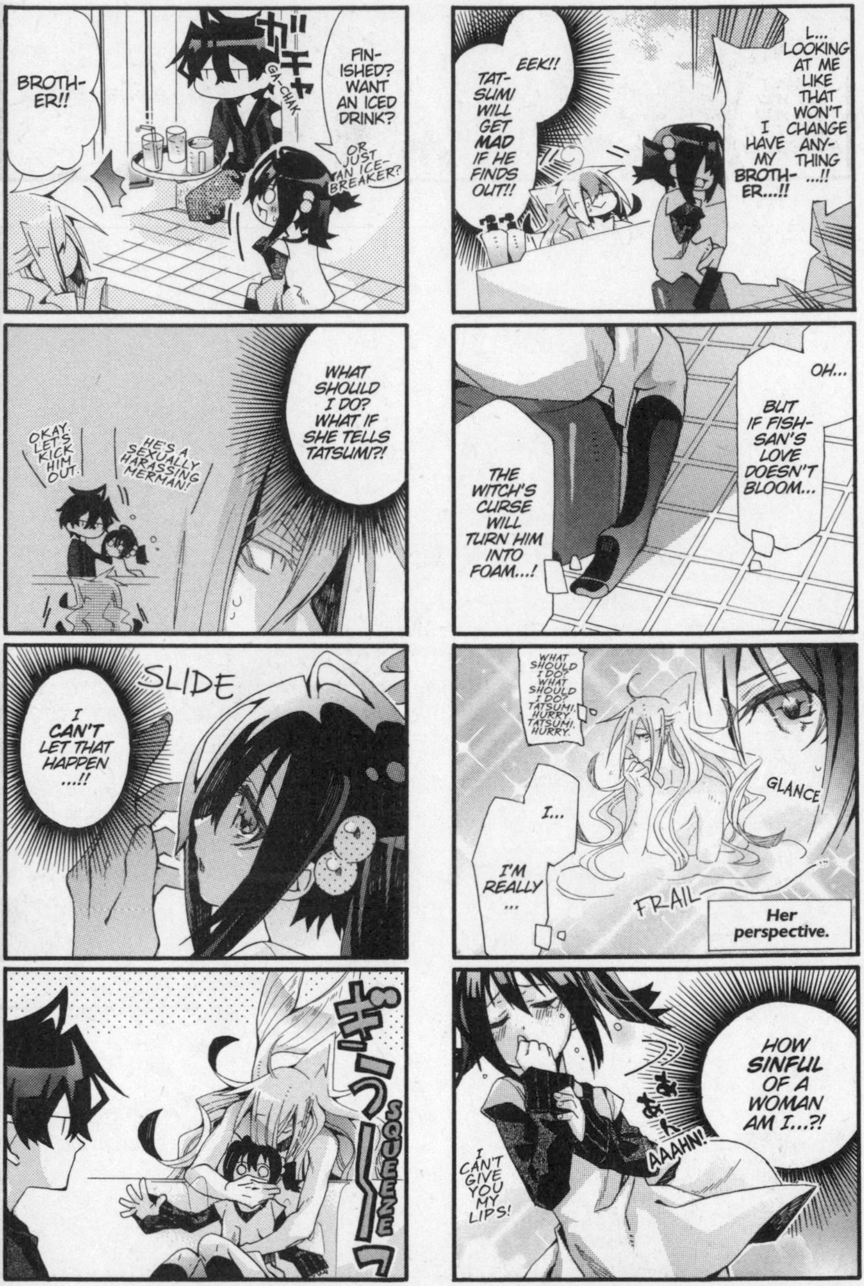

L... LOOKING AT ME LIKE THAT WON'T CHANGE ANYTHING ...!!
I HAVE MY BROTHER...!!
OH...
BUT IF FISH-SAN'S LOVE DOESN'T BLOOM...
THE WITCH'S CURSE WILL TURN HIM INTO FOAM...!
WHAT SHOULD I DO? WHAT SHOULD I DO? TATSUMI, HURRY. TATSUMI, HURRY.
GLANCE
I...
I'M REALLY ...
FRAIL
Her perspective.
HOW SINFUL OF A WOMAN AM I...?!
AAAHN!
I CAN'T GIVE YOU MY LIPS!
BROTHER!!
ガチャ GA-CHAK
FIN-ISHED? WANT AN ICED DRINK?
OR JUST AN ICE-BREAKER?
EEK!!
TAT-SUMI WILL GET MAD IF HE FINDS OUT!!
WHAT SHOULD I DO? WHAT IF SHE TELLS TATSUMI?!
HE'S A SEXUALLY HARASSING MERMAN!
OKAY. LET'S KICK HIM OUT.
SLIDE
I CAN'T LET THAT HAPPEN ...!!
SQUEEZE

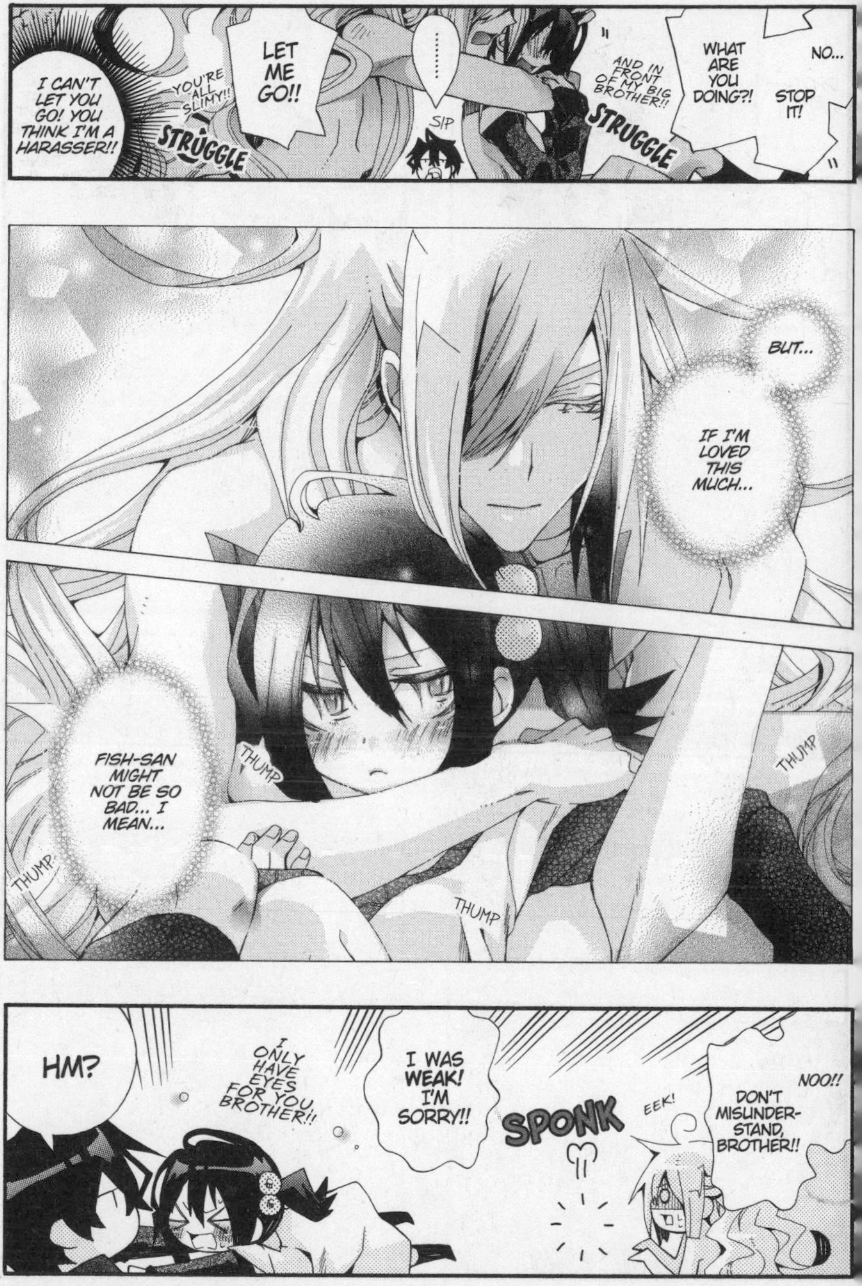
NO...
STOP IT!
WHAT ARE YOU DOING?!
AND IN FRONT OF MY BIG BROTHER!!
STRUGGLE
......
SIP
LET ME GO!!
YOU'RE ALL SLIMY!!
STRUGGLE
I CAN'T LET YOU GO! YOU THINK I'M A HARASSER!!
BUT...
IF I'M LOVED THIS MUCH...
THUMP
THUMP
THUMP
FISH-SAN MIGHT NOT BE SO BAD... I MEAN...
THUMP
NOO!!
DON'T MISUNDERSTAND, BROTHER!!
EEK!
SPONK
I WAS WEAK! I'M SORRY!!
I ONLY HAVE EYES FOR YOU, BROTHER!!
HM?

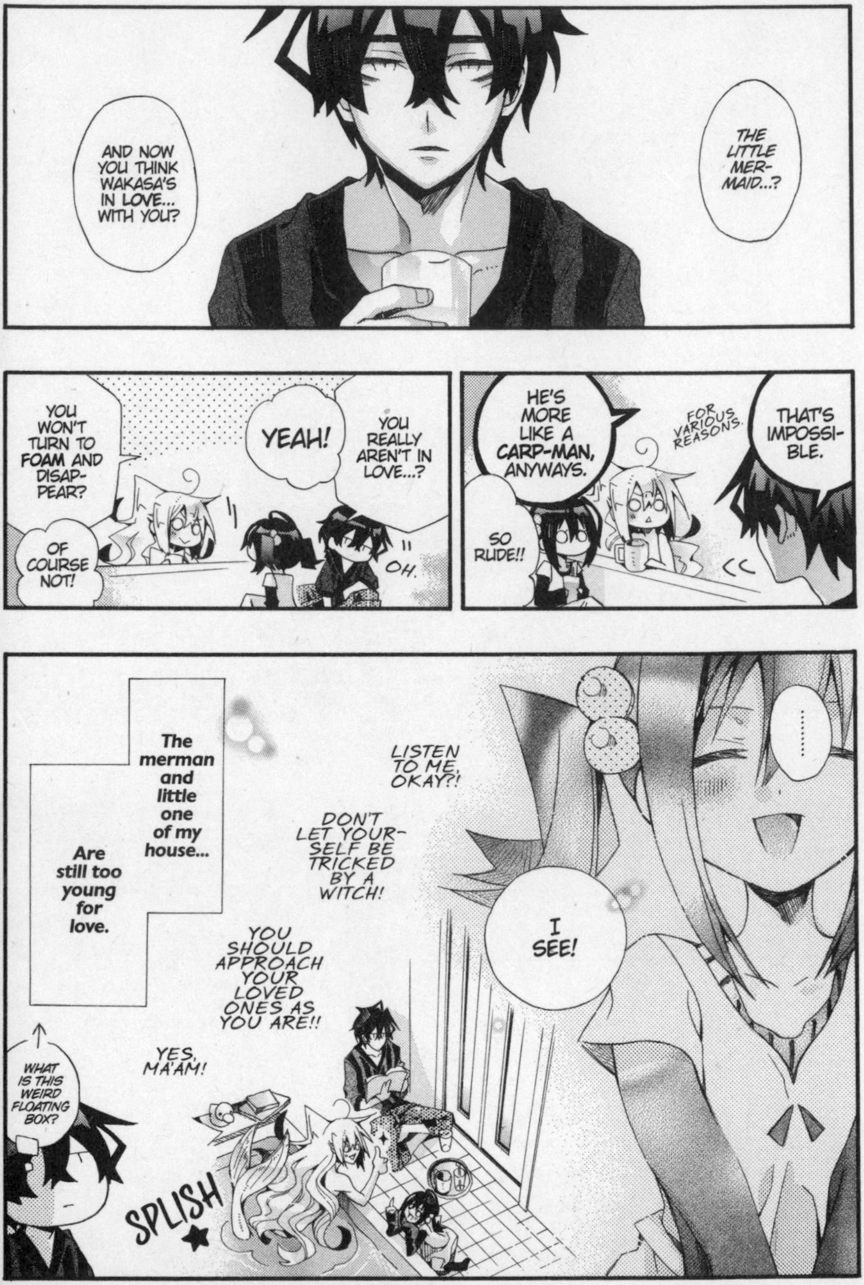

THE LITTLE MERMAID...?
AND NOW YOU THINK WAKASA'S IN LOVE... WITH YOU?
THAT'S IMPOSSIBLE.
FOR VARIOUS REASONS.
HE'S MORE LIKE A CARP-MAN, ANYWAYS.
SO RUDE!!
YOU REALLY AREN'T IN LOVE...?
YEAH!
OH.
YOU WON'T TURN TO FOAM AND DISAPPEAR?
OF COURSE NOT!
......
I SEE!
LISTEN TO ME, OKAY?!
DON'T LET YOURSELF BE TRICKED BY A WITCH!
YOU SHOULD APPROACH YOUR LOVED ONES AS YOU ARE!!
YES, MA'AM!
The merman and little one of my house...
Are still too young for love.
WHAT IS THIS WEIRD FLOATING BOX?
SPLISH

Merman in My Tub

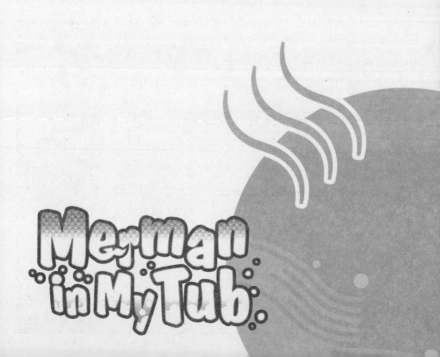

オレん家（ち）のフロ事情

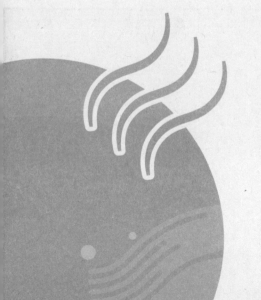

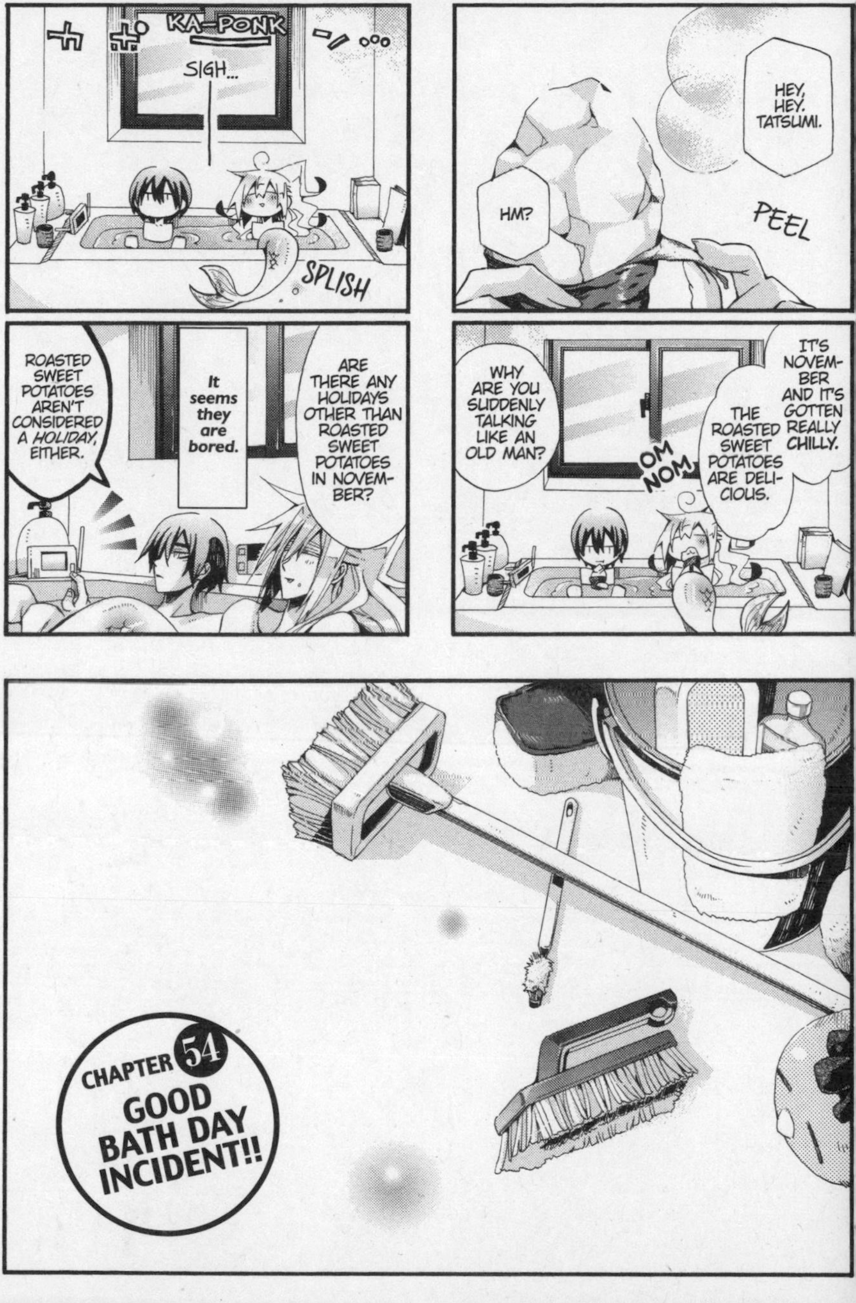
HEY, HEY. TATSUMI.
HM?
PEEL
KA-PONK
SIGH...
SPLISH
IT'S NOVEMBER AND IT'S GOTTEN REALLY CHILLY.
THE ROASTED SWEET POTATOES ARE DELICIOUS.
OM NOM
WHY ARE YOU SUDDENLY TALKING LIKE AN OLD MAN?
ARE THERE ANY HOLIDAYS OTHER THAN ROASTED SWEET POTATOES IN NOVEMBER?
It seems they are bored.
ROASTED SWEET POTATOES AREN'T CONSIDERED A *HOLIDAY*, EITHER.
CHAPTER 54
GOOD BATH DAY INCIDENT!!

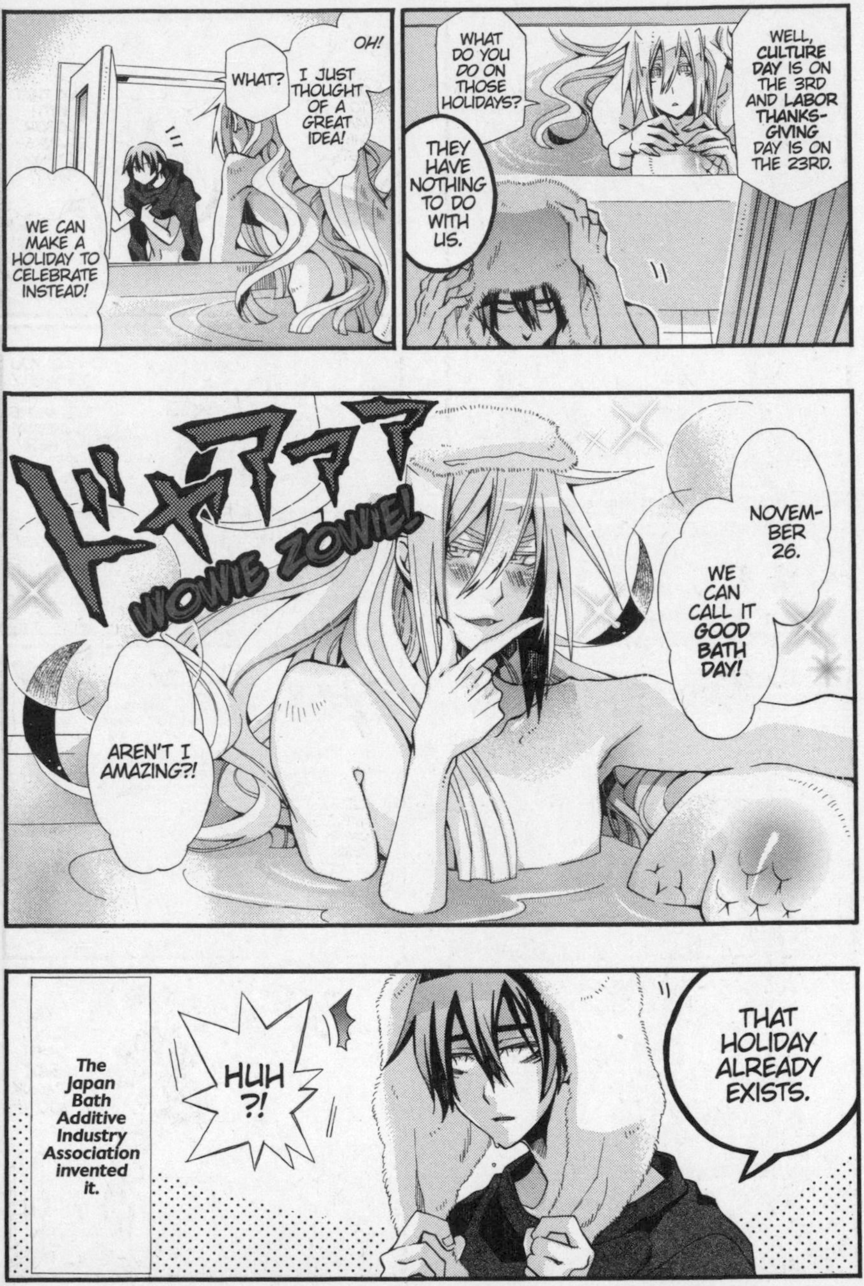
WELL, CULTURE DAY IS ON THE 3RD AND LABOR THANKSGIVING DAY IS ON THE 23RD.
WHAT DO YOU DO ON THOSE HOLIDAYS?
THEY HAVE NOTHING TO DO WITH US.
OH!
I JUST THOUGHT OF A GREAT IDEA!
WHAT?
WE CAN MAKE A HOLIDAY TO CELEBRATE INSTEAD!
NOVEMBER 26.
WE CAN CALL IT GOOD BATH DAY!
ドヤァァァ
WOWIE ZOWIE!
AREN'T I AMAZING?!
THAT HOLIDAY ALREADY EXISTS.
HUH?!
The Japan Bath Additive Industry Association invented it.

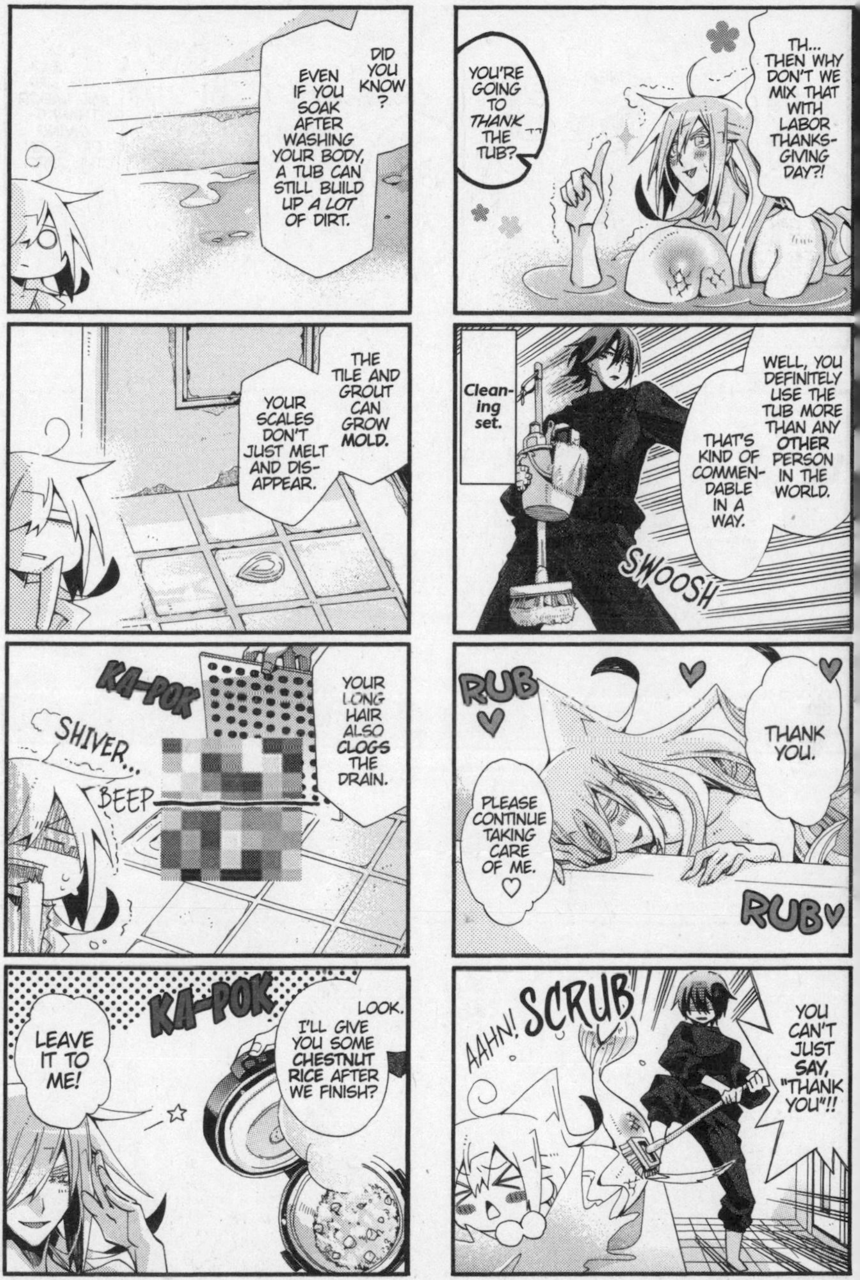
TH... THEN WHY DON'T WE MIX THAT WITH LABOR THANKSGIVING DAY?!
YOU'RE GOING TO *THANK* THE TUB?
WELL, YOU DEFINITELY USE THE TUB MORE THAN ANY OTHER PERSON IN THE WORLD.
THAT'S KIND OF COMMENDABLE IN A WAY.
Cleaning set.
SWOOSH
THANK YOU.
RUB
PLEASE CONTINUE TAKING CARE OF ME. ♡
RUB♡
YOU CAN'T JUST SAY, "THANK YOU"!!
SCRUB
AAHN!
DID YOU KNOW?
EVEN IF YOU SOAK AFTER WASHING YOUR BODY, A TUB CAN STILL BUILD UP *A LOT* OF DIRT.
THE TILE AND GROUT CAN GROW MOLD.
YOUR SCALES DON'T JUST MELT AND DIS-APPEAR.
YOUR LONG HAIR ALSO CLOGS THE DRAIN.
KA-POK
SHIVER...
BEEP
LOOK.
I'LL GIVE YOU SOME CHESTNUT RICE AFTER WE FINISH?
KA-POK
LEAVE IT TO ME!

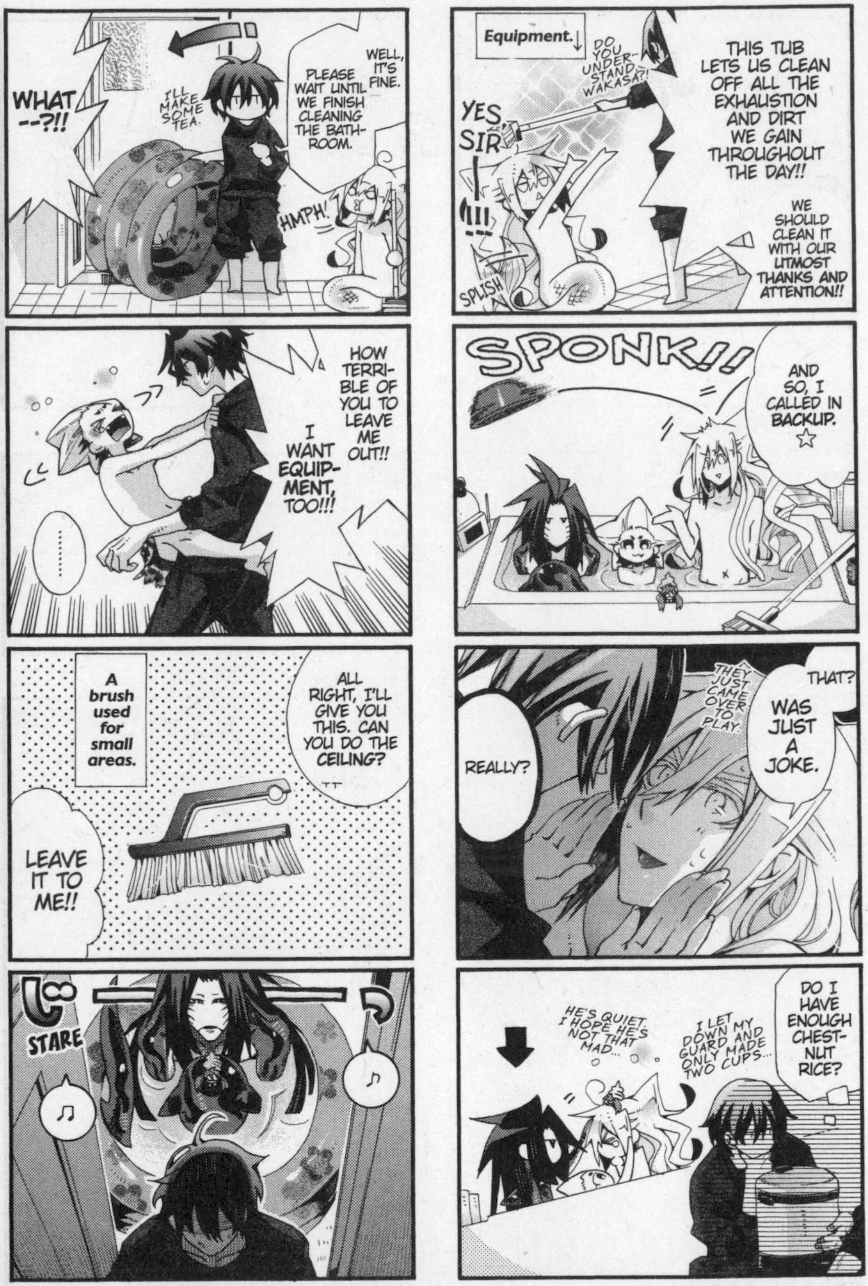

THIS TUB LETS US CLEAN OFF ALL THE EXHAUSTION AND DIRT WE GAIN THROUGHOUT THE DAY!!
WE SHOULD CLEAN IT WITH OUR UTMOST THANKS AND ATTENTION!!
DO YOU UNDERSTAND WAKASA?!
Equipment.↓
YES, SIR!!!
SPLISH
WELL, IT'S FINE.
PLEASE WAIT UNTIL WE FINISH CLEANING THE BATHROOM.
I'LL MAKE SOME TEA.
HMPH!
WHAT--?!!
AND SO, I CALLED IN BACKUP. ☆
SPONK!!
HOW TERRIBLE OF YOU TO LEAVE ME OUT!!
I WANT EQUIPMENT, TOO!!!
......
THAT? WAS JUST A JOKE.
THEY JUST CAME OVER TO PLAY.
REALLY?
ALL RIGHT, I'LL GIVE YOU THIS. CAN YOU DO THE CEILING?
A brush used for small areas.
LEAVE IT TO ME!!
DO I HAVE ENOUGH CHESTNUT RICE?
I LET DOWN MY GUARD AND ONLY MADE TWO CUPS...
HE'S QUIET. I HOPE HE'S NOT THAT MAD...
♪
♫
STARE

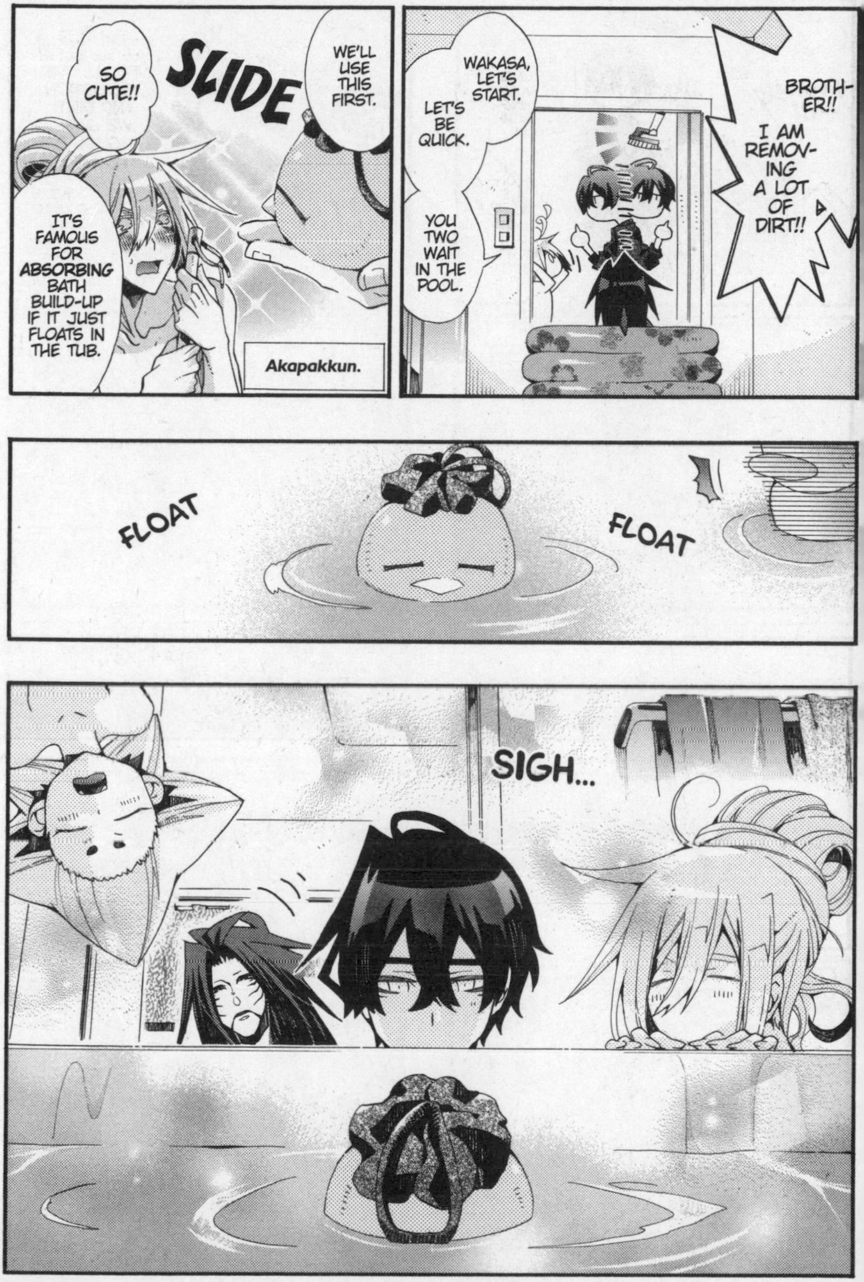
BROTHER!!
I AM REMOVING A LOT OF DIRT!!
WAKASA, LET'S START.
LET'S BE QUICK.
YOU TWO WAIT IN THE POOL.
WE'LL USE THIS FIRST.
SLIDE
SO CUTE!!
IT'S FAMOUS FOR ABSORBING BATH BUILD-UP IF IT JUST FLOATS IN THE TUB.
Akapakkun.
FLOAT
FLOAT
SIGH...

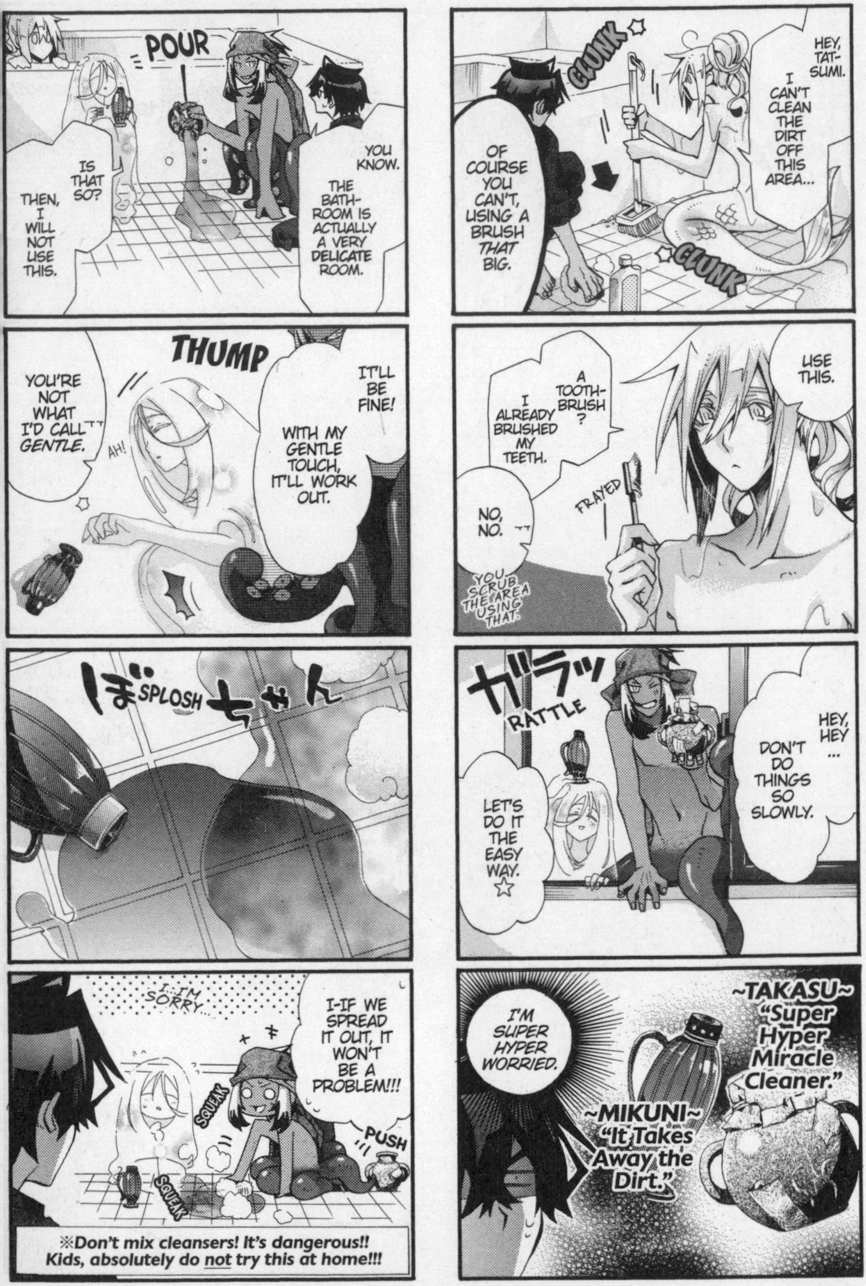
HEY, TAT-SUMI.
I CAN'T CLEAN THE DIRT OFF THIS AREA...
CLUNK
OF COURSE YOU CAN'T, USING A BRUSH *THAT* BIG.
CLUNK
POUR
YOU KNOW.
THE BATH-ROOM IS ACTUALLY A VERY DELICATE ROOM.
IS THAT SO?
THEN, I WILL NOT USE THIS.
USE THIS.
A TOOTH-BRUSH?
I ALREADY BRUSHED MY TEETH.
FRAYED
NO, NO.
YOU SCRUB THE AREA USING THAT.
THUMP
IT'LL BE FINE!
WITH MY GENTLE TOUCH, IT'LL WORK OUT.
AH!
YOU'RE NOT WHAT I'D CALL GENTLE.
ガラッ
RATTLE
HEY, HEY...
DON'T DO THINGS SO SLOWLY.
LET'S DO IT THE EASY WAY. ☆
ぼちゃん
SPLOSH
~TAKASU~ "Super Hyper Miracle Cleaner."
I'M SUPER HYPER WORRIED.
~MIKUNI~ "It Takes Away the Dirt."
I-IF WE SPREAD IT OUT, IT WON'T BE A PROBLEM!!!
I-I'M SORRY...
SQUEAK
PUSH
SQUEAK
※Don't mix cleansers! It's dangerous!! Kids, absolutely do not try this at home!!!

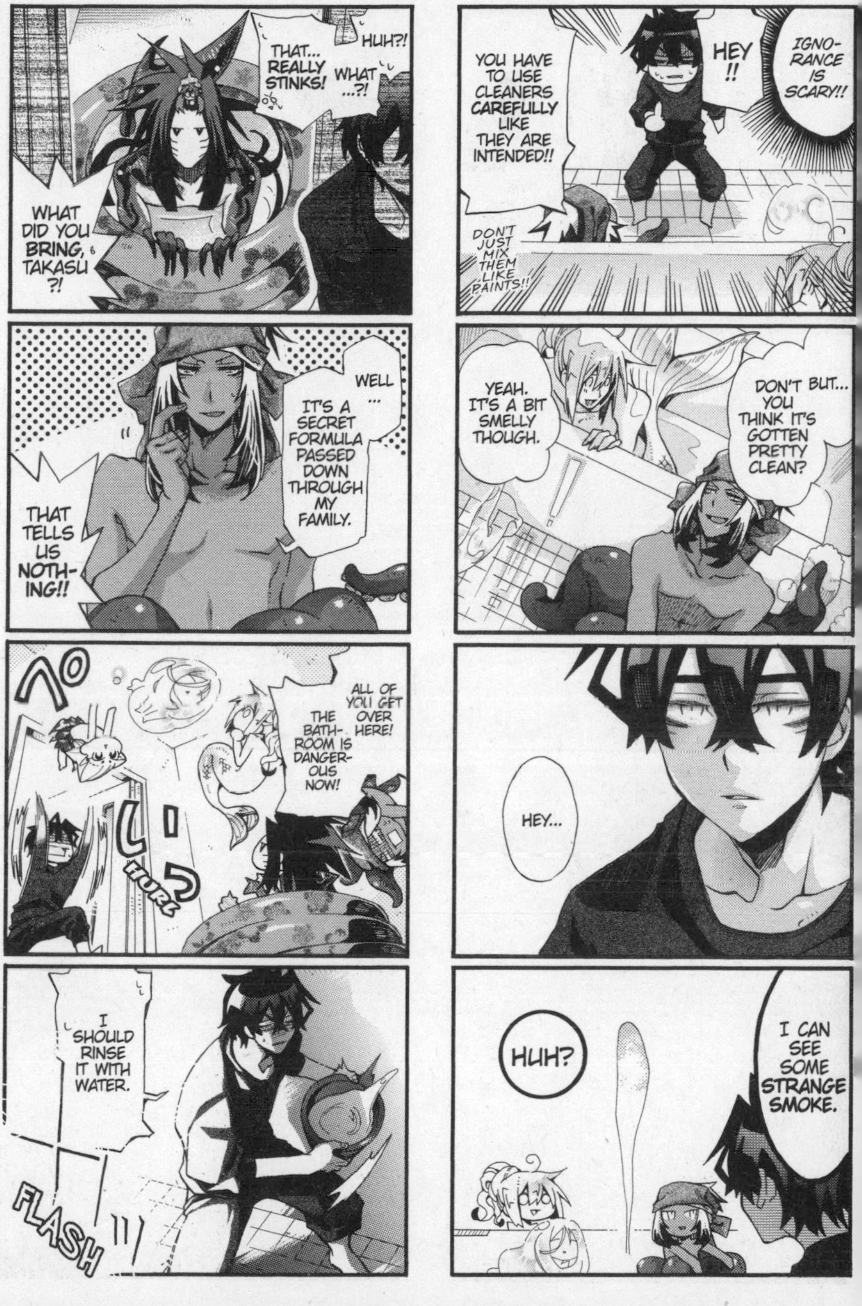
IGNO-RANCE IS SCARY!!
HEY !!
YOU HAVE TO USE CLEANERS CAREFULLY LIKE THEY ARE INTENDED!!
DON'T JUST MIX THEM LIKE PAINTS!!
DON'T BUT... YOU THINK IT'S GOTTEN PRETTY CLEAN?
YEAH. IT'S A BIT SMELLY THOUGH.
HEY...
I CAN SEE SOME STRANGE SMOKE.
HUH?
HUH?!
WHAT ...?!
THAT... REALLY STINKS!
WHAT DID YOU BRING, TAKASU ?!
WELL ...
IT'S A SECRET FORMULA PASSED DOWN THROUGH MY FAMILY.
THAT TELLS US NOTH-ING!!
ALL OF YOU GET OVER HERE!
THE BATH-ROOM IS DANGER-OUS NOW!
HURL
I SHOULD RINSE IT WITH WATER.
FLASH

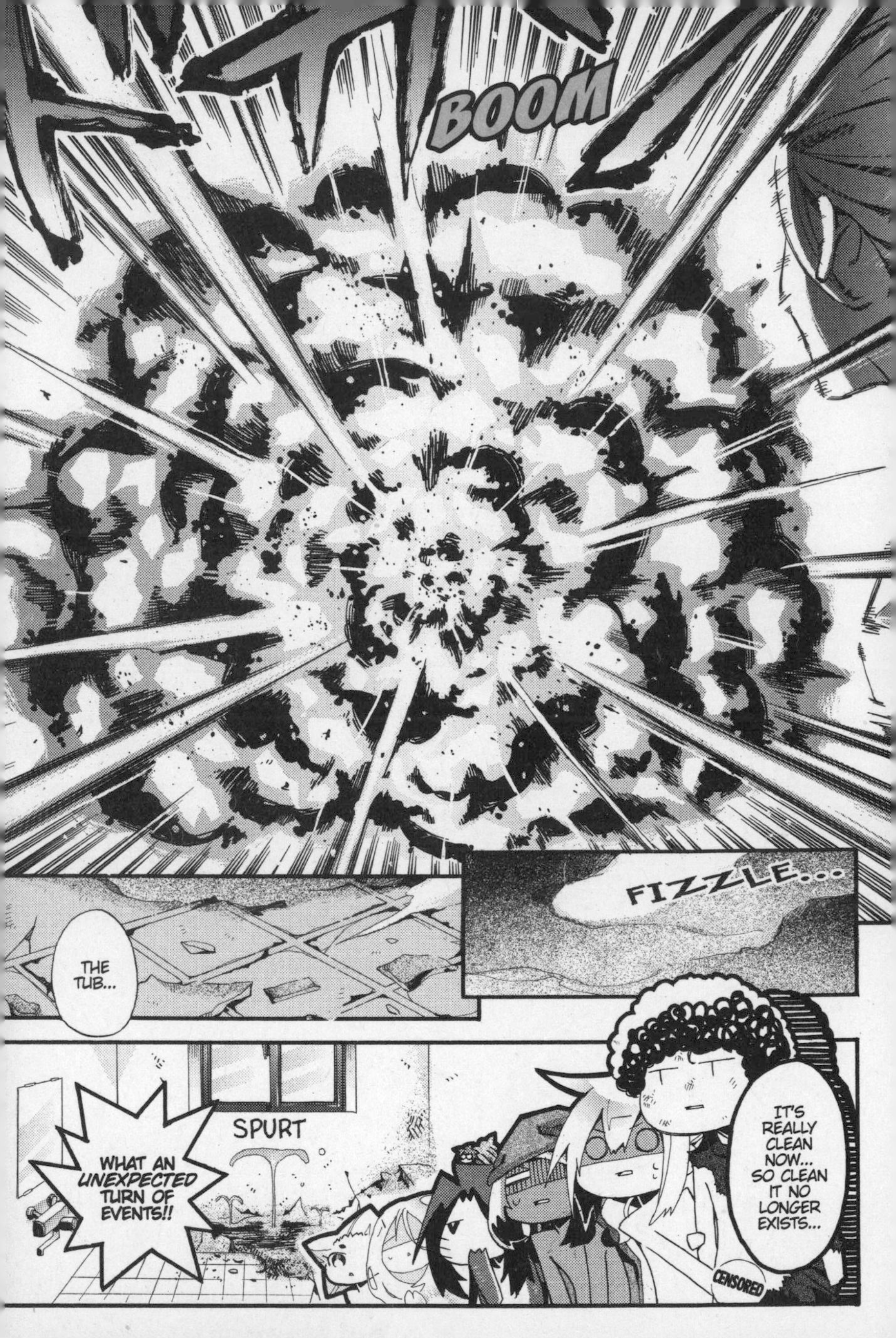
BOOM
FIZZLE...
THE TUB...
IT'S REALLY CLEAN NOW... SO CLEAN IT NO LONGER EXISTS...
CENSORED
SPURT
WHAT AN UNEXPECTED TURN OF EVENTS!!

Merman in My Tub

オレん家のフロ事情

KA-SHUNK

......

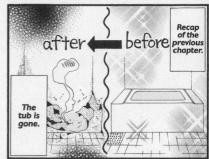

Recap of the previous chapter.

before → after

The tub is gone.

KER-PLUNK

SPLISH

カララ RATTLE

I'LL CALL THE REPAIR-MAN FIRST.

......

CHAPTER 55
NEW ☆ TUB?!

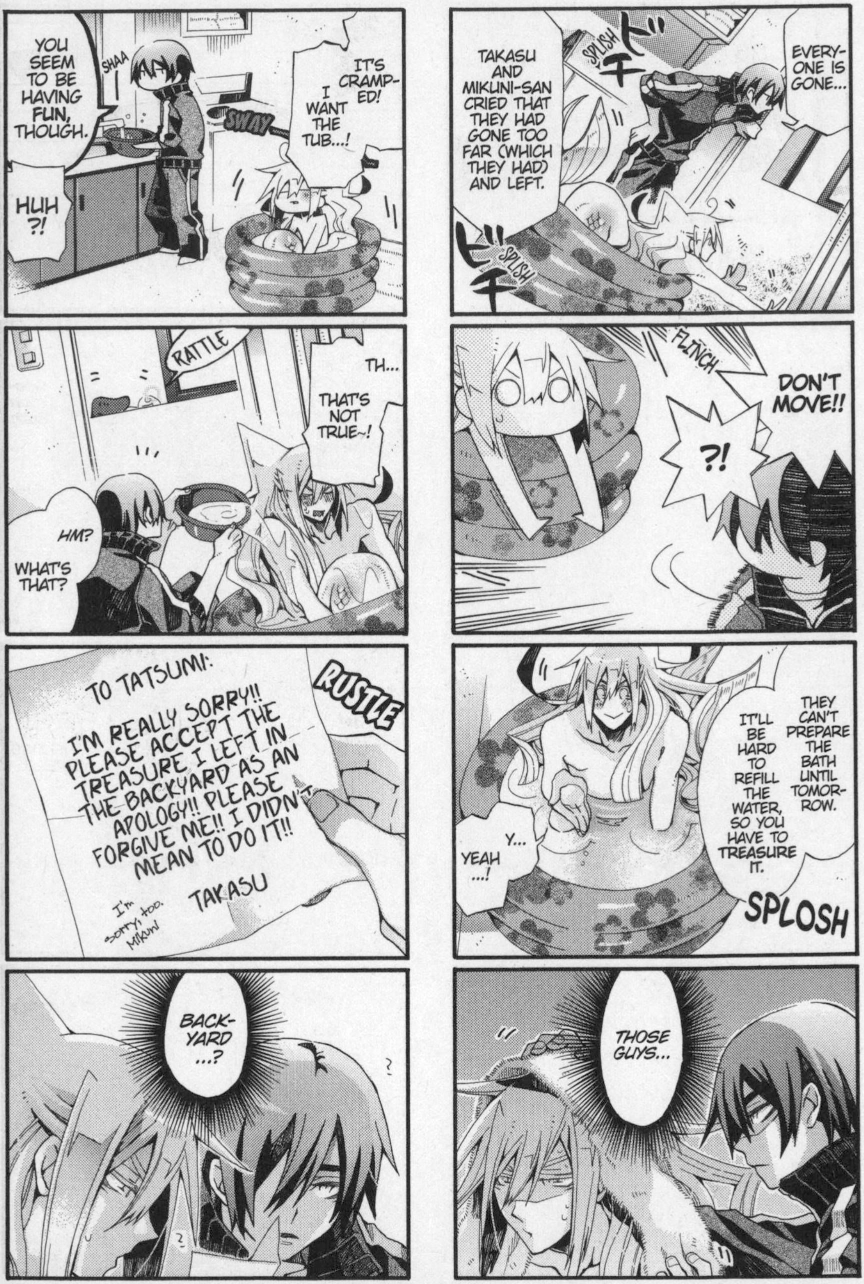
EVERY-ONE IS GONE...
SPLISH
TAKASU AND MIKUNI-SAN CRIED THAT THEY HAD GONE TOO FAR (WHICH THEY HAD) AND LEFT.
SPLISH
IT'S CRAMPED! I WANT THE TUB...!
SWAY
SHAA
YOU SEEM TO BE HAVING FUN, THOUGH.
HUH?!
FLINCH
DON'T MOVE!!
?!
TH... THAT'S NOT TRUE~!
RATTLE
HM? WHAT'S THAT?
THEY CAN'T PREPARE THE BATH UNTIL TOMORROW.
IT'LL BE HARD TO REFILL THE WATER, SO YOU HAVE TO TREASURE IT.
Y... YEAH...!
SPLOSH
RUSTLE
TO TATSUMI:
I'M REALLY SORRY!! PLEASE ACCEPT THE TREASURE I LEFT IN THE BACKYARD AS AN APOLOGY!! PLEASE FORGIVE ME!! I DIDN'T MEAN TO DO IT!!
TAKASU
I'm sorry, too. Mikuni
THOSE GUYS...
BACK-YARD...?

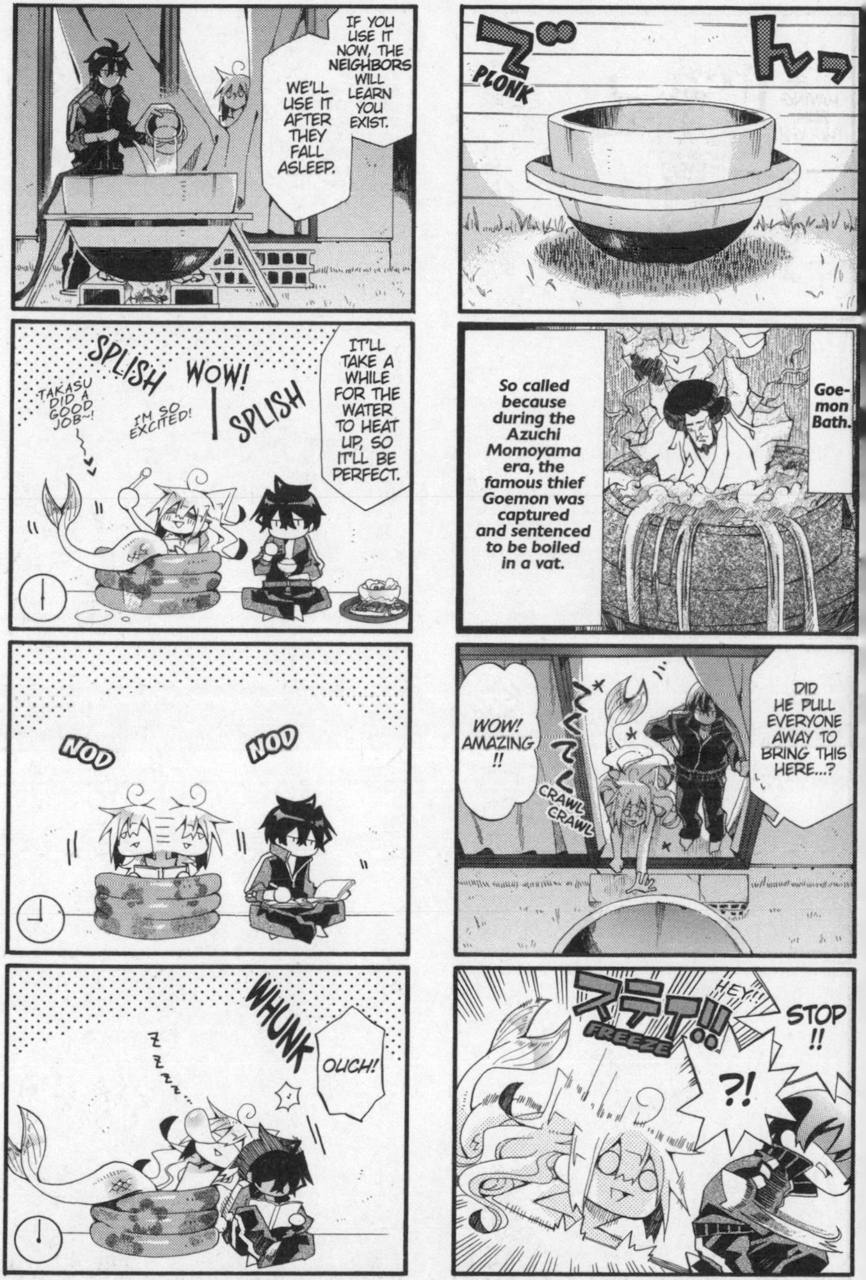
PLONK
Goe-mon Bath.
So called because during the Azuchi Momoyama era, the famous thief Goemon was captured and sentenced to be boiled in a vat.
DID HE PULL EVERYONE AWAY TO BRING THIS HERE...?
WOW! AMAZING!!
CRAWL CRAWL
STOP!!
HEY!!
FREEZE
?!
IF YOU USE IT NOW, THE NEIGHBORS WILL LEARN YOU EXIST.
WE'LL USE IT AFTER THEY FALL ASLEEP.
IT'LL TAKE A WHILE FOR THE WATER TO HEAT UP, SO IT'LL BE PERFECT.
WOW!
SPLISH
SPLISH
I'M SO EXCITED!
TAKASU DID A GOOD JOB~!
NOD
NOD
WHUNK
OUCH!
Z Z Z Z...

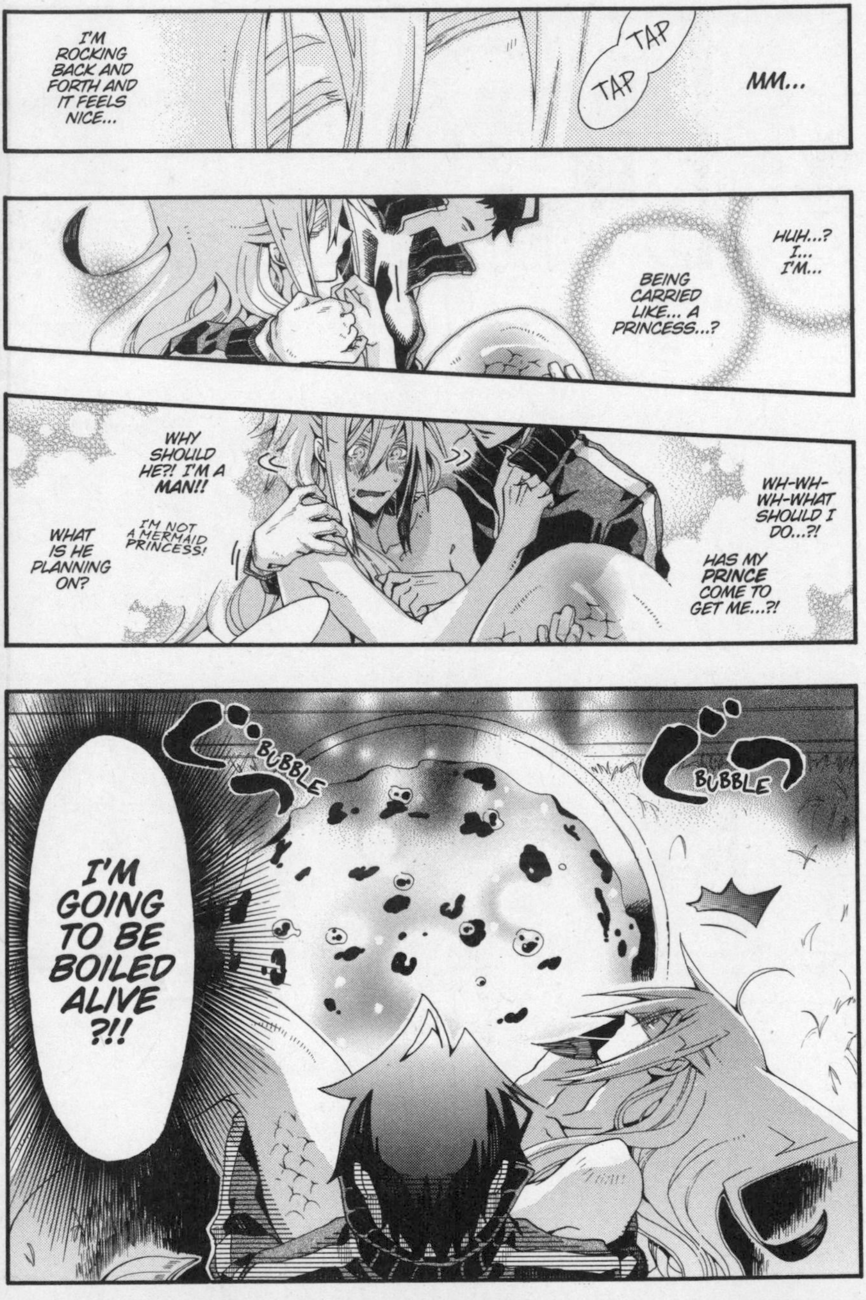
MM...
TAP TAP
I'M ROCKING BACK AND FORTH AND IT FEELS NICE...
HUH...? I... I'M...
BEING CARRIED LIKE... A PRINCESS...?
WH-WH-WH-WHAT SHOULD I DO...?!
HAS MY PRINCE COME TO GET ME...?!
WHY SHOULD HE?! I'M A MAN!!
I'M NOT A MERMAID PRINCESS!
WHAT IS HE PLANNING ON?
BUBBLE
BUBBLE
I'M GOING TO BE BOILED ALIVE?!!

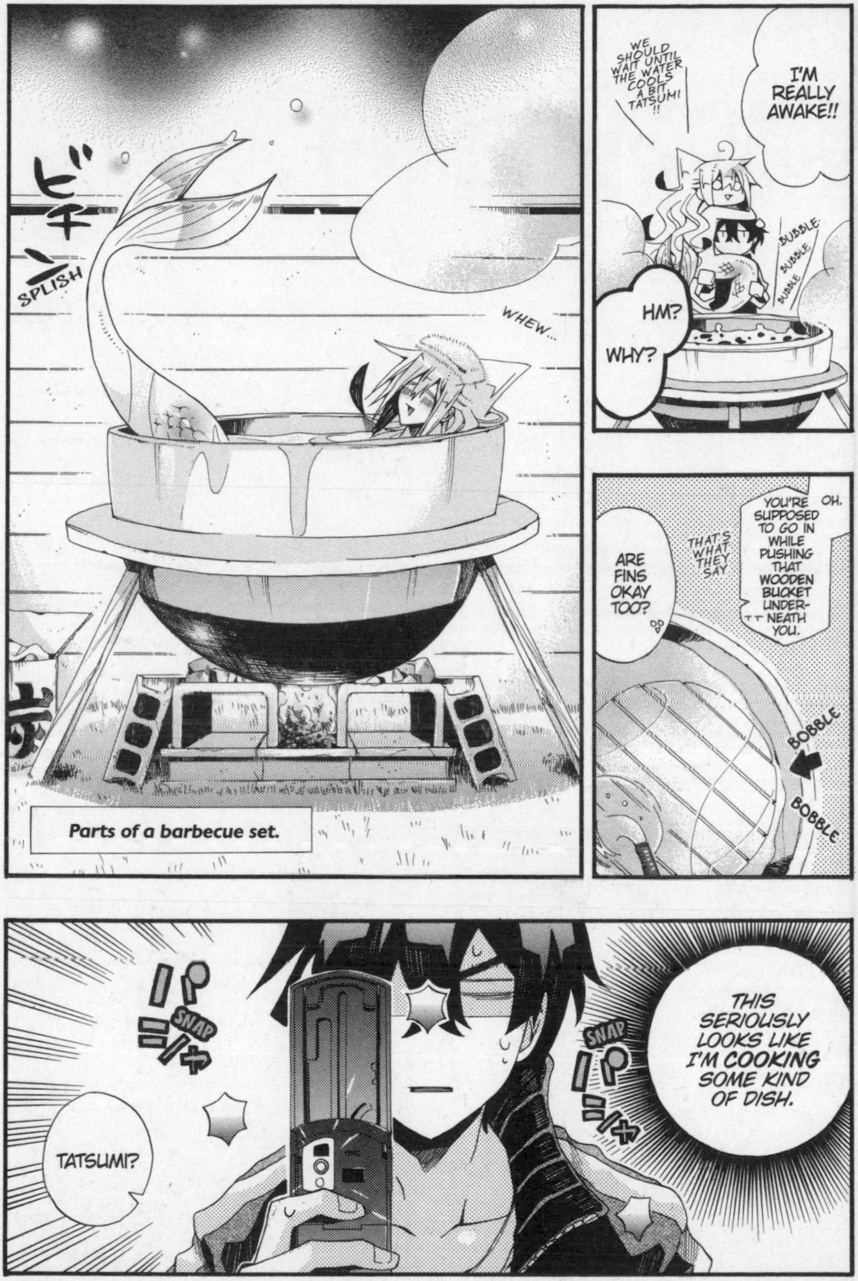
I'M REALLY AWAKE!!
WE SHOULD WAIT UNTIL THE WATER COOLS A BIT, TATSUMI!!
BUBBLE BUBBLE BUBBLE
HM? WHY?
OH.
YOU'RE SUPPOSED TO GO IN WHILE PUSHING THAT WOODEN BUCKET UNDERNEATH YOU.
THAT'S WHAT THEY SAY.
ARE FINS OKAY TOO?
BOBBLE BOBBLE
WHEW...
SPLISH
Parts of a barbecue set.
THIS SERIOUSLY LOOKS LIKE I'M COOKING SOME KIND OF DISH.
SNAP
SNAP
TATSUMI?

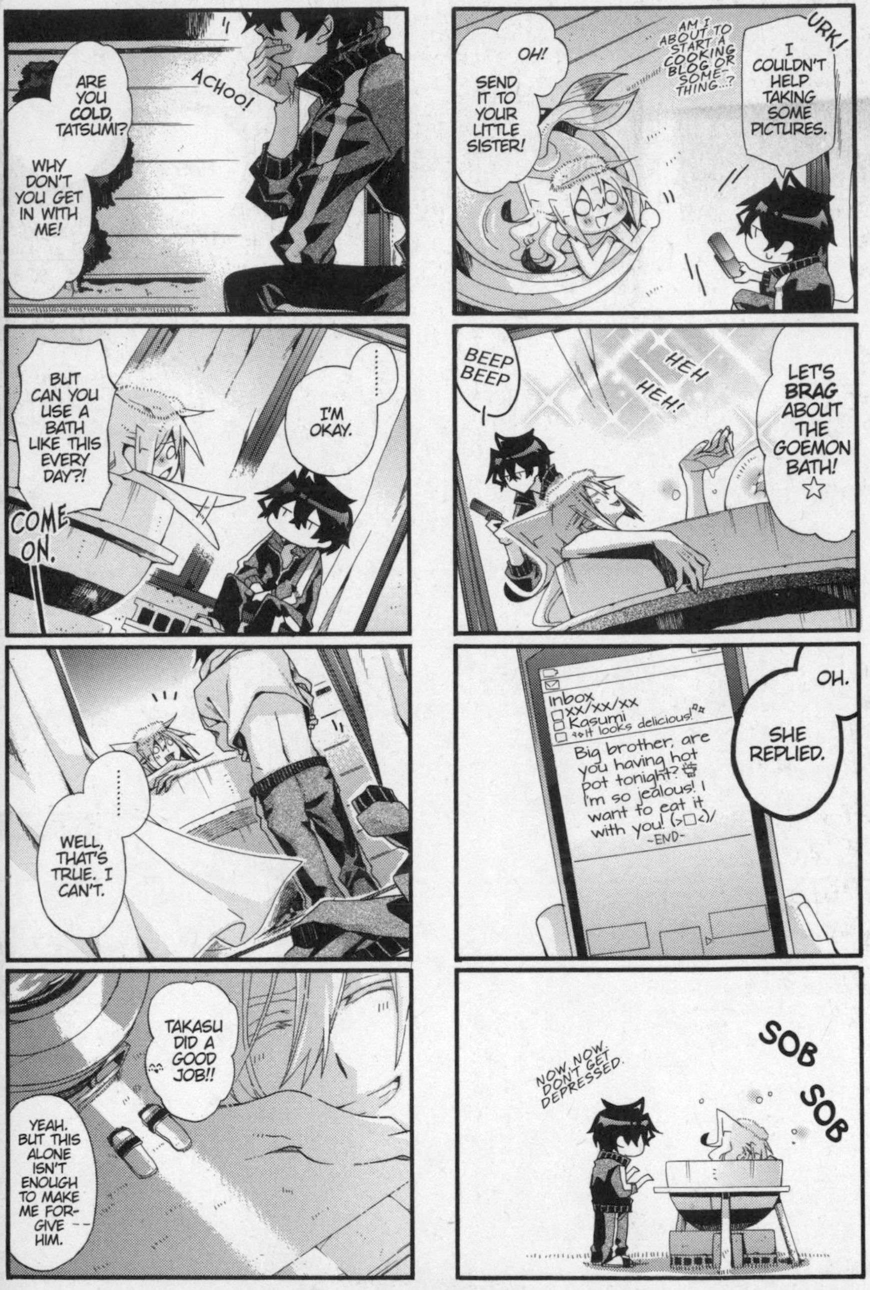
URK!
I COULDN'T HELP TAKING SOME PICTURES.
OH!
SEND IT TO YOUR LITTLE SISTER!
AM I ABOUT TO START A COOKING BLOG OR SOMETHING...?
ACHOO!
ARE YOU COLD, TATSUMI?
WHY DON'T YOU GET IN WITH ME!
LET'S BRAG ABOUT THE GOEMON BATH! ☆
HEH HEH!
BEEP BEEP
......
I'M OKAY.
BUT CAN YOU USE A BATH LIKE THIS EVERY DAY?!
COME ON.
OH.
SHE REPLIED.
Inbox
xx/xx/xx
Kasumi
It looks delicious!
Big brother, are you having hot pot tonight? I'm so jealous! I want to eat it with you! (>□<)/
-END-
......
WELL, THAT'S TRUE. I CAN'T.
SOB SOB
NOW, NOW. DON'T GET DEPRESSED.
TAKASU DID A GOOD JOB!!
YEAH. BUT THIS ALONE ISN'T ENOUGH TO MAKE ME FORGIVE HIM.

HEY, HEY. TATSUMI.
HM?
WHAT CONSTEL-LATION IS THAT?
TAP
TAP
CASSIO-PEIA...?

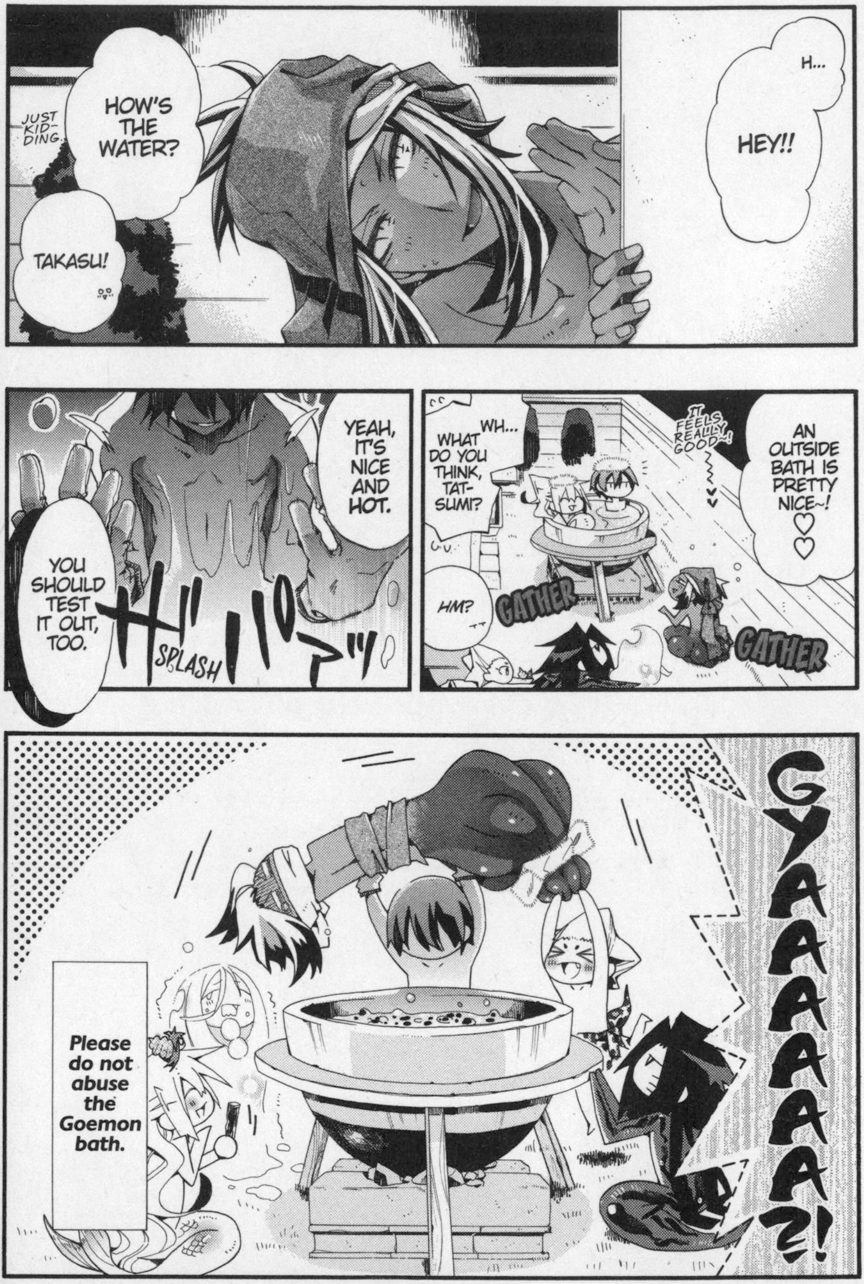
H... HEY!!
HOW'S THE WATER?
JUST KID-DING.
TAKASU!
AN OUTSIDE BATH IS PRETTY NICE~! ♡ ♡
IT FEELS REALLY GOOD~!
WH... WHAT DO YOU THINK, TAT-SUMI?
HM?
GATHER
GATHER
YEAH, IT'S NICE AND HOT.
YOU SHOULD TEST IT OUT, TOO.
SPLASH
GYAAAAAA?!
Please do not abuse the Goemon bath.

Merman
in My Tub

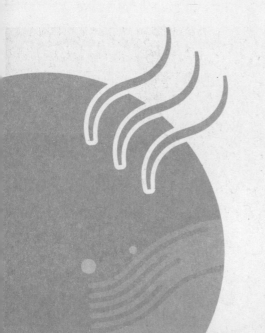

オレん家のフロ事情

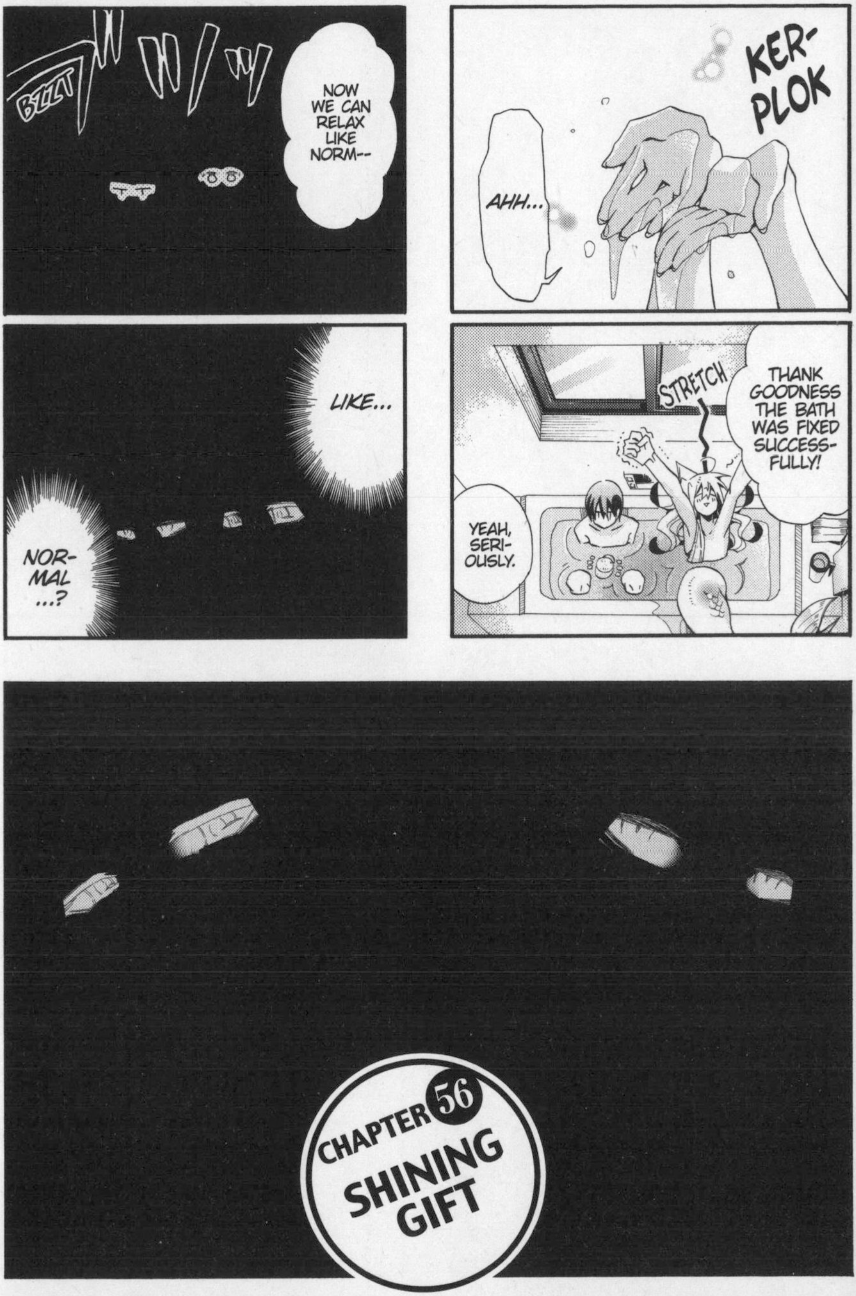
KER-PLOK
AHH...
BZZT
NOW WE CAN RELAX LIKE NORM--
STRETCH
THANK GOODNESS THE BATH WAS FIXED SUCCESS-FULLY!
YEAH, SERI-OUSLY.
LIKE...
NOR-MAL ...?
CHAPTER 56
SHINING GIFT

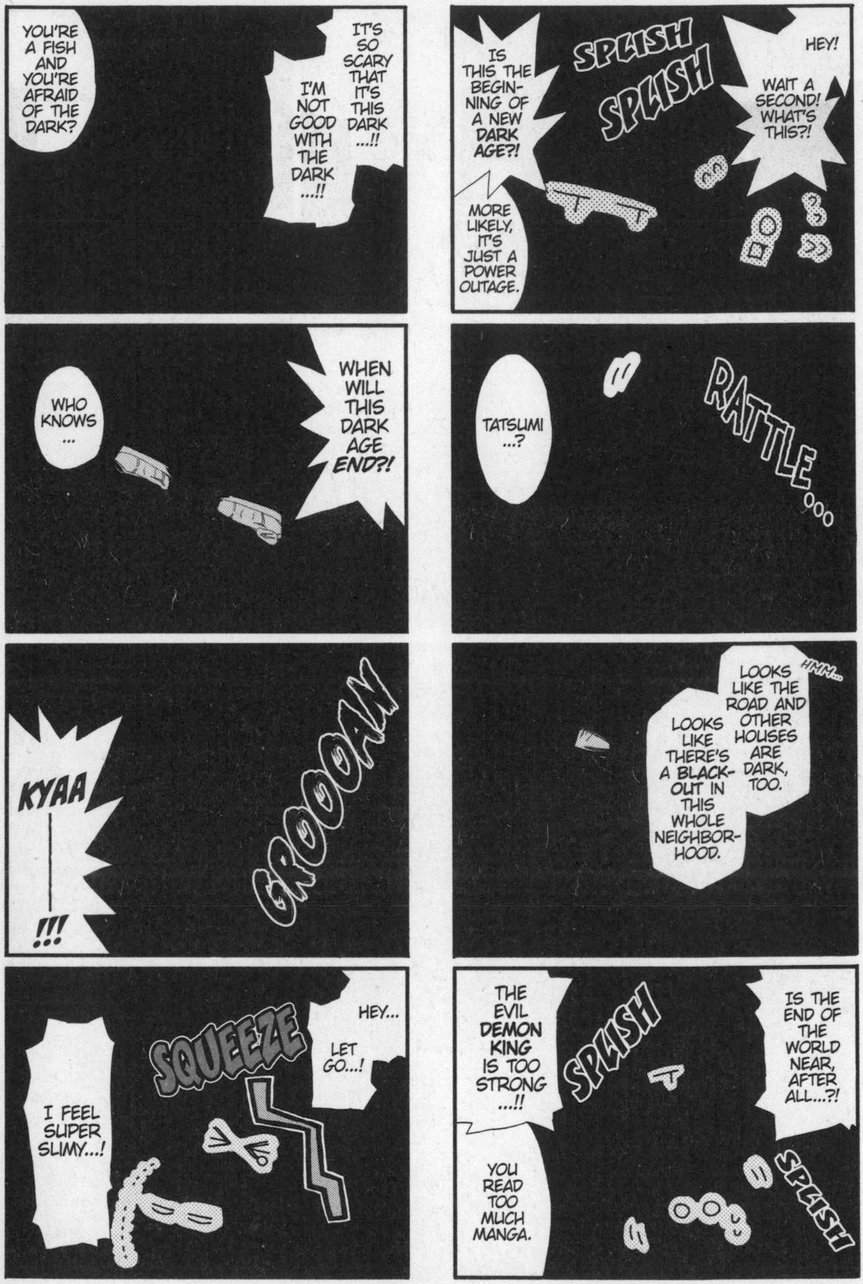
HEY!
WAIT A SECOND! WHAT'S THIS?!
SPLISH
SPLISH
IS THIS THE BEGIN-NING OF A NEW DARK AGE?!
MORE LIKELY, IT'S JUST A POWER OUTAGE.
IT'S SO SCARY THAT IT'S THIS DARK ...!!
I'M NOT GOOD WITH THE DARK ...!!
YOU'RE A FISH AND YOU'RE AFRAID OF THE DARK?
RATTLE...
TATSUMI ...?
WHEN WILL THIS DARK AGE END?!
WHO KNOWS ...
HMM...
LOOKS LIKE THE ROAD AND OTHER HOUSES ARE DARK, TOO.
LOOKS LIKE THERE'S A BLACK-OUT IN THIS WHOLE NEIGHBOR-HOOD.
GROOOAN
KYAA—!!!
IS THE END OF THE WORLD NEAR, AFTER ALL...?!
SPLISH
THE EVIL DEMON KING IS TOO STRONG ...!!
SPLISH
YOU READ TOO MUCH MANGA.
HEY...
LET GO...!
SQUEEZE
I FEEL SUPER SLIMY...!

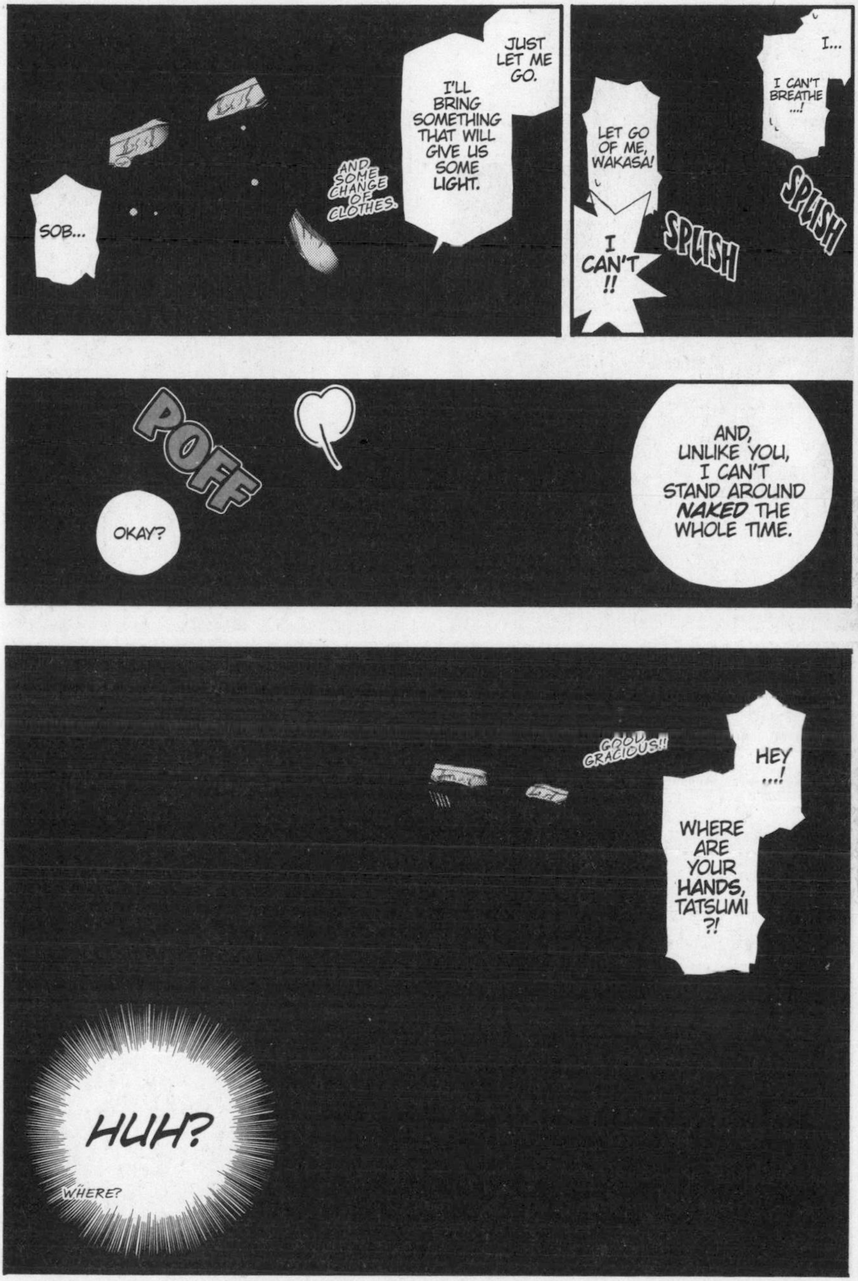
I...
I CAN'T BREATHE ...!
LET GO OF ME, WAKASA!
I CAN'T !!
SPLISH
SPLISH
JUST LET ME GO.
I'LL BRING SOMETHING THAT WILL GIVE US SOME LIGHT.
AND SOME CHANGE OF CLOTHES.
SOB...
AND, UNLIKE YOU, I CAN'T STAND AROUND NAKED THE WHOLE TIME.
POFF
OKAY?
HEY ...!
WHERE ARE YOUR HANDS, TATSUMI ?!
GOOD GRACIOUS!!
HUH?
WHERE?

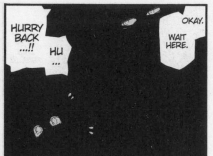

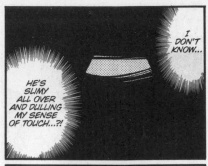

I DON'T KNOW...
HE'S SLIMY ALL OVER AND DULLING MY SENSE OF TOUCH...?!
OKAY. WAIT HERE.
HURRY BACK ...!!
HU ...
ANY-WAY, MOVE !! I NEED TO GET SOME GLOVES ON!!
SPLISH
NO!! DON'T LEAVE ME ALONE!!
SPLISH
SPLISH
HMM...
RUMMAGE
DIDN'T I HAVE SOME-THING?
RUMMAGE
THEN DECIDE WHETHER YOU WANT TO STAY STILL WITH NO LIGHT...
STIFFEN
OR DEAL WITH SOME INCONVE-NIENCE, SO I CAN LIGHT SOME-THING?
OH. I HAVE A SINGLE CANDLE.
BWOOSH
!!!!
SPLASH
SPLISH
AND IT'S GONE ... AND THE MATCHES ARE SOAKED, TOO.
SPLISH
IT...!
IT'S YOUR FAULT FOR SCARING ME LIKE THAT...!

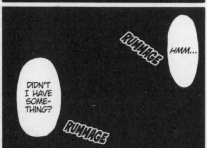

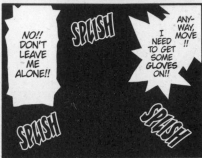

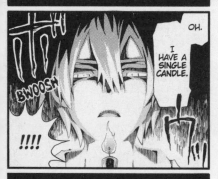

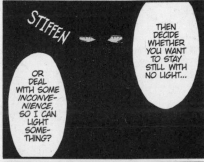

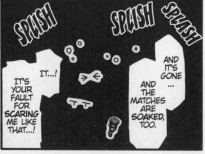

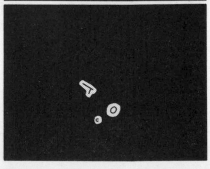

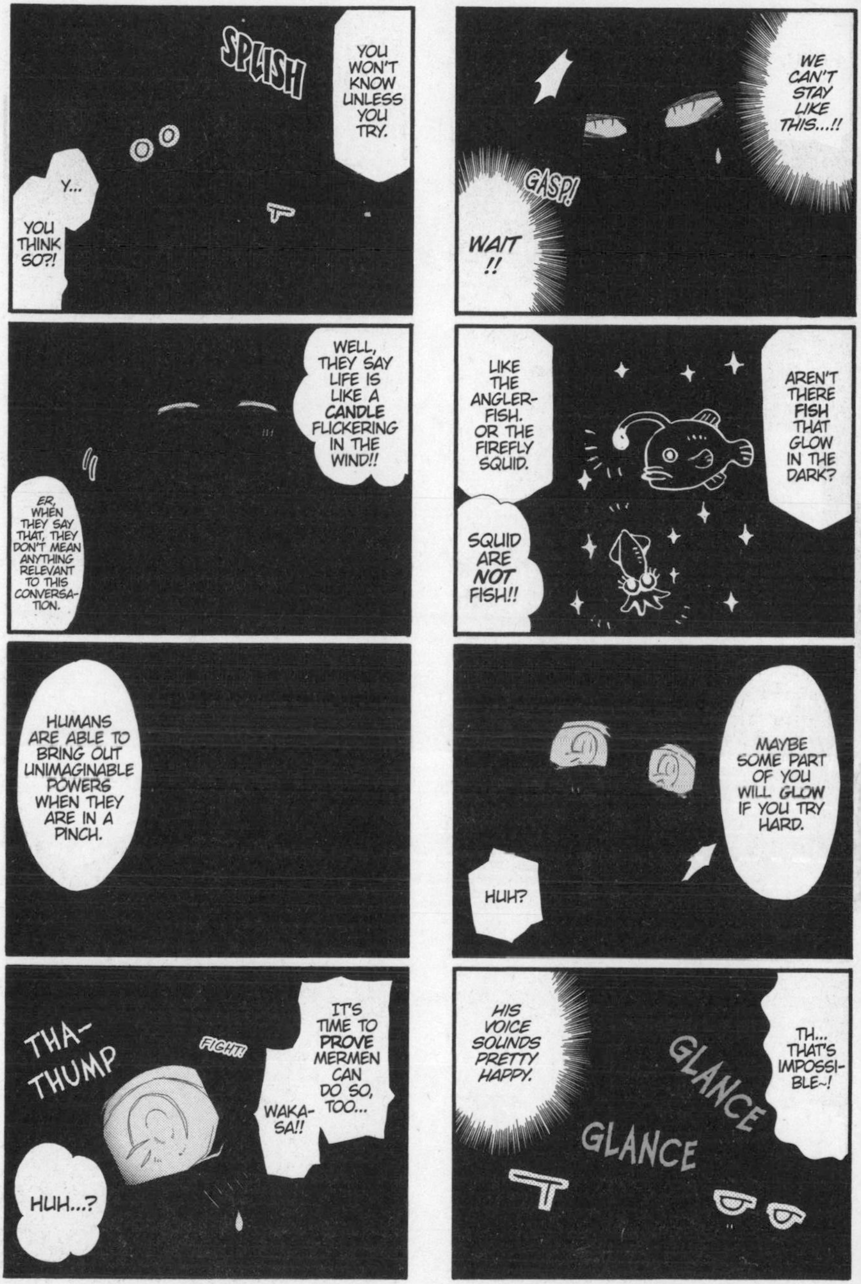
WE CAN'T STAY LIKE THIS...!!
GASP!
WAIT !!
YOU WON'T KNOW UNLESS YOU TRY.
SPLISH
Y...
YOU THINK SO?!
AREN'T THERE FISH THAT GLOW IN THE DARK?
LIKE THE ANGLER-FISH. OR THE FIREFLY SQUID.
SQUID ARE NOT FISH!!
WELL, THEY SAY LIFE IS LIKE A CANDLE FLICKERING IN THE WIND!!
ER, WHEN THEY SAY THAT, THEY DON'T MEAN ANYTHING RELEVANT TO THIS CONVERSA-TION.
MAYBE SOME PART OF YOU WILL GLOW IF YOU TRY HARD.
HUH?
HUMANS ARE ABLE TO BRING OUT UNIMAGINABLE POWERS WHEN THEY ARE IN A PINCH.
TH... THAT'S IMPOSSI-BLE~!
GLANCE
GLANCE
HIS VOICE SOUNDS PRETTY HAPPY.
IT'S TIME TO PROVE MERMEN CAN DO SO, TOO...
FIGHT!
WAKA-SA!!
THA-THUMP
HUH...?

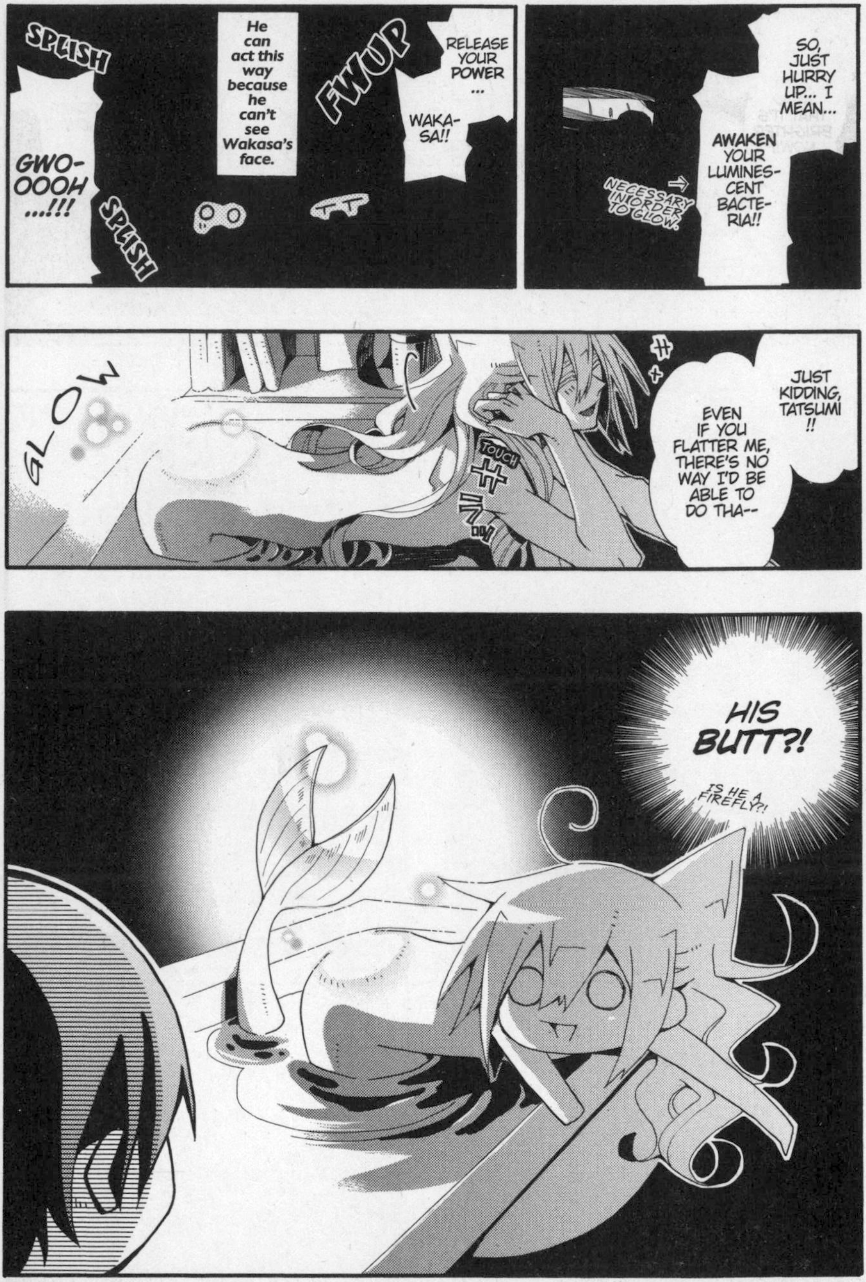
SO, JUST HURRY UP... I MEAN...
AWAKEN YOUR LUMINES-CENT BACTE-RIA!!
NECESSARY IN ORDER TO GLOW.
RELEASE YOUR POWER ...
WAKA-SA!!
FWUP
He can act this way because he can't see Wakasa's face.
SPLISH
GWO-OOOH ...!!!
SPLISH
JUST KIDDING, TATSUMI !!
EVEN IF YOU FLATTER ME, THERE'S NO WAY I'D BE ABLE TO DO THA--
TOUCH
GLOW
HIS BUTT?!
IS HE A FIREFLY?!

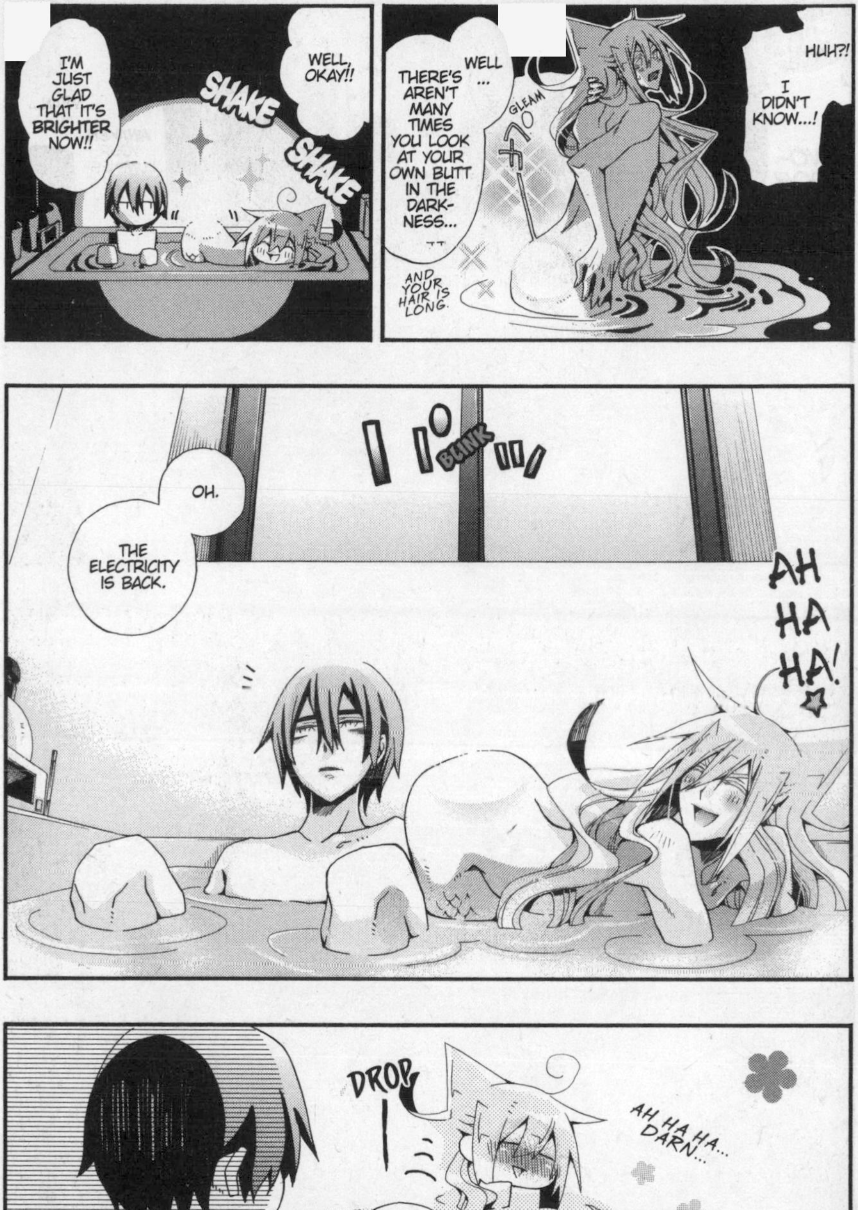
HUH?!
I DIDN'T KNOW...!
WELL ... THERE'S AREN'T MANY TIMES YOU LOOK AT YOUR OWN BUTT IN THE DARKNESS...
GLEAM
AND YOUR HAIR IS LONG.
WELL, OKAY!!
SHAKE
SHAKE
I'M JUST GLAD THAT IT'S BRIGHTER NOW!!
BLINK
OH.
THE ELECTRICITY IS BACK.
AH HA HA!
AH HA HA... DARN...
DROP

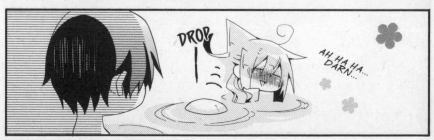

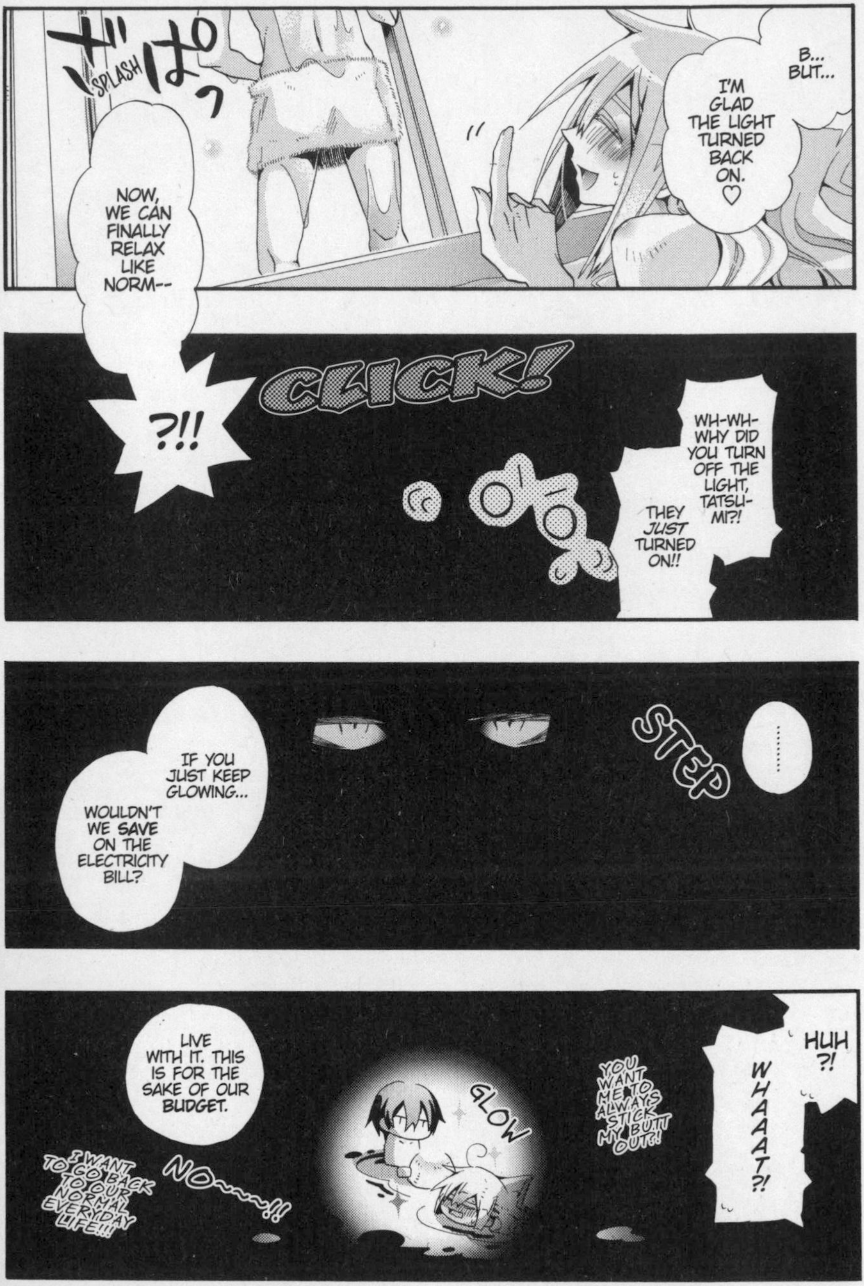
B... BUT... I'M GLAD THE LIGHT TURNED BACK ON. ♡
ザぱっ
SPLASH
NOW, WE CAN FINALLY RELAX LIKE NORM--
CLICK!
?!!
WH-WH-WHY DID YOU TURN OFF THE LIGHT, TATSUMI?! THEY JUST TURNED ON!!
......
STEP
IF YOU JUST KEEP GLOWING... WOULDN'T WE SAVE ON THE ELECTRICITY BILL?
HUH?!
WHAAAAT?!
YOU WANT ME TO ALWAYS STICK MY BUTT OUT?!
GLOW
LIVE WITH IT. THIS IS FOR THE SAKE OF OUR BUDGET.
NO~~~!!
I WANT TO GO BACK TO OUR NORMAL EVERYDAY LIFE!!!

Merman in My Tub

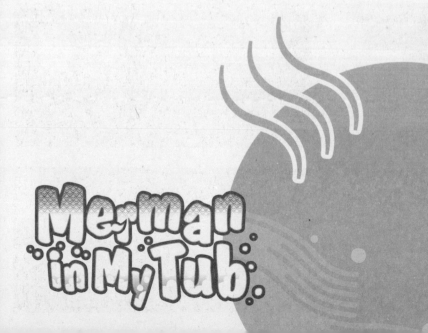

オレん家（ち）のフロ事情

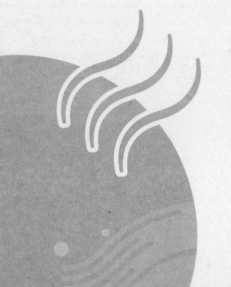

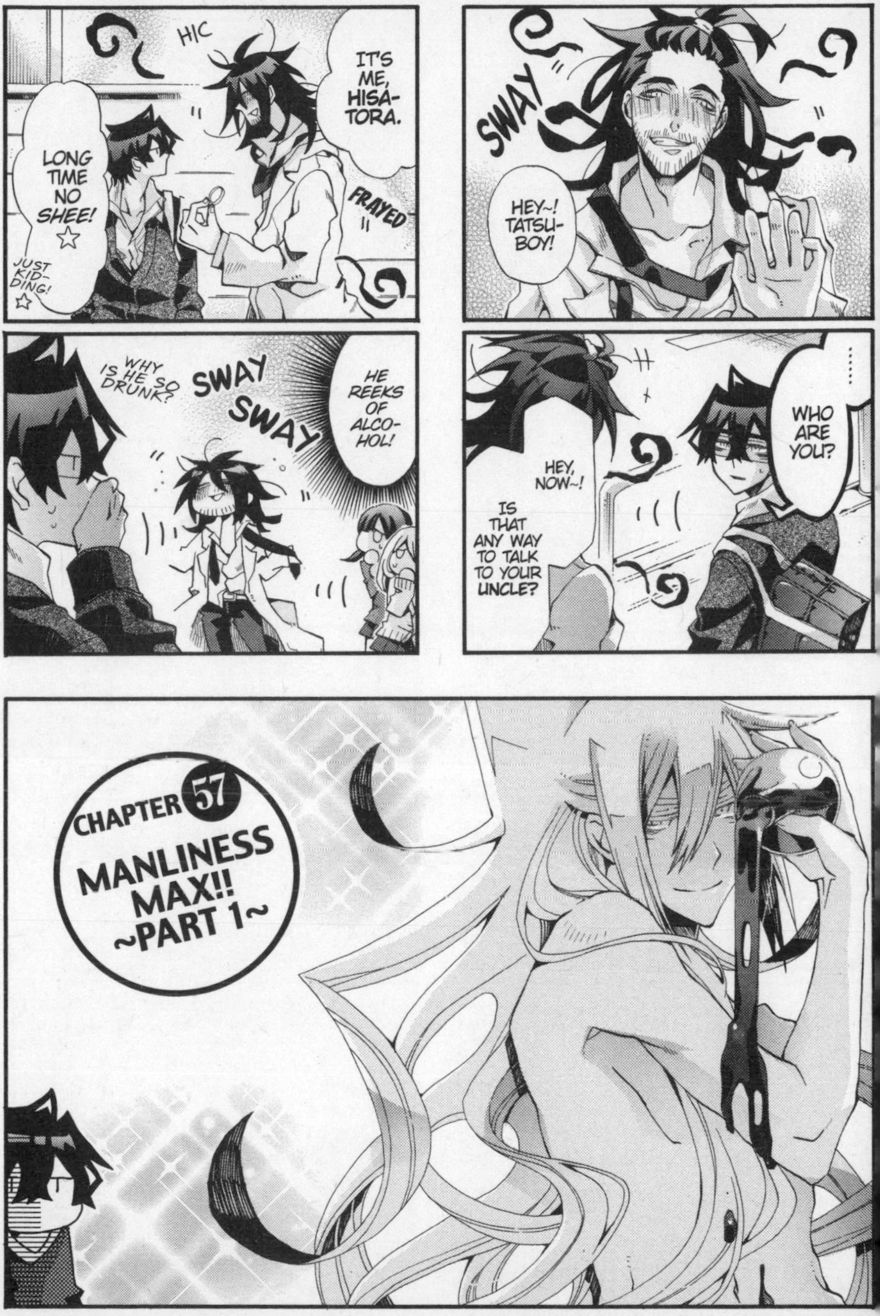
SWAY
HEY~! TATSU-BOY!
IT'S ME, HISA-TORA.
HIC
LONG TIME NO SHEE! ☆
FRAYED
JUST KID-DING! ☆
......
WHO ARE YOU?
HEY, NOW~!
IS THAT ANY WAY TO TALK TO YOUR UNCLE?
HE REEKS OF ALCO-HOL!
SWAY SWAY
WHY IS HE SO DRUNK?
CHAPTER 57
MANLINESS MAX!! ~PART 1~

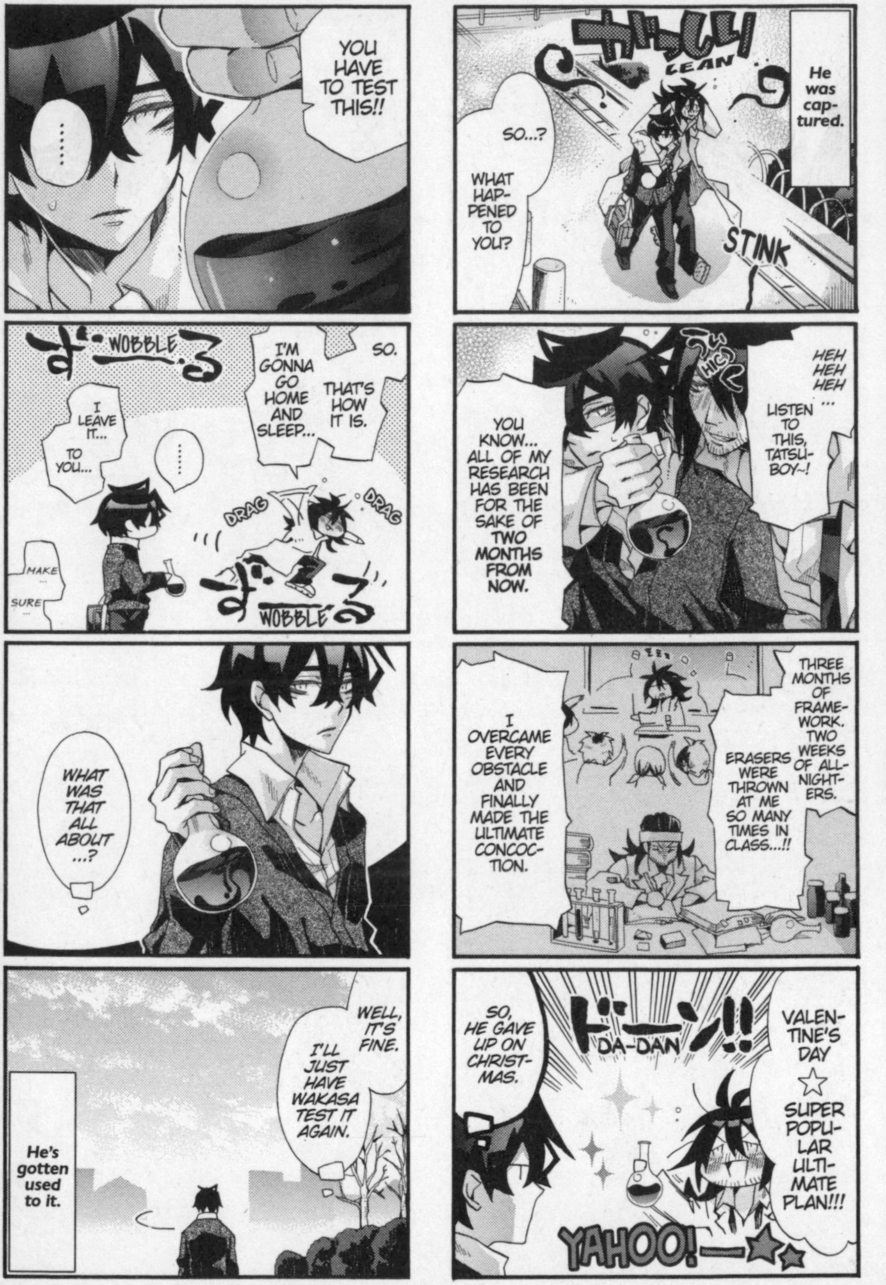He was cap-tured.
LEAN
SO...?
WHAT HAP-PENED TO YOU?
STINK
HEH HEH HEH ...
LISTEN TO THIS, TATSU-BOY~!
HIC
YOU KNOW... ALL OF MY RESEARCH HAS BEEN FOR THE SAKE OF TWO MONTHS FROM NOW.
THREE MONTHS OF FRAME-WORK. TWO WEEKS OF ALL-NIGHT-ERS.
ERASERS WERE THROWN AT ME SO MANY TIMES IN CLASS...!!
I OVERCAME EVERY OBSTACLE AND FINALLY MADE THE ULTIMATE CONCOC-TION.
VALEN-TINE'S DAY ☆ SUPER POPU-LAR ULTI-MATE PLAN!!!
DA-DAN
SO, HE GAVE UP ON CHRIST-MAS.
YAHOO!
YOU HAVE TO TEST THIS!!
......
SO.
THAT'S HOW IT IS.
I'M GONNA GO HOME AND SLEEP...
I LEAVE IT...
TO YOU...
......
WOBBLE
DRAG
DRAG
WOBBLE
MAKE ...
SURE ...
WHAT WAS THAT ALL ABOUT ...?
WELL, IT'S FINE.
I'LL JUST HAVE WAKASA TEST IT AGAIN.
He's gotten used to it.

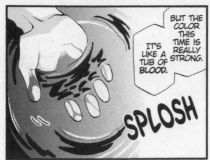

I'M HOME.
GA-CHAK
SPLISH
WEL-COME HOME!
YOU GOT SOME-THING AGAIN !!
SPLISH
BUT THE COLOR THIS TIME IS REALLY STRONG.
IT'S LIKE A TUB OF BLOOD.
SPLOSH
WHAT IS IT THIS TIME?
IT ALWAYS TURNS OUT TERRI-BLE.
THIS TIME...
SO?
DID IT HAVE ANY KIND OF EFFECT?
WAKA--
GRAB
?
I WON-DER.
HE SAID HE MADE IT FOR VALEN-TINE'S DAY.
IT'S SOMETHING THAT'S SUPPOSED TO MAKE YOU... POPULAR?
GLARE
DOO DEE DOO.
POOOOUR
?!

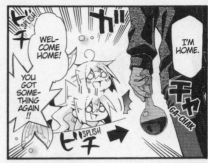

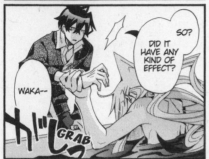

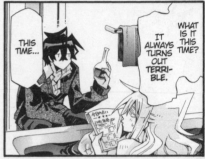

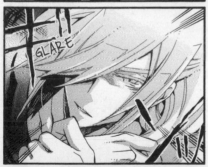

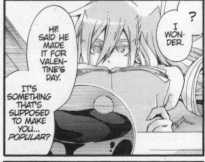

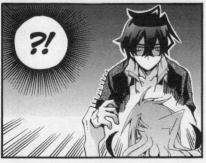

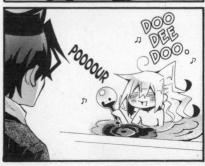

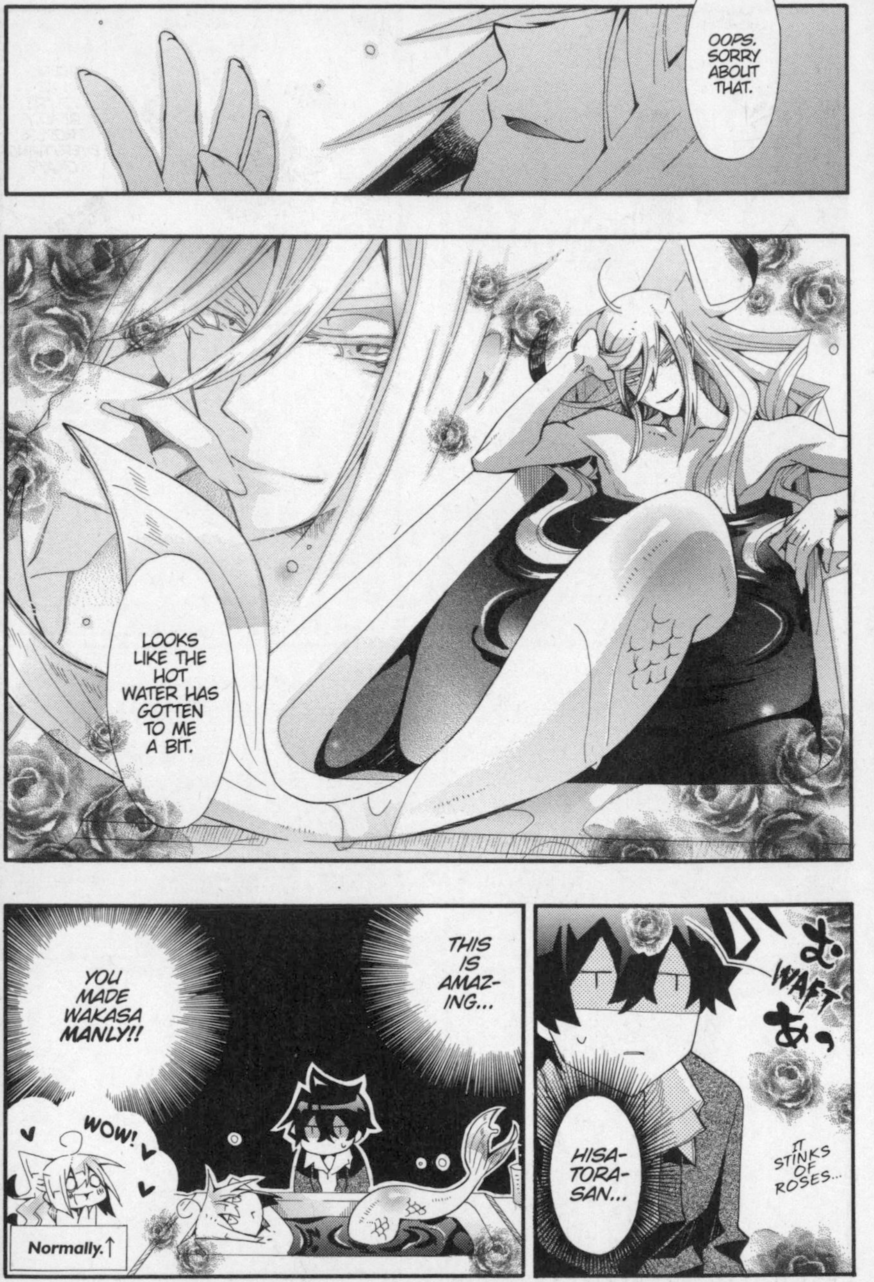
OOPS. SORRY ABOUT THAT.
LOOKS LIKE THE HOT WATER HAS GOTTEN TO ME A BIT.
WAFT
HISATORA-SAN...
IT STINKS OF ROSES...
THIS IS AMAZ-ING...
YOU MADE WAKASA MANLY!!
WOW!
Normally.↑

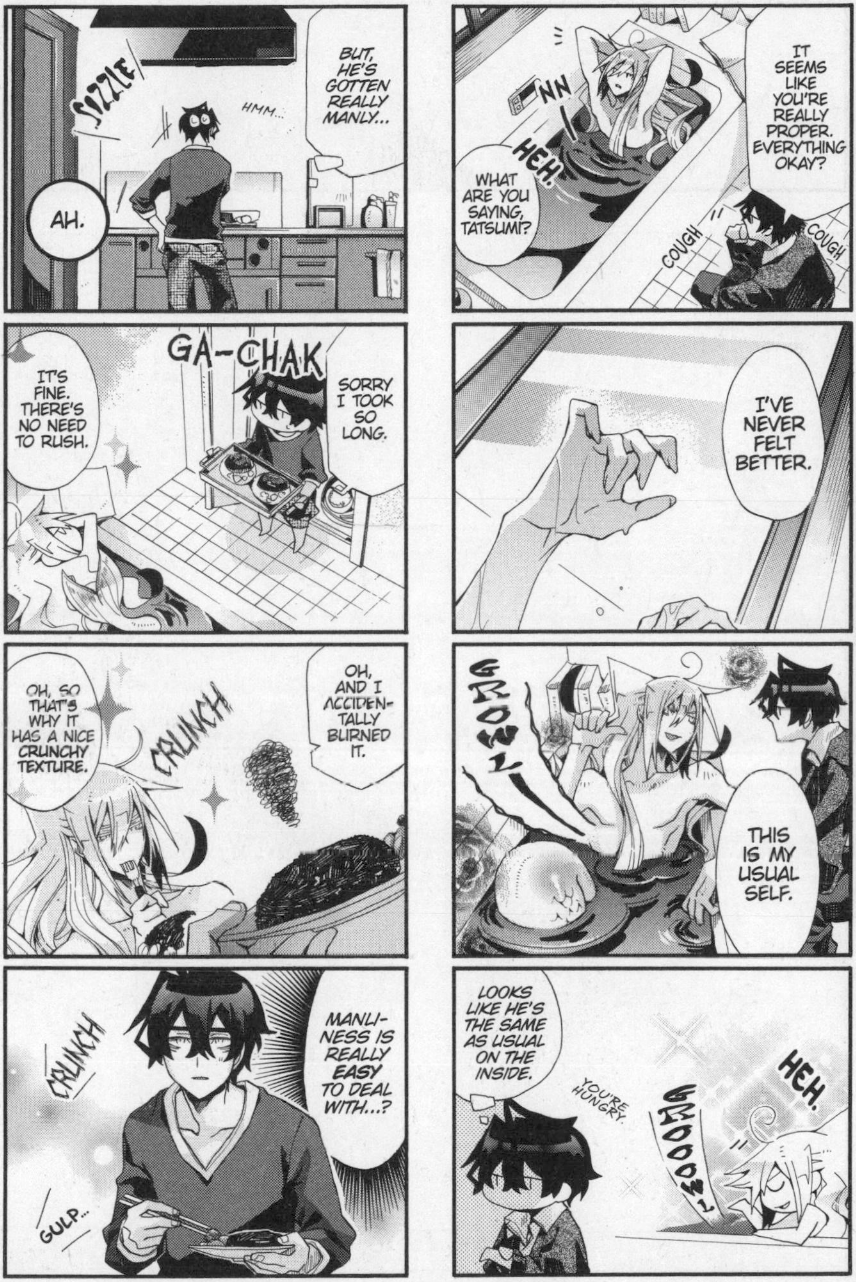

IT SEEMS LIKE YOU'RE REALLY PROPER. EVERYTHING OKAY?
NN
HEH.
WHAT ARE YOU SAYING, TATSUMI?
COUGH
COUGH
I'VE NEVER FELT BETTER.
GROWL
THIS IS MY USUAL SELF.
LOOKS LIKE HE'S THE SAME AS USUAL ON THE INSIDE.
HEH.
GROOOWL
YOU'RE HUNGRY.
BUT, HE'S GOTTEN REALLY MANLY...
HMM...
SIZZLE
AH.
GA-CHAK
SORRY I TOOK SO LONG.
IT'S FINE. THERE'S NO NEED TO RUSH.
OH, AND I ACCIDENTALLY BURNED IT.
CRUNCH
OH, SO THAT'S WHY IT HAS A NICE CRUNCHY TEXTURE.
MANLINESS IS REALLY EASY TO DEAL WITH...?
CRUNCH
GULP...

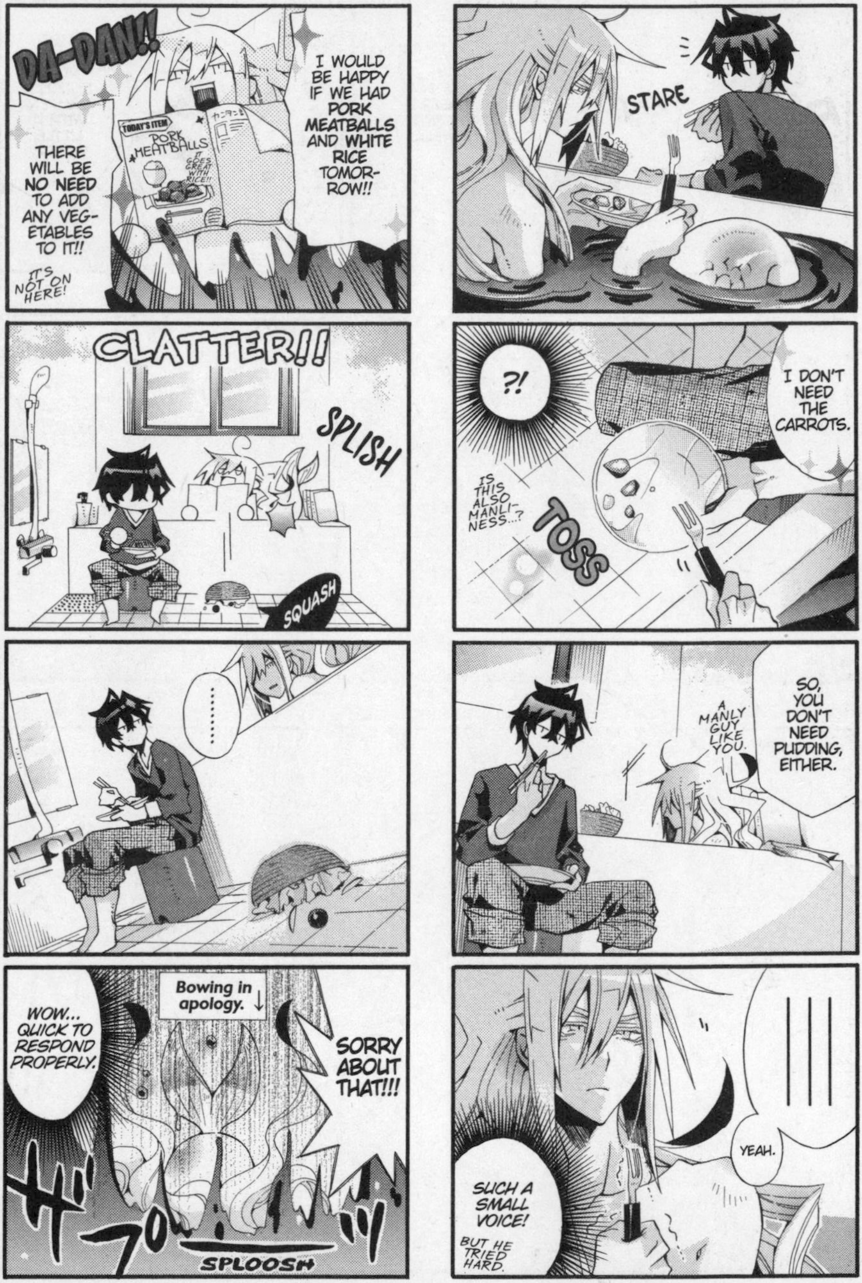
STARE
DA-DAN!!
I WOULD BE HAPPY IF WE HAD PORK MEATBALLS AND WHITE RICE TOMORROW!!
TODAY'S ITEM
PORK MEATBALLS
IT GOES GREAT WITH RICE!!
THERE WILL BE NO NEED TO ADD ANY VEGETABLES TO IT!!
IT'S NOT ON HERE!
I DON'T NEED THE CARROTS.
?!
IS THIS ALSO MANLINESS...?
TOSS
CLATTER!!
SPLISH
SQUASH
SO, YOU DON'T NEED PUDDING, EITHER.
A MANLY GUY LIKE YOU.
....
YEAH.
SUCH A SMALL VOICE!
BUT HE TRIED HARD.
SORRY ABOUT THAT!!!
Bowing in apology.
WOW... QUICK TO RESPOND PROPERLY.
SPLOOSH

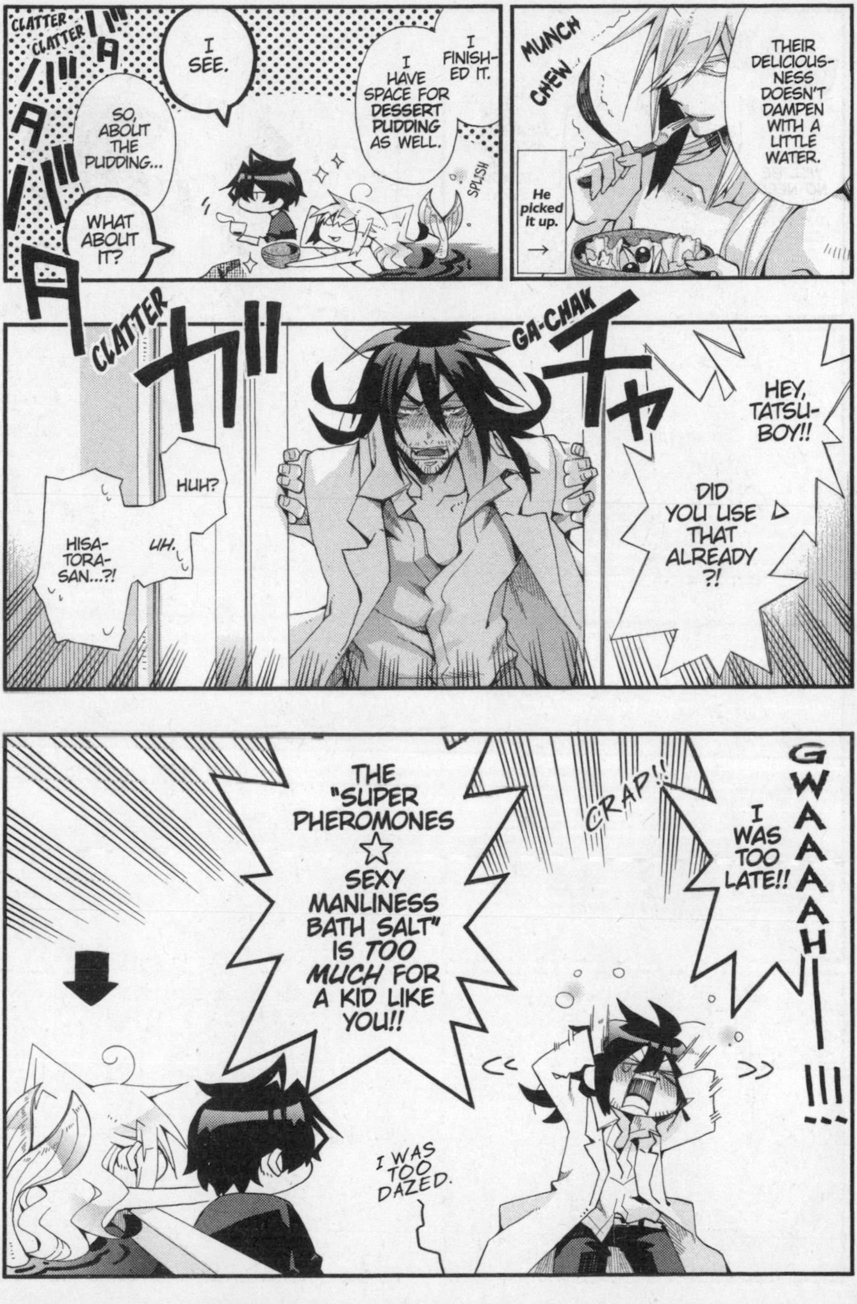
MUNCH
CHEW
THEIR DELICIOUSNESS DOESN'T DAMPEN WITH A LITTLE WATER.
He picked it up. →
I FINISHED IT.
I HAVE SPACE FOR DESSERT PUDDING AS WELL.
SPLISH
I SEE.
SO, ABOUT THE PUDDING...
WHAT ABOUT IT?
CLATTER CLATTER
GA-CHAK
CLATTER
HEY, TATSU-BOY!!
DID YOU USE THAT ALREADY?!
HUH?
UH.
HISATORA-SAN...?!
GWAAAAAH—!!!
I WAS TOO LATE!!
CRAP!!
THE "SUPER PHEROMONES ☆ SEXY MANLINESS BATH SALT" IS *TOO MUCH* FOR A KID LIKE YOU!!
I WAS TOO DAZED.

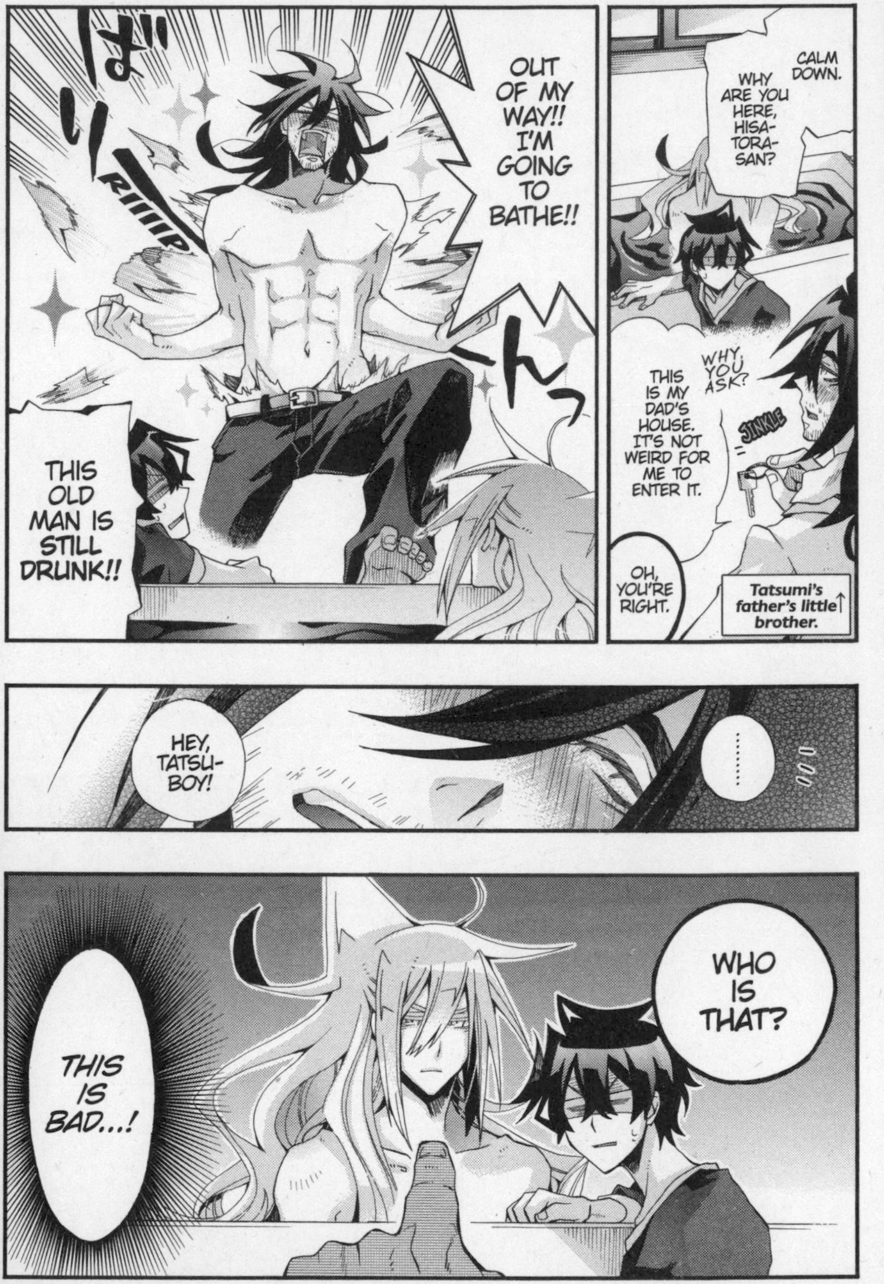

CALM DOWN.
WHY ARE YOU HERE, HISA-TORA-SAN?
WHY, YOU ASK?
THIS IS MY DAD'S HOUSE. IT'S NOT WEIRD FOR ME TO ENTER IT.
JINKLE
OH, YOU'RE RIGHT.
Tatsumi's father's little↑ brother.
RIIIIIP
OUT OF MY WAY!! I'M GOING TO BATHE!!
THIS OLD MAN IS STILL DRUNK!!
......
HEY, TATSU-BOY!
WHO IS THAT?
THIS IS BAD...!

Merman in My Tub

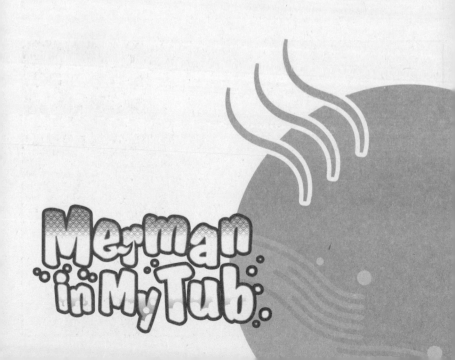

オレん家のフロ事情

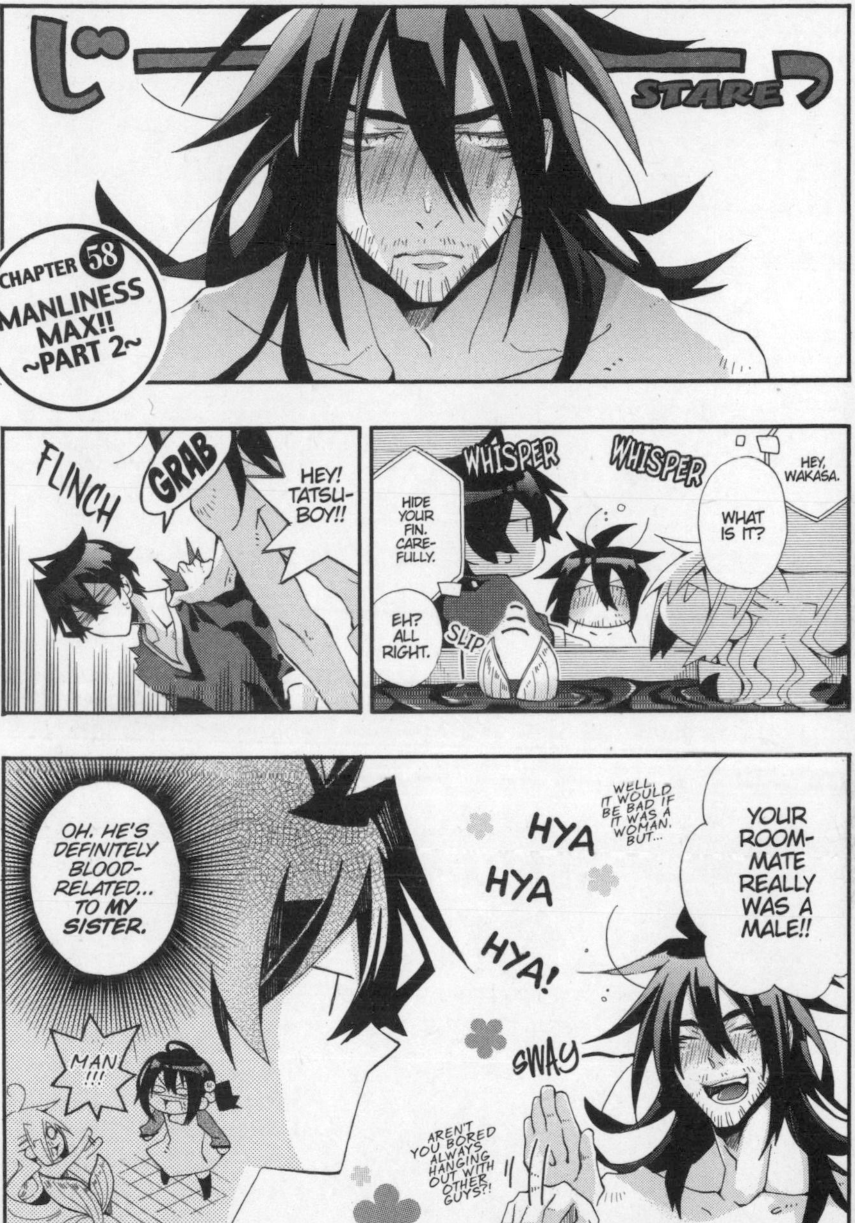
じー
STARE
CHAPTER 58
MANLINESS MAX!! ~PART 2~
WHISPER
WHISPER
HEY, WAKASA.
WHAT IS IT?
HIDE YOUR FIN. CAREFULLY.
EH? ALL RIGHT.
SLIP
HEY! TATSU-BOY!!
GRAB
FLINCH
YOUR ROOMMATE REALLY WAS A MALE!!
WELL, IT WOULD BE BAD IF IT WAS A WOMAN, BUT...
HYA
HYA
HYA!
SWAY
AREN'T YOU BORED ALWAYS HANGING OUT WITH OTHER GUYS?!
OH. HE'S DEFINITELY BLOOD-RELATED... TO MY SISTER.
MAN!!!
Little sister's response. ↑

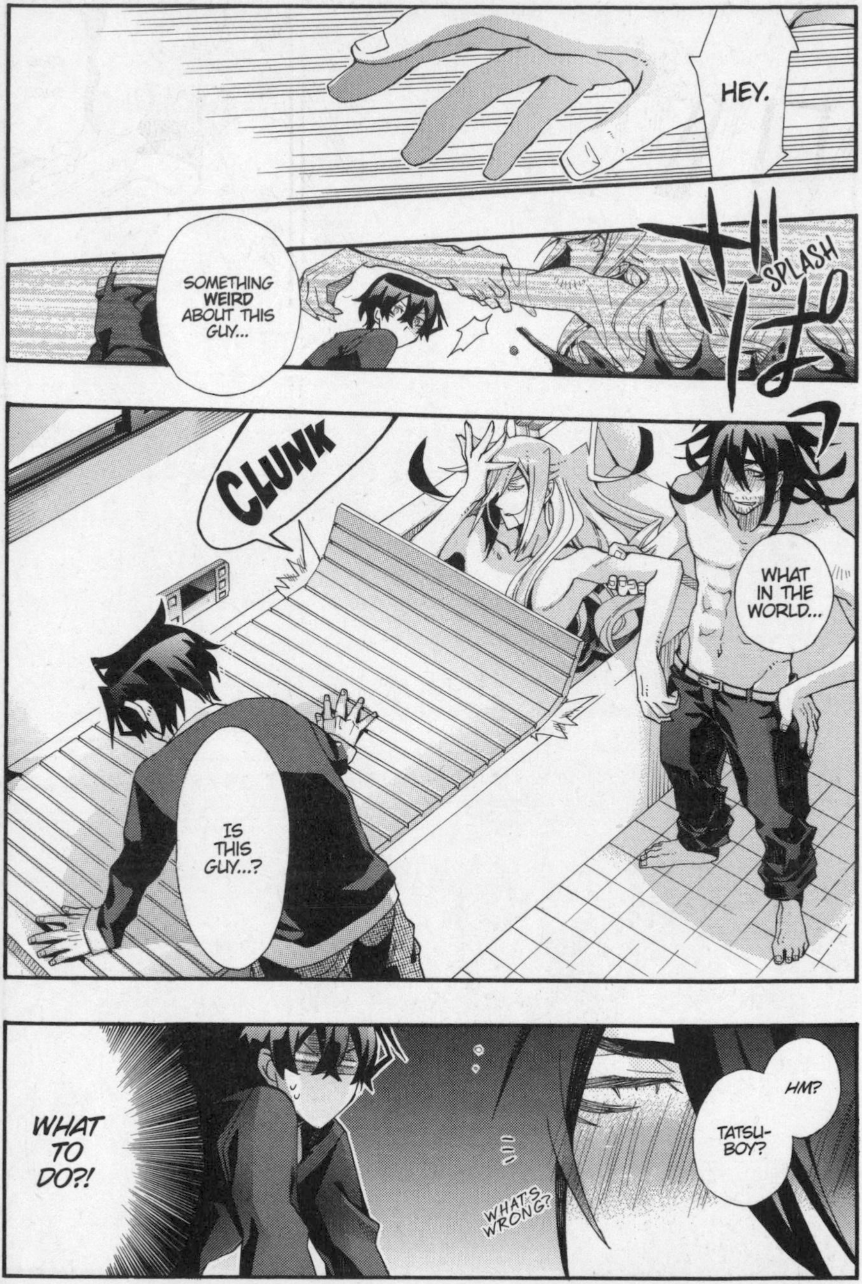
HEY.
SPLASH
SOMETHING WEIRD ABOUT THIS GUY...
WHAT IN THE WORLD...
CLUNK
IS THIS GUY...?
HM?
TATSU-BOY?
WHAT'S WRONG?
WHAT TO DO?!

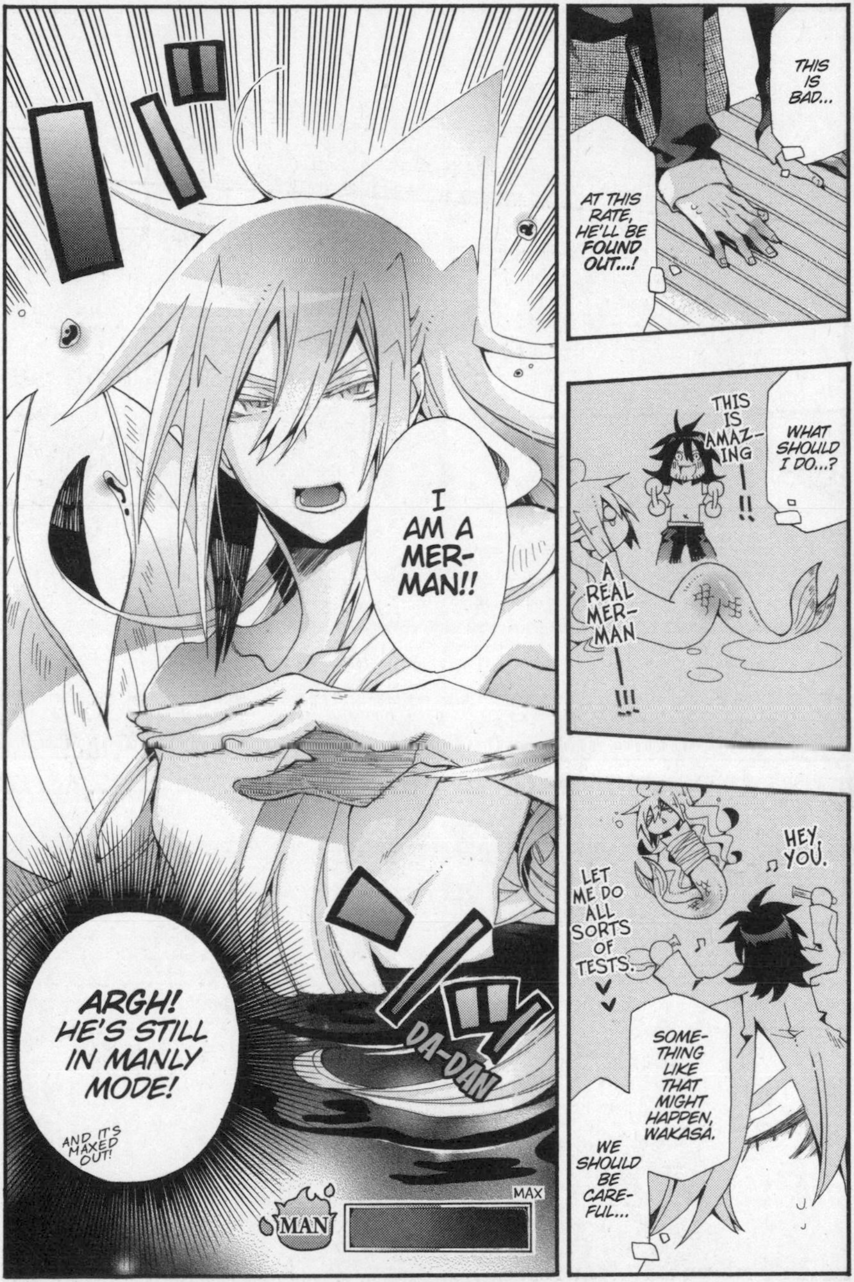
THIS IS BAD...
AT THIS RATE, HE'LL BE FOUND OUT...!
WHAT SHOULD I DO...?
THIS IS AMAZING—!!
A REAL MERMAN—!!!
HEY, YOU. ♪
LET ME DO ALL SORTS OF TESTS. ♥♥
SOMETHING LIKE THAT MIGHT HAPPEN, WAKASA.
WE SHOULD BE CAREFUL...
I AM A MERMAN!!
DA-DAN
ARGH! HE'S STILL IN MANLY MODE!
AND IT'S MAXED OUT!
MAN
MAX

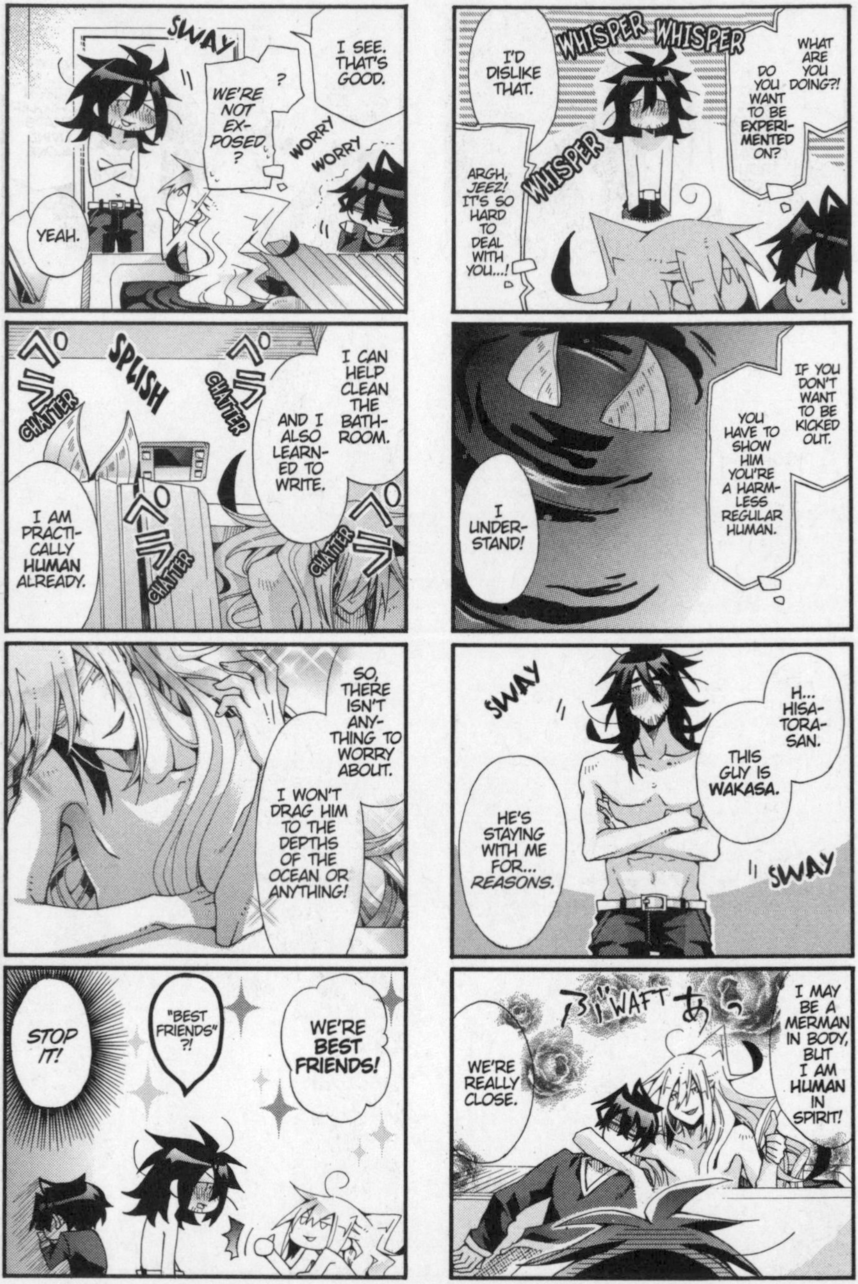
WHAT ARE YOU DOING?!
DO YOU WANT TO BE EXPERIMENTED ON?
WHISPER WHISPER
I'D DISLIKE THAT.
WHISPER
ARGH, JEEZ! IT'S SO HARD TO DEAL WITH YOU...!
I SEE. THAT'S GOOD.
SWAY
?
WE'RE NOT EXPOSED?
WORRY WORRY
YEAH.
IF YOU DON'T WANT TO BE KICKED OUT.
YOU HAVE TO SHOW HIM YOU'RE A HARMLESS REGULAR HUMAN.
I UNDERSTAND!
I CAN HELP CLEAN THE BATHROOM.
AND I ALSO LEARNED TO WRITE.
CHATTER
SPLISH
CHATTER
CHATTER
CHATTER
I AM PRACTICALLY HUMAN ALREADY.
H... HISATORA-SAN.
THIS GUY IS WAKASA.
SWAY
HE'S STAYING WITH ME FOR... REASONS.
SWAY
SO, THERE ISN'T ANYTHING TO WORRY ABOUT.
I WON'T DRAG HIM TO THE DEPTHS OF THE OCEAN OR ANYTHING!
I MAY BE A MERMAN IN BODY, BUT I AM HUMAN IN SPIRIT!
WAFT
WE'RE REALLY CLOSE.
WE'RE BEST FRIENDS!
"BEST FRIENDS"?!
STOP IT!

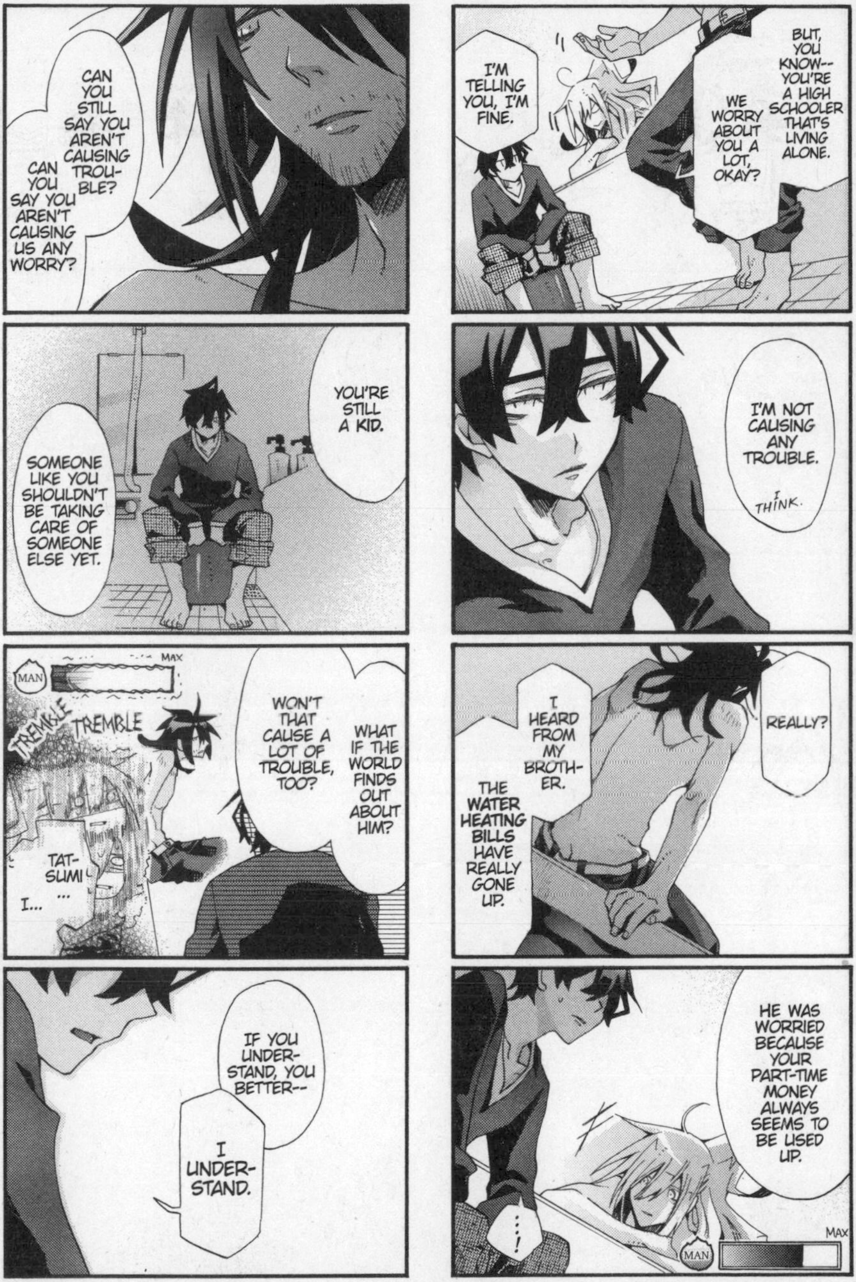
BUT, YOU KNOW-- YOU'RE A HIGH SCHOOLER THAT'S LIVING ALONE.
WE WORRY ABOUT YOU A LOT, OKAY?
I'M TELLING YOU, I'M FINE.
CAN YOU STILL SAY YOU AREN'T CAUSING TROUBLE?
CAN YOU SAY YOU AREN'T CAUSING US ANY WORRY?
I'M NOT CAUSING ANY TROUBLE.
I THINK.
YOU'RE STILL A KID.
SOMEONE LIKE YOU SHOULDN'T BE TAKING CARE OF SOMEONE ELSE YET.
REALLY?
I HEARD FROM MY BROTHER.
THE WATER HEATING BILLS HAVE REALLY GONE UP.
WHAT IF THE WORLD FINDS OUT ABOUT HIM?
WON'T THAT CAUSE A LOT OF TROUBLE, TOO?
MAX
MAN
TREMBLE TREMBLE
TAT-SUMI ...
I...
HE WAS WORRIED BECAUSE YOUR PART-TIME MONEY ALWAYS SEEMS TO BE USED UP.
...!
MAX
MAN
IF YOU UNDERSTAND, YOU BETTER--
I UNDERSTAND.

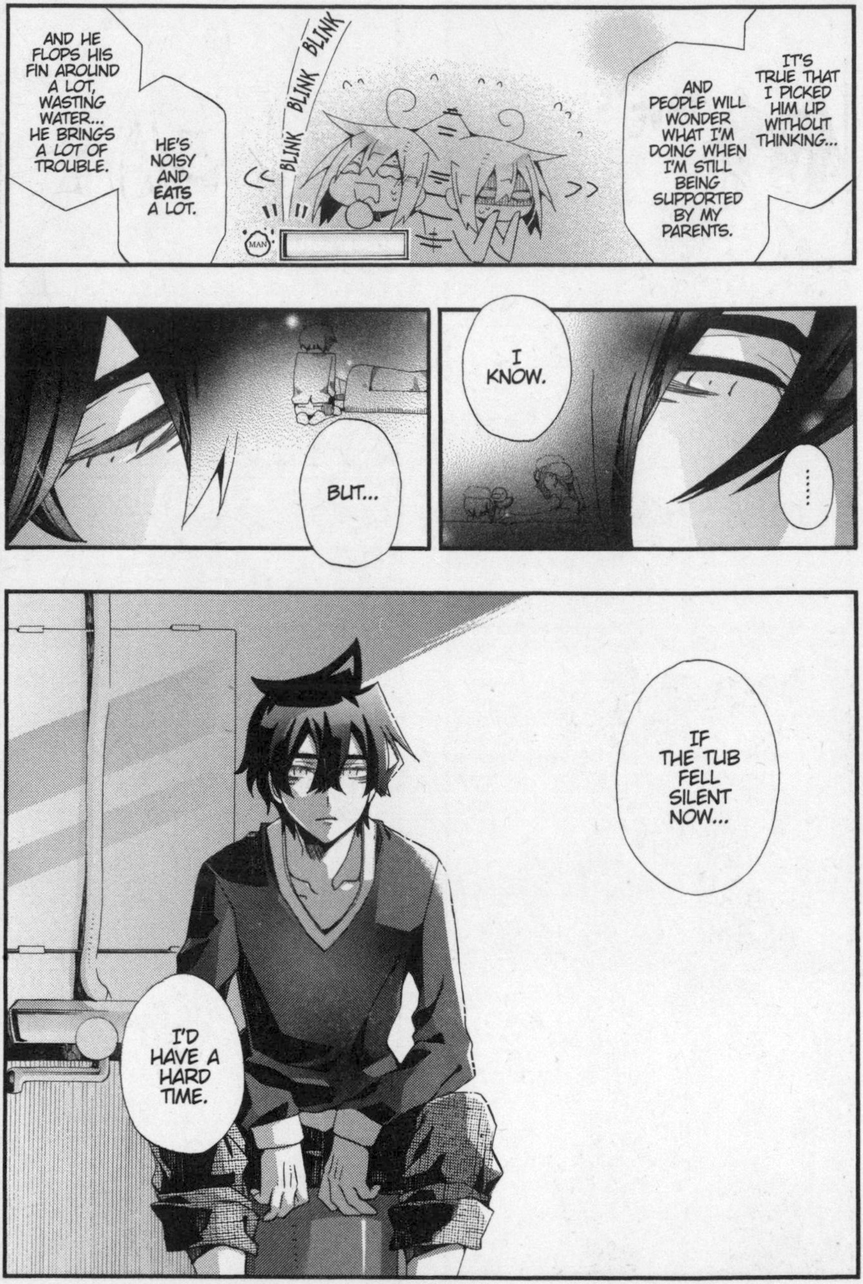
IT'S TRUE THAT I PICKED HIM UP WITHOUT THINKING...
AND PEOPLE WILL WONDER WHAT I'M DOING WHEN I'M STILL BEING SUPPORTED BY MY PARENTS.
BLINK BLINK BLINK
MAN
HE'S NOISY AND EATS A LOT.
AND HE FLOPS HIS FIN AROUND A LOT, WASTING WATER... HE BRINGS A LOT OF TROUBLE.
I KNOW.
......
BUT...
IF THE TUB FELL SILENT NOW...
I'D HAVE A HARD TIME.

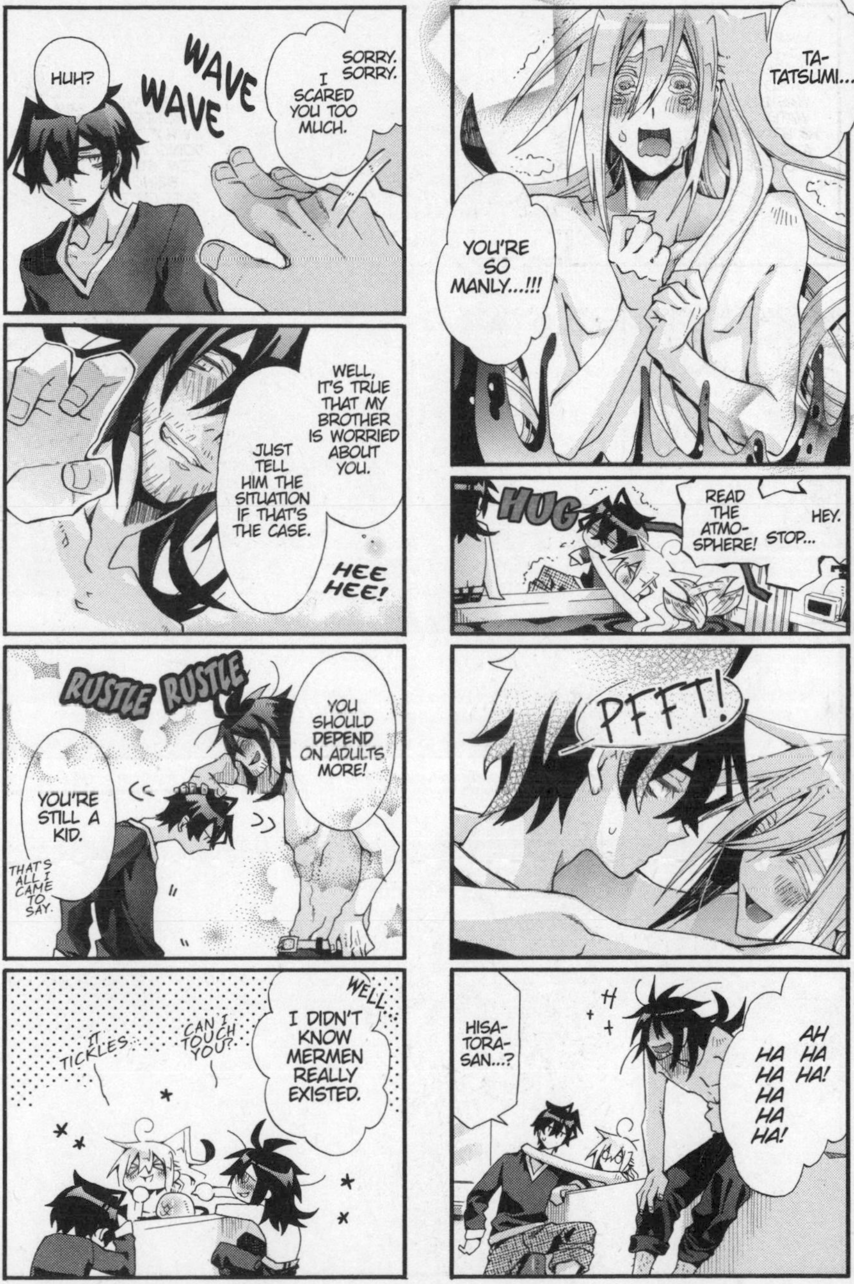
TA-TATSUMI...!
YOU'RE SO MANLY...!!!
HUG
HEY. STOP...
READ THE ATMOSPHERE!
PFFT!
AH HA HA HA HA HA HA HA HA!
HISA-TORA-SAN...?
SORRY. SORRY. I SCARED YOU TOO MUCH.
WAVE WAVE
HUH?
WELL, IT'S TRUE THAT MY BROTHER IS WORRIED ABOUT YOU.
JUST TELL HIM THE SITUATION IF THAT'S THE CASE.
HEE HEE!
RUSTLE RUSTLE
YOU SHOULD DEPEND ON ADULTS MORE!
YOU'RE STILL A KID.
THAT'S ALL I CAME TO SAY.
WELL...
I DIDN'T KNOW MERMEN REALLY EXISTED.
CAN I TOUCH YOU?
IT TICKLES...

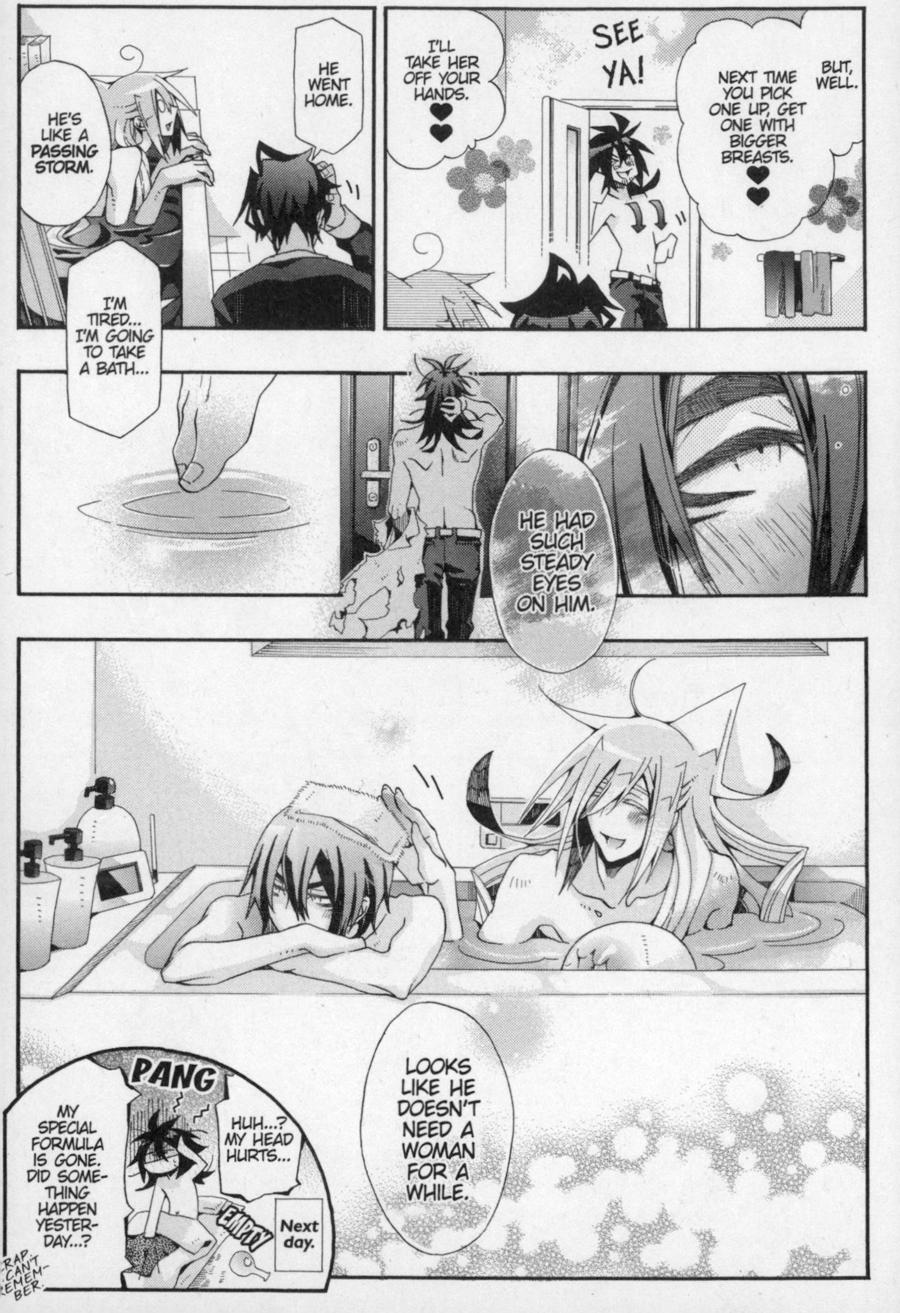
SEE YA!
BUT, WELL.
NEXT TIME YOU PICK ONE UP, GET ONE WITH BIGGER BREASTS. ♥ ♥
I'LL TAKE HER OFF YOUR HANDS. ♥ ♥
HE WENT HOME.
HE'S LIKE A PASSING STORM.
HE HAD SUCH STEADY EYES ON HIM.
I'M TIRED... I'M GOING TO TAKE A BATH...
LOOKS LIKE HE DOESN'T NEED A WOMAN FOR A WHILE.
Next day.
EMPTY
HUH...? MY HEAD HURTS...
PANG
MY SPECIAL FORMULA IS GONE. DID SOMETHING HAPPEN YESTERDAY...?
RAP. CAN'T EMEM-BER.

To be continued...

オレん家のフロ事情

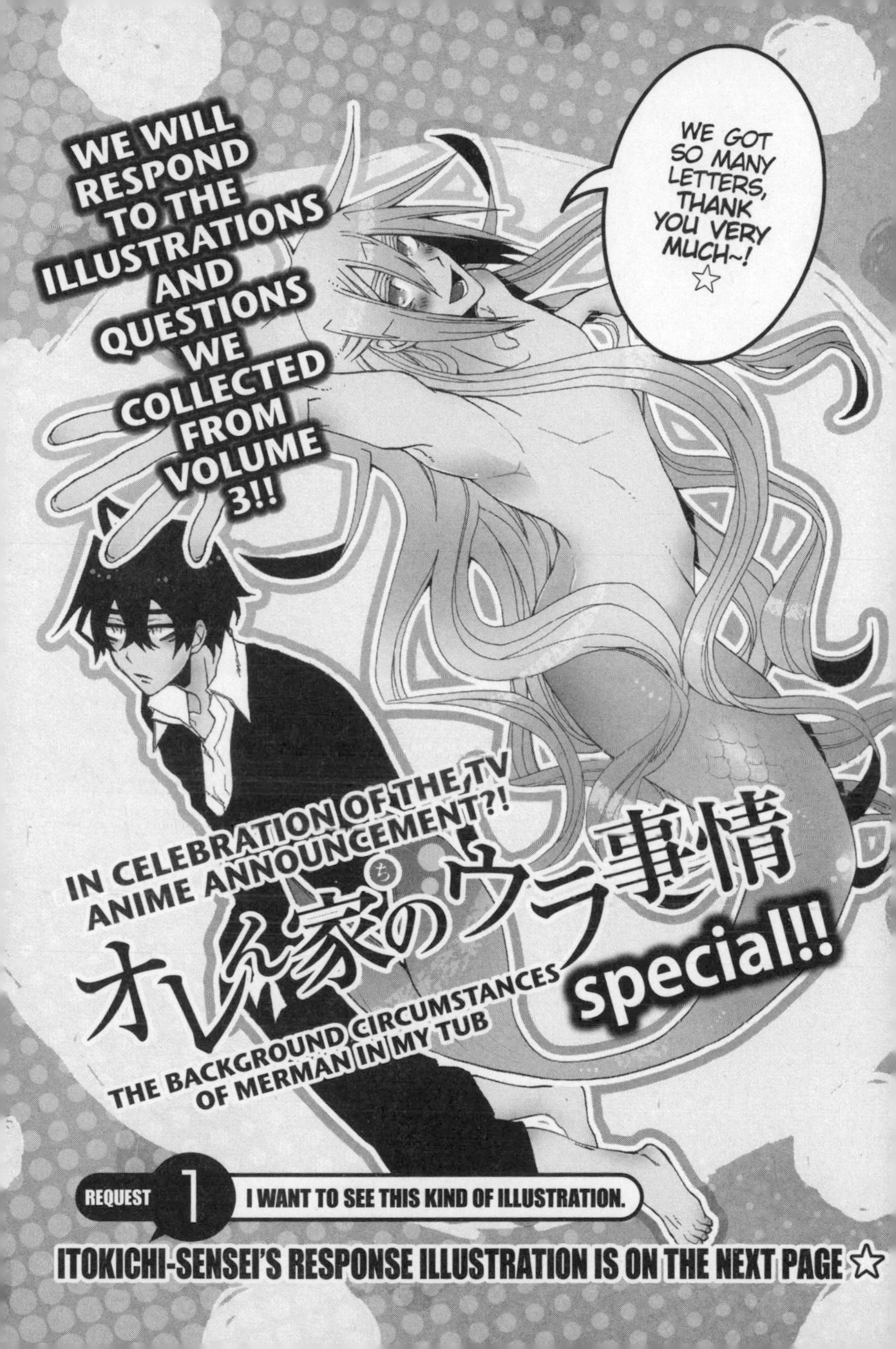
WE GOT SO MANY LETTERS, THANK YOU VERY MUCH~! ☆
WE WILL RESPOND TO THE ILLUSTRATIONS AND QUESTIONS WE COLLECTED FROM VOLUME 3!!
IN CELEBRATION OF THE TV ANIME ANNOUNCEMENT?!
オレん家のウラ事情 special!!
THE BACKGROUND CIRCUMSTANCES OF MERMAN IN MY TUB
REQUEST 1 I WANT TO SEE THIS KIND OF ILLUSTRATION.
ITOKICHI-SENSEI'S RESPONSE ILLUSTRATION IS ON THE NEXT PAGE ☆

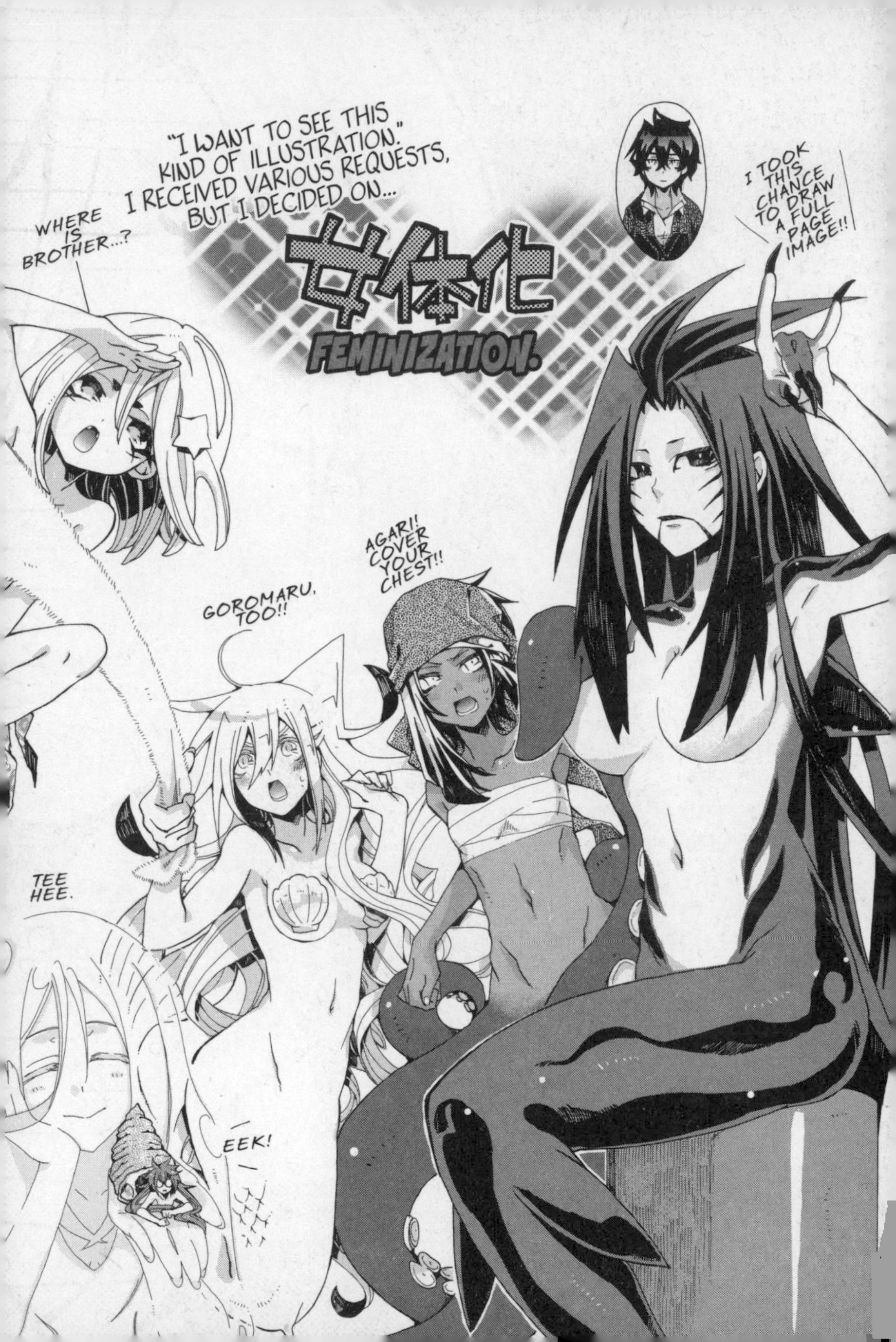

"I WANT TO SEE THIS KIND OF ILLUSTRATION." I RECEIVED VARIOUS REQUESTS, BUT I DECIDED ON...
女体化
FEMINIZATION.
I TOOK THIS CHANCE TO DRAW A FULL PAGE IMAGE!!
WHERE IS BROTHER...?
AGARI!! COVER YOUR CHEST!!
GOROMARU, TOO!!
TEE HEE.
EEK!

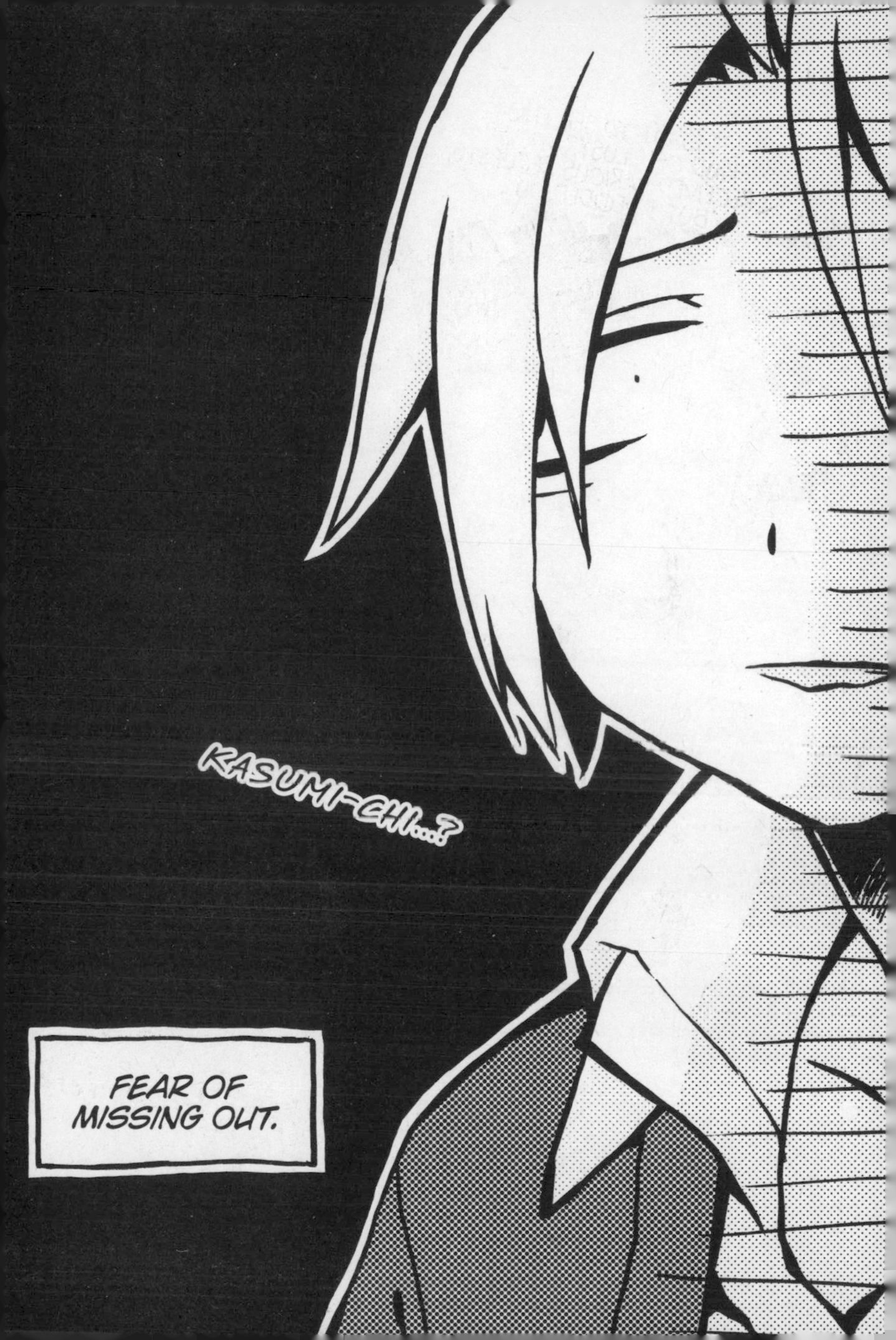
KASUMI-CHI...?
FEAR OF MISSING OUT.

REQUEST 2 READER'S ILLUSTRATION CORNER

I'D LIKE TO SHOW YOU SOME OF THE WONDERFUL ART PEOPLE HAVE SENT ME!!

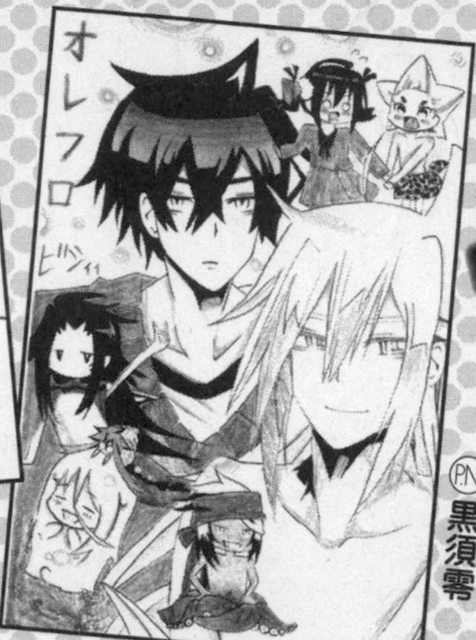

オレフロ

P.N 黒須雫

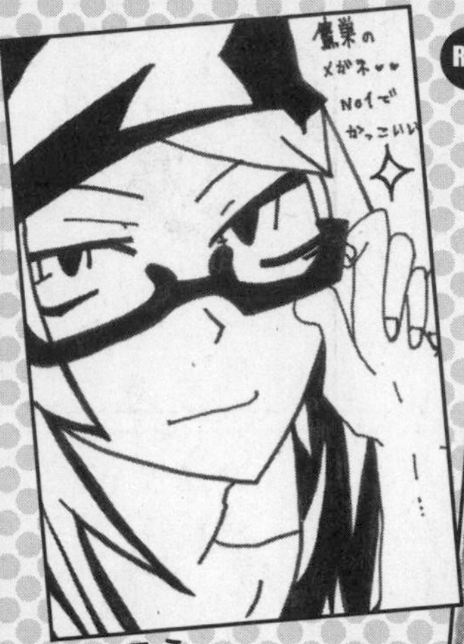

No1でかっこいい

P.N たろう

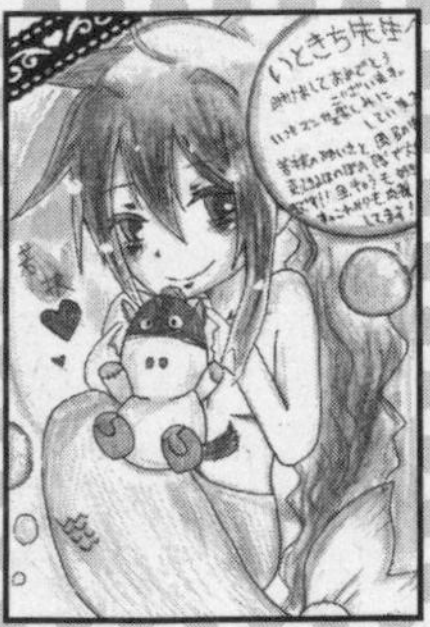
P.N 木内充紀

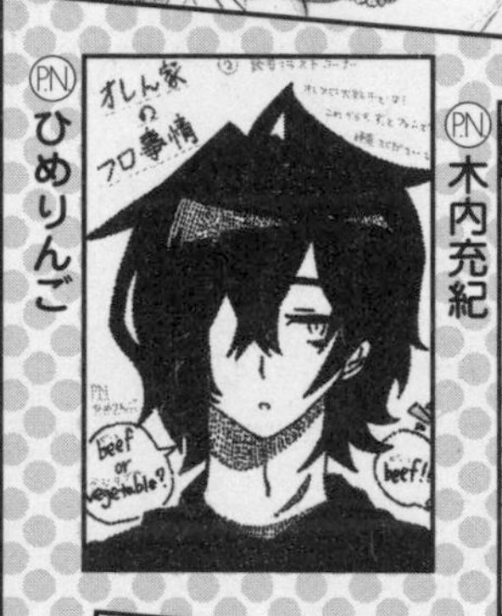

オレん家のフロ事情
beef or vegetable?
beef!!

P.N ひめりんご

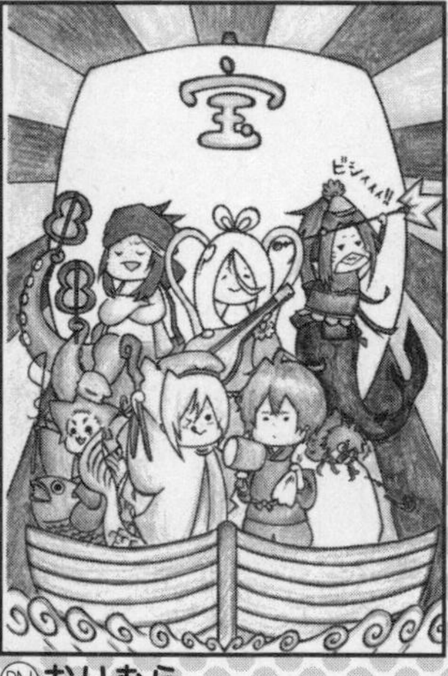

宝

P.N おりむら

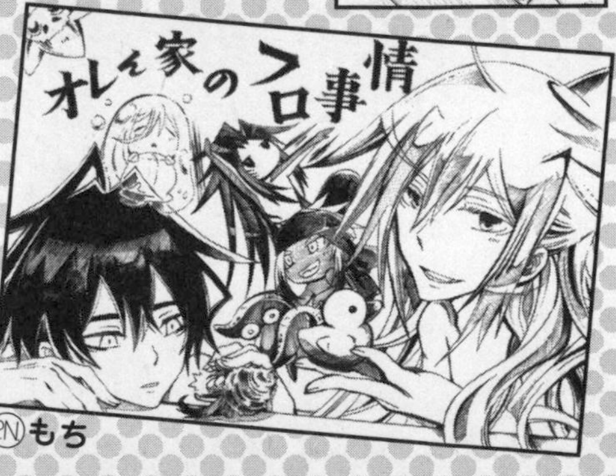

オレん家のフロ事情

P.N もち

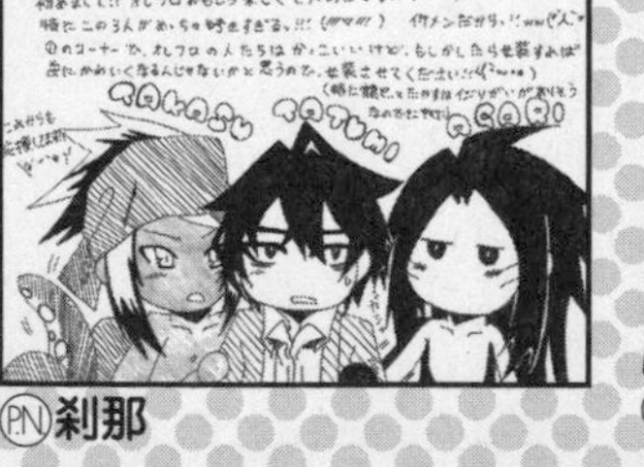
P.N 刹那

P.N. 彰無契

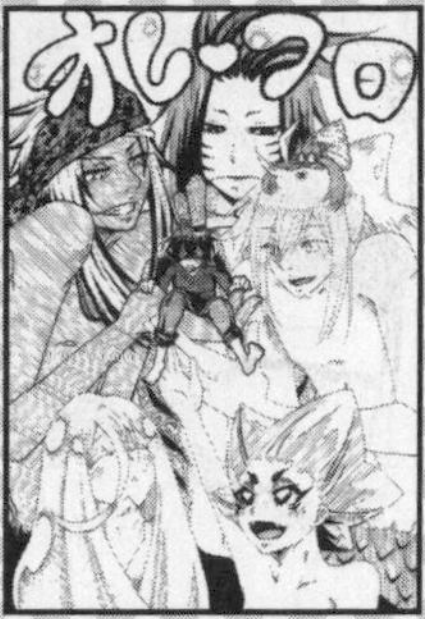
オレフロ

P.N. ちる

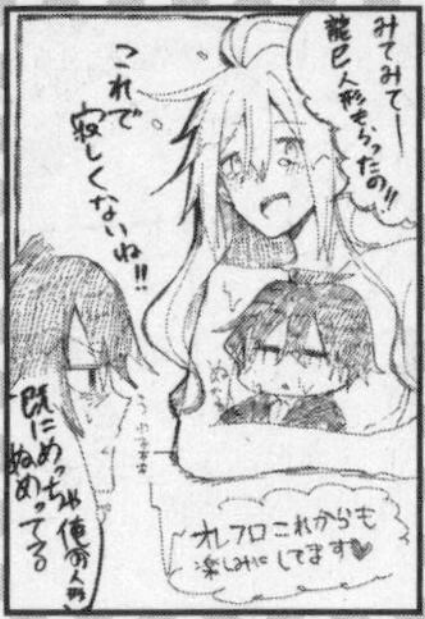
みてみてー 龍巳人形もらったの!!
これで寂しくないね!!
既にめっちゃ俺の人形ぬめってる
オレフロこれからも楽しみにしてます♥

P.N. ミサ吉

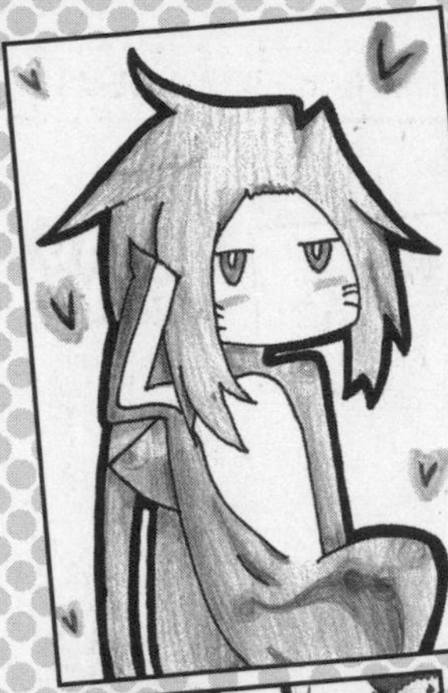

P.N. 柚木矢代

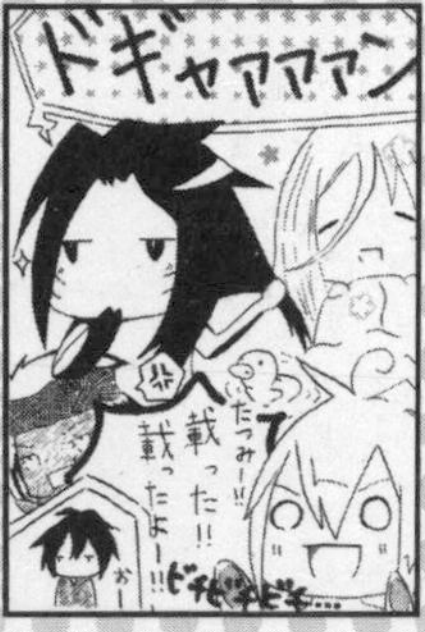
ドギャアアアアン
たつみー!! 載った!! 載ったよー!!
おー

P.N. たち

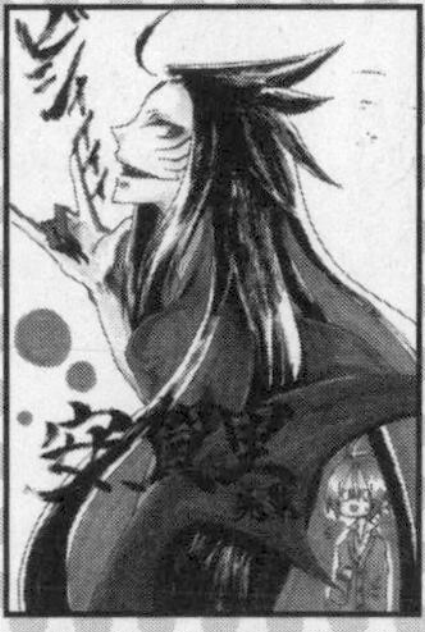

P.N. 内藤みなみ

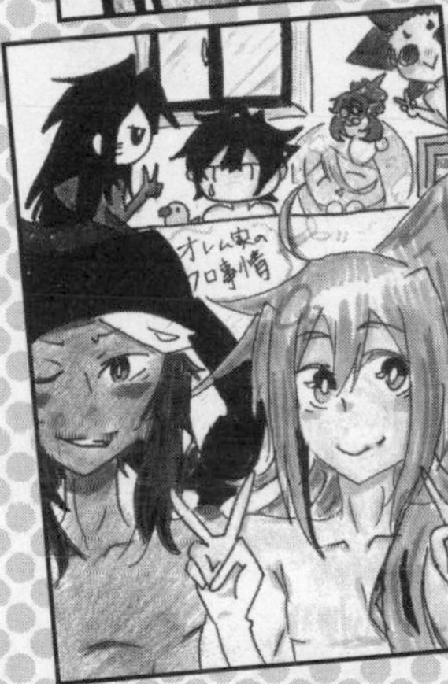
オレん家のフロ事情

P.N. NATTACHA

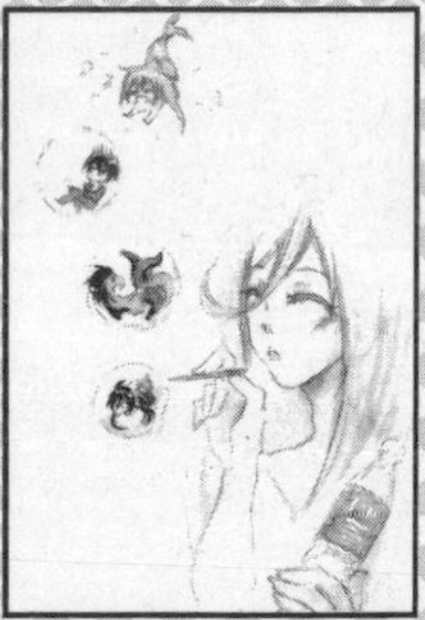

P.N. 冬いち

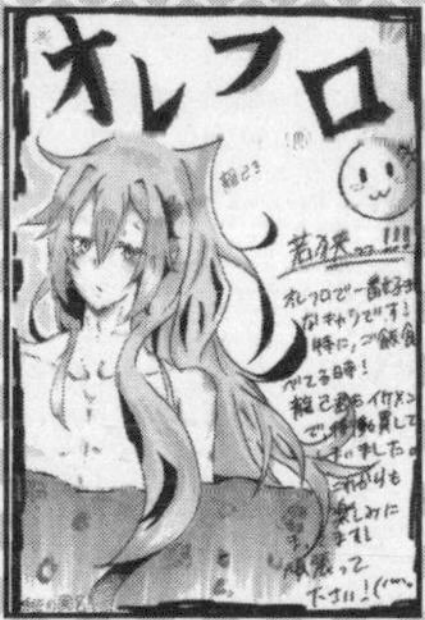
オレフロ
オレフロで一番好きなキャラです!
特に、ご飯食べてる時!
これからも楽しみにしてます!
頑張って下さい!

P.N. Tu10vemomo

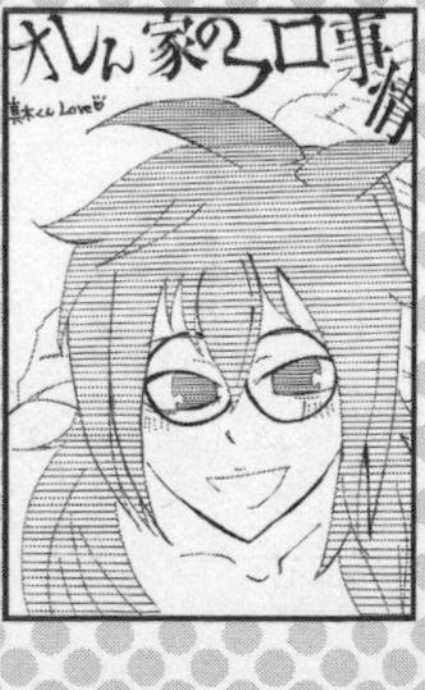
オレん家のフロ事情
真木くんLove

P.N. 鳥羽居綾

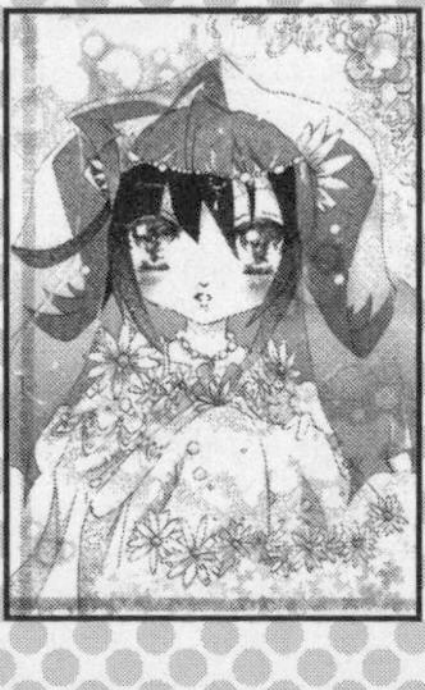

P.N. カルハ

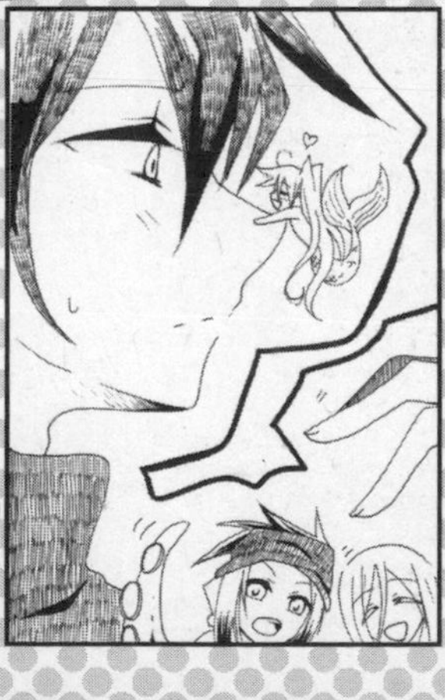

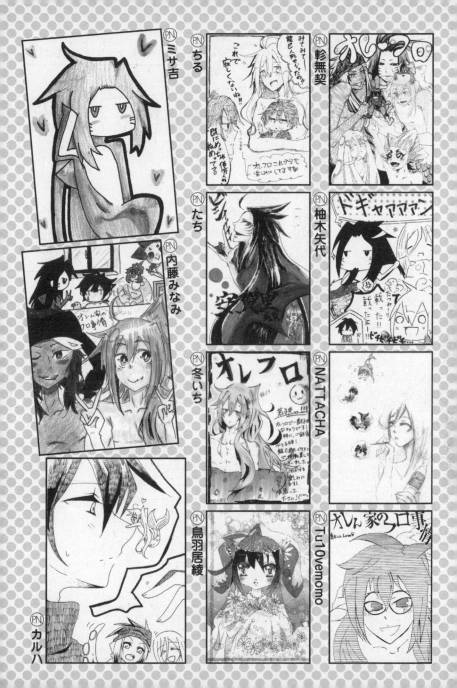

REQUEST 3 — QUESTIONS FOR ITOKICHI-SENSEI

ITOKICHI-SENSEI WILL ANSWER EVERYONE'S QUESTIONS! ♪

Q1 — WHO IS YOUR FAVORITE CHARACTER?

A — I love Kasumi the best. I also love drawing her the most. Next would be Takasu.

Q2 — MIKUNI-SAN'S HAIR IS DRAWN CURLED TO THE RIGHT THEN CURLED TO THE LEFT IN THE NEXT PANEL SOMETIMES. WHAT'S UP WITH THAT? (PN. NEKOKABURI)

A — This... I didn't realize it until you said something...! That's what it was all about... Let's leave it at that... (laugh)

Q3 — IN A PREVIOUS CHAPTER, TAKASU-SAN GAVE TATSUMI-SAN HIS OWN LEG, SAYING, "THIS SHOULD HELP YOU OUT!" DID HE EAT THAT? DIDN'T IT HURT? (CRY) TAKASU'S MANLINESS IS VERY COOL!!

A — He didn't eat it. Tatsumi is very polite so he only thanked him for the offer. Life can bring you pain, but as long as you have manliness you can overcome it!

Q4 — I REALLY WANT TO KNOW KASUMI-CHAN'S AGE!! I ALSO WANT TO KNOW HOW BIG MAKI-SAN IS INSIDE HIS SHELL? HE STRETCHES A LOT AND I'M CURIOUS. (PN. YUKISA)

A — Kasumi is a second grader! (Decided during the anime meeting) Maki's shell is about 7 cm [3 inches] and his body wraps about inside of it. How big he is... I leave it to your imagination. (laugh)

Q5 — MAKI-SAN'S BODY STRETCHED A LOT DURING THE ONE HUNDRED PEOPLE, ONE POEM TOURNAMENT. HOW FAR CAN HE STRETCH? (PN. MOMIJI)

A — If he tries hard he can stretch twice his body length!

Q6 — PLEASE TELL ME THE PROFILES OF ALL YOUR CHARACTERS. ♪ I REALLY WANT TO KNOW!! ESPECIALLY THEIR BIRTHDAYS~! ♪

A — When I asked them about that, they replied, "How does someone know the day they were born?" Sorry!

Q7 — I THINK KURAYAMA-SAN IS REALLY CUTE AND LOVE HER. I WAS WONDERING IF YOU CAN GIVE ME (OR SET) HER DETAILED PROFILE! (PN. KURUMI)

A — Thank you very much! That makes me so happy! Kurayama-san's profile is at the top.

Q8 **WILL KASUMI MEET TAKASU AND THE OTHERS? (PN. KIMERA)**

A - No. If they met her, she could get into a situation that may get me kicked out of the publishing company.

Q9 **ARE SOUSUKE'S BIG SISTERS FUJOUSHI? (PN. ITOU)**

A - His big sisters love cute boys.

Q10 **WHO IS THE STRONGEST IN ARM WRESTLING AMONG THE MERMAN IN MY TUB CHARACTERS?**

A - Agari > Wakasa > Tatsumi > Takasu > Sousuke > Mikuni > Goromaru > Unbeatable Hurdle > Maki.

Q11 **WHAT IS THE POINTY PART OF WAKASA'S HEAD? (PN. PUKUPUKU)**

A - That is the top of his ponytail, but the point got stronger as I continued drawing... It's a drawing issue.

Q12 **EVERYONE WHO APPEARS IN MERMAN IN MY TUB IS FROM THE "SEA" BUT WILL ANYONE FROM RIVERS OR LAKES APPEAR? FOR INSTANCE, TURTLES, GOLDFISH, FRESHWATER CRABS... I RECOMMEND THE MEXICAN SALAMANDER! THOUGH, IT'S THE KIND OF SLIMY THING THAT TATSUMI HATES. (CRY) (PN. TATSUBOSHI)**

A - Wakasa lived in the sea for a long time, so all of his friends and acquaintances are from there. Mexican salamanders... I love them so it makes me want them to appear too...

Q13 **ISN'T KURAYAMA-SAN TOO CUTE?? (PN. MIKU)**

A - Thank you very much.

Q14 **PLEASE EXPLAIN AGARI-NESE TO ME!!**

A - A) Snaap (This is) Snaaaap (the basics) Snaaaap (of Agari-nese).

Q15 **HOW DO YOU START DRAWING YOUR CHARACTERS? (FROM THE FACE, EYES~!) (PN. YUNE)**

A - From the face. First I make the general head, then the nose, then mouth, then eyes, then hair. I am bad at mouths and noses!

Q16 **IS WAKASA A SALTWATER FISH? FRESHWATER? HE HAS LIVED IN THE RIVERS, BUT HAS FRIENDS FROM THE SEA. I WORK AT A SUSHI RESTAURANT AND I AM VERY CURIOUS.**

A - He is more of a saltwater fish. But his top half is human so he can go into any type of water. Please work hard at your job! (Sushi... [drool])

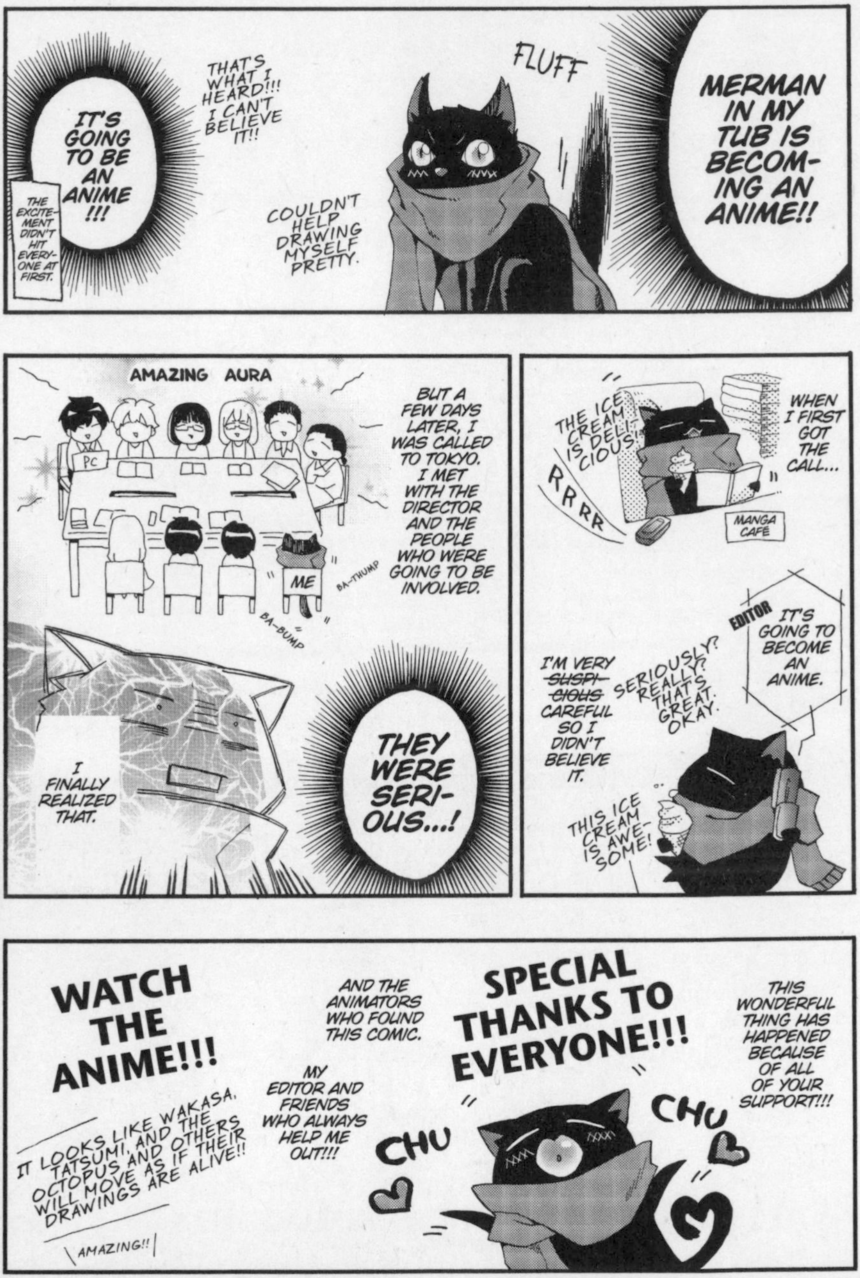
MERMAN IN MY TUB IS BECOMING AN ANIME!!
FLUFF
COULDN'T HELP DRAWING MYSELF PRETTY.
THAT'S WHAT I HEARD!!! I CAN'T BELIEVE IT!!
IT'S GOING TO BE AN ANIME!!!
THE EXCITEMENT DIDN'T HIT EVERYONE AT FIRST.
WHEN I FIRST GOT THE CALL...
THE ICE CREAM IS DELICIOUS!!
RRRRR
MANGA CAFÉ
EDITOR
IT'S GOING TO BECOME AN ANIME.
SERIOUSLY? REALLY? THAT'S GREAT. OKAY.
I'M VERY ~~SUSPICIOUS~~ CAREFUL SO I DIDN'T BELIEVE IT.
THIS ICE CREAM IS AWESOME!
BUT A FEW DAYS LATER, I WAS CALLED TO TOKYO. I MET WITH THE DIRECTOR AND THE PEOPLE WHO WERE GOING TO BE INVOLVED.
AMAZING AURA
PC
ME
BA-THUMP
BA-BUMP
THEY WERE SERIOUS...!
I FINALLY REALIZED THAT.
THIS WONDERFUL THING HAS HAPPENED BECAUSE OF ALL OF YOUR SUPPORT!!!
SPECIAL THANKS TO EVERYONE!!!
AND THE ANIMATORS WHO FOUND THIS COMIC.
MY EDITOR AND FRIENDS WHO ALWAYS HELP ME OUT!!!
CHU
CHU
WATCH THE ANIME!!!
IT LOOKS LIKE WAKASA, TATSUMI, AND THE OCTOPUS AND OTHERS WILL MOVE AS IF THEIR DRAWINGS ARE ALIVE!!
AMAZING!!

Merman in My Tub

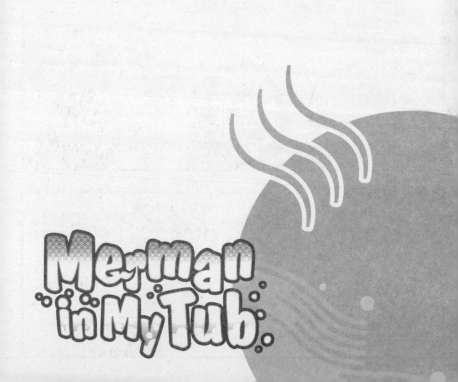

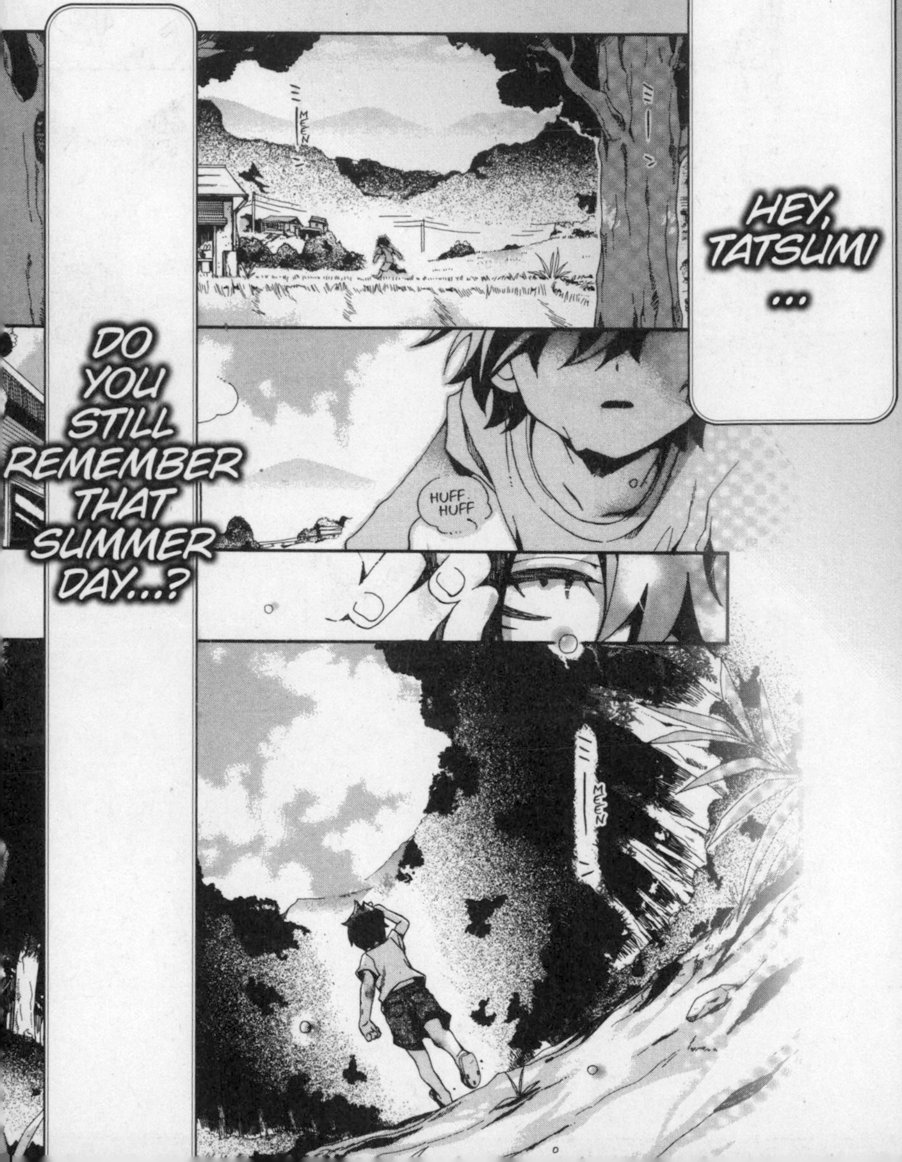

HEY, TATSUMI ...
MEEN
HUFF HUFF
MEEN
DO YOU STILL REMEMBER THAT SUMMER DAY...?